SHOWA JAPAN

For Kay Cotter

with best wishes—

Hans Brinckmann
3/29/09

For H

SHOWA JAPAN

The Post-War Golden Age and Its Troubled Legacy

Hans Brinckmann

Photographs by
Ysbrand Rogge and **Hans Brinckmann**

TUTTLE PUBLISHING
Tokyo • Rutland, Vermont • Singapore

Published by Tuttle Publishing, an imprint of Periplus Editions (HK) Ltd., with editorial offices at 364 Innovation Drive, North Clarendon, Vermont 05759 U.S.A.

Text copyright © 2008 by Hans Brinckmann
Photographs © Hans Brinckmann unless otherwise noted

The photographs on pages 4 (bottom) and 6 of this book's color insert were first published in 2005 by Global Oriental, Folkestone, UK, in the author's Japan memoir *The Magatama Doodle* and are reproduced here with their kind permission.

Library of Congress Cataloging-in-Publication Data
Brinckmann, Hans, 1932–
  Showa Japan : the post-war golden age and its troubled legacy / Hans Brinckmann ; photographs by Ysbrand Rogge and Hans Brinckmann.
      p. cm.
  Includes index.
  ISBN 978-4-8053-1002-1 (hardcover : alk. paper)
  1. Japan—History—1945–1989. I. Rogge, Ysbrand. II. Title.
  DS889.B675 2008
  952.04—dc22

                            2008016959

ISBN-13: 978-4-8053-1002-1

Distributed by

North America, Latin America & Europe
Tuttle Publishing
364 Innovation Drive
North Clarendon, VT 05759-9436 U.S.A.
Tel: 1 (802) 773-8930; Fax: 1 (802) 773-6993
info@tuttlepublishing.com
www.tuttlepublishing.com

Asia Pacific
Berkeley Books Pte. Ltd.
61 Tai Seng Avenue #02-12
Singapore 534167
Tel: (65) 6280-1330; Fax: (65) 6280-6290
inquiries@periplus.com.sg
www.periplus.com

Japan
Tuttle Publishing
Yaekari Building, 3rd Floor
5-4-12 Osaki, Shinagawa-ku
Tokyo 141 0032
Tel: (81) 3 5437-0171; Fax: (81) 3 5437-0755
tuttle-sales@gol.com

First edition
12 11 10 09 08   10 9 8 7 6 5 4 3 2 1

Printed in Hong Kong

TUTTLE PUBLISHING® is a registered trademark of Tuttle Publishing, a division of Periplus Editions (HK) Ltd.

Contents

Preface

Japan—A Case Apart

There is hardly an affluent country in the world today that is not going through a reappraisal of its core identity and a search for the least hazardous course to follow to secure its future. Around the world, once stable nations are in a state of flux, struggling to unite disparate populations and redefine themselves for this modern era.

The United Kingdom is confronted domestically by the forces of devolution and restive ethnic minorities, while internationally it attempts to redefine its role as a military power and its place in the European Union. France—like Germany, the Netherlands, and several other European nations—is facing the consequences of easy-going immigration policies of the past, while battling rising xenophobia with belated attempts to integrate the country's sizable population of ethnic minorities. And what about the United States? Once a model of successful integration of diverse ethnic elements and a beacon to the oppressed of the world, as of early 2008 it is enmeshed in two messy wars, a huge influx of illegal aliens, an assertive religious ascendancy, and the aftermath of heinous terrorist attacks on its soil. All of these factors have led to an agonizing reexamination of its national priorities and international commitments.

Against this restless backdrop of turmoil and instability, Japan seems an island of calm and reason. With its exemplary infrastructure, largely homogeneous population, apparently well-distributed prosperity and peaceful policies, it is the envy of many.

Yet Japan is facing some serious challenges of its own, challenges that differ fundamentally from those facing the West in that they are largely not the result of external threats or internal conflict but of deep-seated, historical uncertainties. Below its placid exterior lies a welter of undigested experiences and conflicting value systems.

The root cause of these tensions can perhaps be traced back to Japan's sudden post-war conversion from a largely post-feudal, militarist, class-ridden society into a formally democratic and peace-loving one. The notions of individual freedom and equality and the power of the ballot box were largely unfamiliar to a nation that for centuries had been ruled by various forms of authoritarian regime. The decade-long, rather stormy, experiment with multiparty democratic government that followed the First World War in Japan was genuine and promising, but its roots were shallow and it collapsed with the ascendancy of the military in the early 1930s.

When General Douglas MacArthur, the American commander of the allied forces that occupied Japan in August 1945, declared, soon after his arrival, that he intended to bring democracy to Japan, his announcement was widely welcomed. And he meant business: the first general election was held in April 1946, seven months after Japan's surrender.

This tight timetable left Japan's people and leaders no meaningful pause for a conscientious postmortem of their crushing defeat. They had to swallow democracy whole, so to speak, without the benefit of a thorough grounding in its principles and responsibilities. Perhaps as a result, the traditional Japanese values—such as self-denial, nonassertiveness, group identity, and deference to superiors—which had survived the brief pre-war democratic period and been reinforced under the military regime, were not fully eradicated. They were allowed, indeed subtly encouraged, to coexist with the new notions of classlessness and rule by ballot.

To this day, these time-honored standards of "correct" behavior constantly compete with the newer ideas of individual rights, freedom of expression, and open competition. These contrasting requirements have apparently left many Japanese bewildered and parents uncertain what to pass on to their offspring. Three indicators—among many—point to the resulting existential problems.

The first concerns personal fulfillment and happiness. In a 2006 UNICEF survey of "subjective well-being" among children eleven to fifteen years old, an astounding 30 percent of Japanese children said they "felt lonely," three times the next highest-scoring country, Iceland, and *ten times* the rate in the Netherlands, which scored lowest. An additional 18 percent of the Japanese children felt "awkward and out of place."

Nor do the grown-ups feel much better, as evidenced by the next indicator. Recent surveys rank Japan almost uniformly at the low end of highly developed countries in terms of such criteria as individual happiness, life satisfaction, pride in their nationality, and—significantly—people's political engagement and confidence in their parliament. In the latter two categories, Japan scored lowest among seventeen developed countries surveyed by World Values Survey, a nonprofit organization devoted to understanding ongoing global social changes.[1]

Japan's consistently high suicide rate (over 30,000 a year, the highest among rich nations) is yet another indication of the prevalence of depression and hopelessness in Japanese society.

Even granted that surveys and statistics such as these must be viewed with caution, the consistency with which Japan ranks low on almost every scale purporting to measure values and attitudes relating to lifestyle and sociopolitical engagement cannot but indicate some deep-seated uncertainties.

If personal and social factors lie at the base of these "unhappiness indicators," there is another, hardly less worrisome, problem in urgent need of addressing. It has to do with Japan's historic sense of isolation and alienation from the rest of Asia, including its direct neighbors, the two Koreas and China. In the distant past, China and Korea were Japan's mentors, but beginning in the late nineteenth century that image was firmly replaced by one that elevated Japan in its own eyes to a position of almost divine superiority. It was this exalted self-image that provided the moral justification for annexing Korea, attacking the United States, and occupying most of East and Southeast Asia before and during the Pacific War.

Defeat destroyed that image—at least the tangible evidence of it, if not the underlying belief in the minds of many Japanese (notably some of those in positions of power) that Japan's cause was a righteous one. The pressing need to rebuild the country and prevent it from turning Communist in the immediate post-war years of Cold War confrontation understandably concentrated Japan's collective mind on the exigencies of the present, leaving little room for a postmortem on their ill-fated Asian conquest.

But even after political stability and economic success were achieved, little was done to face up to history and repair Japan's damaged relationships with its neighboring countries. While Germany did its utmost to demonstrate its contrition and develop normal, equal relationships with the countries it had occupied or been at war with, Japan's post-war leaders and the population at large effectively glossed over their mainland Asia experience, tainted as it was with the shame of defeat. The legacy of this emotional neglect and refusal to acknowledge wartime atrocities is a lingering regional dislike for and suspicion of Japan at a time when Japan can ill afford it.

China's inexorable rise as a major new world power confronts Japan with perhaps its greatest challenge since the end of the Second World War. But China, with its juggernaut tactics and authoritarian rule has yet to earn the credentials to be Asia's leader. By rights, that role belongs to Japan, with its more than half a century of democratic rule, successful economy, and generally exemplary observance of international laws and treaties. Unfortunately, failure to confront its past and recent nationalistic stirrings have complicated its efforts to be seen as Asia's most trustworthy and deserving major power. Its reluctant diplomacy does not help either.

Of course, Japan's leaders are well aware of these and other issues bedeviling their nation. Indeed, there have been repeated indications, these past few years, of political acknowledgment of the need both to inspire the young and to improve the country's regional and world standing. But the manner in which these matters are being approached has raised eyebrows both in Japan and elsewhere.

Japan has failed to capitalize on its undoubted economic and social accomplishments and peaceful policies over the past sixty years and make them a linchpin for a more truly open, trust-inspiring internationalist vision. Instead, Japan's ruling elite in recent years has been chasing after some kind of purification of the national soul by instilling "patriotism" in the nation's young and glorifying the country's history and culture. At the same time, persistent efforts are being made to amend Article 9 of its pacifist "American-imposed" constitution, enacted in 1947, which forbids the maintenance of military forces and the use of war to settle disputes. This provision has long since been undermined by the creation of a sizable Self-Defense Force. The ruling Liberal Democratic Party's plan to legitimize the status of its armed forces by amending the constitution faces vehement resistance from the political opposition and has caused considerable unease in Korea and China.

To most observers such an agenda must seem puzzling, even perverse. But there is much in Japan's culture and history to suggest that its present course is very much in character. Japan has always been an insular society, both in geographic fact and from what we might call conditioned inclination. From the early seventeenth to the middle nineteenth centuries, it completely isolated itself from the world, not permitting anyone to leave or enter the country. Until 1945 it had never been invaded, defeated, or occupied. Its social and political institutions were substantially home-grown. The introduction of Western science and governing systems in the late nineteenth century were desperate measures necessitated by foreign pressure and in any case given a distinctly Japanese twist. The ultimate goal was always to preserve the "unique" Japanese way and identity substantially intact.

In that sense, current efforts to revitalize Japanese society by turning inward and to the past rather than outward and to the future could be said to be in line with the historic pattern. Japan's general direction is largely regressive, with an emphasis on flag and obedience that seems curiously out of step with today's world.

Will the efforts succeed? The endemic docility of the electorate would suggest that, as always, it will continue to rubber stamp anything their leaders decide to do. But the conservative leadership can no longer ignore the political opposition, which vehemently resists any slide back to the past and now controls the House of Councilors—which, along with the House of Representatives constitutes the

National Diet of Japan, the nation's parliament. In addition there are social forces at work, which in time may yet lead to the dinosaurs' demise: a new generation of Japanese whose independent (or merely freewheeling) lifestyle is at sharp variance with the official line that demands a return to traditional values. But unless these dissidents join the political discourse to confront the country's sclerotic leadership, there is little chance of fundamental change.

All of these issues collide in this book's subject, the post-war part of Japan's sixty-three-year long Showa era and its challenging, often tumultuous, ongoing aftermath. Showa began in 1926, when Hirohito became emperor, but it is the latter two-thirds of the era, ending with his death in 1989, that is relevant for this analysis—not only because it is, without doubt, the formative period of today's Japan but also because I didn't arrive in Japan until 1950, and I chose to make my observations largely from a personal perspective.

This book explores some of the social changes and accompanying "moods" that have occurred in Japan over the past half-century. During this time, Japan went through five more-or-less distinct periods: reconstruction (until 1960), economic growth (the 1960s and 1970s), high growth leading to a spectacular price bubble (the 1980s), the collapse of the bubble followed by deflation and extensive restructuring (1989 to 2003), and the still-continuing economic upturn, accompanied by an apparent revival of nationalistic sentiments.

We begin in Part One with an evaluation of first two of these periods: post-war reconstruction and the following era of economic growth. The current nostalgia for the whole of that period is examined in some detail.

Part Two focuses more specifically on the hubris that brought about the 1980s bubble economy, with its wild spending and excesses in every field, and the calamitous effects of its collapse, coinciding with the death of the Showa emperor in 1989. Then follows, in Part Three, a detailed discussion of conditions in the country around 2002, as Japan worked to recover from the decade-old bust. This part is based on extensive first-hand research and interviews with over one hundred Japanese.

The concluding section, Part Four, scrutinizes present conditions in Japan as it agonizes over how to meet the serious challenges it faces. The relevance of the "Showa nostalgia" to present concerns is examined, as are the country's recent nationalistic leanings.

The book ends on a note of caution: that self-absorption has its price. Unless Japan attends to some serious, and to me self-evident, "unfinished business," it will do a disservice to its future generations and miss what may well prove to be its last chance to fulfill its destiny as a major player in Asia and, indeed, on the world stage.

I do not pretend to know what is "best for Japan"—only the Japanese can and should address that question. But given Japan's vast importance as one of the world's economic superpowers and its strategic position in the fast-growing East Asian region, its political direction and social health are matters of huge concern to all of us.

Part One
A Showa Perspective

As we have seen, Showa is the name of the reign of Japan's previous emperor, Hirohito. The Showa era began in 1926 with his accession to the Chrysanthemum Throne at the age of twenty-five and ended sixty-three years later, on January 7, 1989, when he died at the age of eighty-seven. The Common or Christian era is a division of time fairly widely used in Japan, but most Japanese are more comfortable with their nation's own traditional and still dominant system of naming and numbering the years for the reign of the incumbent emperor. Thus, 1945 was "Showa 20," and 1985 was "Showa 60."

It is said that Hirohito (referred to posthumously as the Emperor Showa) personally chose the name by which his reign was to be known: Showa, "Enlightened Peace." The Showa era turned out to be the most momentous, calamitous, successful, and glamorous period in the modern history of Japan. The formative era of modern Japan, it was a period in which the nation went from fledgling democracy to military dictatorship to a disastrous war and from there, at an ever more dizzying pace, to the exalted position of the world's second largest economy.

Post-war Showa is now honored as much in nostalgic memory as it is in new, deliberate efforts to reshape Japanese society into some kind of amalgam of Showa values, globalization, and certain pre-Showa conceptions of nationhood and national identity.

Looking back today at the 1950s through the mid-1970s—what might be called quintessential Showa—the era seems to have acquired a sepia coloring, a character that is both distinct in time and not a little quaint. The contrasts with today's Japan can hardly be exaggerated. Intimate neighborhoods and low-rise office blocks have made way for spectacular, large-scale urban developments, which have catapulted Tokyo and several other Japanese cities into the front ranks of architectural importance in the world. Neighborhood shopping has been largely replaced by supermarkets, huge malls, and department stores. Dusty country roads are now major highways, and urban sprawl has obliterated hundreds, perhaps thousands, of once-rural or semi-rural communities.

These are exciting and impressive accomplishments. But to a Western observer the cost in terms of the lost quality of life—life on a human scale—seems disproportionately high, especially in the cities. Of course, Europe and America have not stayed put either—but in none of the five advanced countries on four continents I have lived in during the intervening years has the physical transformation been as sweeping as in Japan. In the cities, a house more than thirty or forty years old is unusual, and the few noteworthy buildings remaining from the Meiji (1868–1912), Taisho (1912–1926), and early Showa eras have become protected relics. It is only a slight exaggeration to say that most Japanese cities—Tokyo foremost—are essentially new creations, which have sprung up since I left in 1974.

The countryside, too, has experienced massive change. As a consequence of half a century of relentless industrialization and urban sprawl, rural areas have virtually disappeared from many coastal regions.

Yet the Japanese people seem to have taken the drastic makeover of their cities and much of their countryside in their stride, rarely openly lamenting what was lost. Perhaps the venerable temple complexes of Kyoto, Nara, and elsewhere and the local shrines and temples and surviving farmhouses up and down the country make up for the lack of a richer patrimony, not to mention the steady supply of films and television costume dramas showing what Showa and pre-Showa Japan was like.

But I am not sure. The discontinuity in the tangible living environment is bound to affect one's identity and must be especially hard on older people. The palpable longing of many sensitive Japanese for Europe's traditional low-rise urban vistas, with their long history and incomparable artistic and architectural heritage (a longing that was nurtured in the 1920s during Japan's brief experience with democracy and a more internationalist outlook) suggests a need that the homeland can no longer satisfy. State-of-the-art developments such as Tokyo's trendy Roppongi Hills, Fukuoka's Canal City, or the spectacular Kyoto Station complex leave visitors awestruck. But they fail to arouse deep feelings.

On the other hand, the absence of an old urban heartland to care for and muse on also frees the country to face its future with a progressive mindset. When design and technology are not held back by the demands of conservation, society may well benefit in terms of greater comfort and efficiency.

Is the trade-off a good one? Most Japanese would probably not want to waste time trying to answer a rhetorical question like that. Considering the what-ifs of life or bemoaning the mistakes or misfortunes of the past does not easily fit the Japanese psyche, which is more attuned to dealing with the actuality of the present. Looking back nostalgically to the past, as is now the case with the Showa era, however, is a different matter. The Japanese are a surprisingly *sentimental* people.

Chapter 1

Japan's Golden Age

In spite of the era's official start date, most Japanese tend to equate the term *Showa* with the latter two-thirds of Hirohito's long reign, the period after 1945, when their defeated nation embarked belatedly on the road to peace and progress. It is that benign image of the Showa Era—the Showa of hard work, clear goals, unparalleled economic success and regained national pride embedded in pacifist ideals—that comes to mind when they think of Showa.

This period is widely regarded as Japan's "Golden Age"—an era of great achievements and unprecedented world stature. Some American commentators at the time even predicted that the twenty-first century would be the Japanese century.

Since then, Showa has come to stand for all that was good and decent and secure about Japan before the bursting of the great speculative bubble of the late 1980s confronted its people with new and harsh realities—at just about the time that Hirohito passed from the scene. It was, in a double sense, the end of an era.

That, in the long run, the ruinous crash of property and stock values that marked the end of this bubble economy in the late 1980s and early 1990s might turn out to have been a necessary alert to help prepare Japan for the unvarnished facts of globalization has not been widely appreciated, and it is beside the point anyway. Nostalgia breeds on perception, not fact.

For the Showa era has become for many Japanese an object of nostalgia, even veneration. Some of those too young to have personal memories of the period find it evocative of an attractive "mood" even as they seek to distance themselves from their parents' values in their own lives. The faddish popularity of 1960s and 1970s retro fashions is one expression of this fascination.

Older people remember early post-war Showa with affection for its small pleasures, its family cohesion, the sense that life could only get better. It is remembered for low-rise cities, streetcars, princess skirts, and wild rivers before they were dammed and lined with concrete. Showa was when you ate dinner at low tables, seated on *tatami* mats, and endured the summer heat in your starched cotton kimono with the help of electric fans and shaved ice, while listening to the shrilling of the cicadas or the chirping of the crickets. For the breadwinner, Sundays on the golf course were his only chance to get away. Holidays were not taken. Bonuses were saved, not spent. Showa was about dedication and hope. Showa was about achievement and the fruits of hard work: undreamed-of prosperity and worldwide recognition.

Showa was also about manners and consideration. You didn't eat or attend to your makeup in public, and if you owned a car, you dimmed your lights when you stopped at the traffic signal as a courtesy to oncoming drivers. On the sidewalk, you made way for others.

The ugly side of Showa—air pollution, hideously overcrowded trains, inhumanly long working hours, substandard housing, chronic political corruption—is not part of the Showa nostalgia, except when caught in artistic black-and-white photographs. Even the life of the emperor who gave the era its name is not really part of it, for "Showa" is not about a person. It is about a feeling.

Perhaps, in the final analysis, the memory of Showa is the memory of youth—that vital phase of life when you discover that beauty can be found in little things, and that friendship and togetherness and personal discipline can yield great rewards. The way youth should be, and mostly was, but, in a world awash with gadgets and television and ready-made entertainment, so seldom is anymore. It is also the memory of belonging—to a family and an employer and a firm social structure, all for life. That security too has gone.

In 2007, the enduring significance of Showa was permanently enshrined in the nation's consciousness with the introduction of a new national holiday, Showa Day. The only other emperor similarly honored was Meiji, Hirohito's highly influential grandfather. Repurposed as Culture Day after the post-war adoption of Japan's new constitution, this national holiday marked both Meiji's birthday and the era—and constitution—he represented.

But few Japanese today will still think of Emperor Meiji or the Meiji era when they enjoy Culture Day as a welcome day off work. By contrast, Showa Day honors an era that most Japanese remember and cherish. In the following chapter we will assess the significance of this new holiday.

A Personal Perspective

I was born in the seventh year of Showa, 1932, and arrived in Japan in 1950, five years after military control of Japan ended. I was there when, in 1953, Emperor Showa passed my office in a boxy limousine. And thirty-six years later I was on hand after his death to place my signature "as an objective witness" in the register at the Tokyo Imperial Palace, which had been opened within hours of his passing to enable the public to offer their condolences. I left Japan in 1974, but returned fifteen times thereafter, until I once again became a resident in 2003.

Though a Westerner, I am in some ways as much a product of Showa as my Japanese contemporaries. Many of the thoughts and images presented here betray this particular conditioning, this tendency to see things as if through Japanese eyes. I do not consider this an achievement or even a special talent. It is merely the way I felt as a young man, and there are moments even now when this old sensitivity suddenly reasserts itself, and I am once again back in the sober but warm cocoon of those long-gone days of Showa.

The New Urban Lifestyle

The Showa era visibly and permanently altered both the people and the geography of Japan. For most of post-war Showa, say until the mid-1970s, the national focus was on production for export. Consumption and personal comfort had to be postponed. Prestige projects such as the 1964 Tokyo Olympics and the 1970 Osaka Expo did necessitate some very intrusive urban surgery. However, wholesale demolition of old housing to make way for modern apartment blocks and the construction of new business districts did not really take off until the mid-1970s, when Prime Minister Kakuei Tanaka launched an ambitious nationwide construction program. The government provided the financing for massive infrastructure projects, while the banks were permitted, for the first time, to make available personal mortgages to the rising middle classes.

Showa laid the foundation for a constant quest for the newest and the most innovative that has become a national characteristic. Like much of the world, Japan remade itself during the past fifty years: from rural to urban, from part of nature to self-perceived master of the natural world. But in contrast to most of Europe and North America, resistance to the destruction of familiar neighborhoods and venerable city centers was hardly ever an issue.

While nurturing an apparently inescapable nostalgia for the lost "mood" of Showa, *materially* the Japanese have shown a remarkable readiness not to linger over what will never return. In modern Japan, newness is prized more than venerable age. The forces of conservation and thoughtful planning have been too weak to resist the government's pork barrel projects or the commercial schemes of the developers, who for their part not only found a ready market but could always count on the "understanding" of the bureaucrats and politicians—at a price—

whenever zoning regulations loomed as potential obstacles. The result is a society that has relegated the remains of its visible past to the confines of museums and temples, while savoring to the full the thrill of high-tech, high-rise, high-fashion, high-speed living.

Not everyone, though, has the money to participate in the life of that new Japan. As the twenty-first century approaches the end of its first decade, the world-brand boutiques of Tokyo's many high-class retail quarters are doing a roaring business catering to the expensive tastes of the burgeoning numbers of the newly rich. But for an increasing segment of the population, it is not shopping at the Ginza or selecting a new state-of-the-art apartment that occupies their minds. It is the struggle to make a living in a society that is a far cry from the more egalitarian ideals of Showa. Either way, it is not surprising that many Japanese feel nostalgic for those more innocent days of Showa.

But was Showa really that wonderful? Or is there perhaps a tendency to idealize an era that—while seemingly safe and solid—actually bore the seeds of future problems?

To understand the true import of Showa, it needs to be scrutinized through the unclouded prism of Heisei—Showa's unruly successor, now two decades old. In the chapters that follow we will examine the impact that the Showa era—and its aftermath—has had on various aspects of Japanese society.

Chapter 2

The Real Significance of the
Showa Celebrations

When Japan's National Holiday Law was promulgated in 1948, at a time when the country was still groaning under the aftermath of its lost war, it declared nine national holidays, perhaps to bring some cheer into the gloom. Today Japan has fifteen national holidays, more than any other advanced country. It's as if Japan wants to prove to itself and the world that, as the world's second-largest economic power, it can afford to give its workers some extra days off. (Actually, for most workers these national holidays are the *only* days they get off during the year, as the annual vacations they are entitled to are rarely taken.)

For those curious what all these holidays are, here is the list: New Year's Day, the current Emperor's Birthday, Greenery Day, the Spring and Autumn Equinoxes, and separate holidays variously honoring Children, Coming-of-Age, Labor, the Aged, the Constitution; the (mythical) date of the Nation's Founding, Culture, the Ocean, and Health and Sports. The fifteenth holiday was added in 2007. It's the one called Showa Day, and it falls on April 29, replacing Greenery Day, which has been moved to another date.

It is this new holiday that is of special interest in the context of our analysis. As provided by the National Holiday Law, April 29 originally was a holiday celebrating the birthday of the Showa emperor, Hirohito. After his death in 1989, the date remained a national holiday but was renamed Greenery Day. Not until 2007 was its reference to Showa reinstated, which is of considerable symbolic significance. It undoubtedly reflects the importance and sense of nostalgia that the Japanese people in general attach to the historical period represented by that emperor's reign, especially its post-war part. On another level, it could be seen as the government's way of implicitly treating the entire Showa era—from 1926 to 1989—as an integral and honorable whole, thereby effectively exonerating the Showa emperor and those who acted in his name from any lasting guilt or blame for the acts of war for which they are still held responsible in certain foreign and domestic circles. As we have seen, these acts include the invasion of China and the atrocities committed there, the occupation of most of Southeast Asia in the 1930s and 1940s, and, of course, the surprise attack on Pearl Harbor, to name the most serious events.

In addition, the new holiday provides those who seek to reinstill a sense of patriotism and national pride in the younger generation a useful peg to hang the day's lesson on. That lesson could well contain this message: "The Showa era was Japan's Golden Age, when we all worked toward the same goal: Japan's greatness. We must never forget the values that we then held high."

A New Beginning?

In contrast with Showa Day's memorialization of a past seen through rose-colored glasses, in 2005 the sixtieth anniversary of the end of the Second World War in Japan came to represent a different yearning—one for a fresh start. It provided a further impetus to reflective assessment of the whole post-war period against the very different realities of today's Japan.

In Japanese tradition, age sixty represents a full cycle, the completion of one's active life. Sixty was the age at which men formally retired, not only from employment but also from the headship of the extended family, yielding their place to the eldest son. This was common practice at a time when three generations typically lived together under the same roof, a tradition that has gradually lapsed during the past two or three decades as families became more mobile and younger people set up their own households. But when the tradition was still observed, the retiring (grand-)father (and his wife) moved to a quiet part of the house to devote himself to his hobbies and perhaps the contemplation of nature. It was not the end of life but a new beginning, a rebirth, symbolized by a red bib or undergarment the man was given to wear when he reached sixty. That charming tradition is still observed, though it is now seldom more than an empty gesture. The "head of the family" concept has been all but abandoned, and retirement at sixty is now seen more as a burden than a privilege.

Yet for the country as a whole that sixtieth anniversary of the war's end was commemorated using the familiar language of a sixty-year cycle: a closure (of the "post-war" era), a time to stop talking (and apologizing) about the past, a new beginning. Apart from numerous column inches and TV programs devoted to the subject, the mood was made concrete by persistent government-sponsored efforts to remove any references to "atrocities" committed by Japan's wartime military from school textbooks and, somewhat belatedly, by ex–prime minister Abe's patriotic policies centering on the revision of the constitution and the image of a "beautiful Japan," as discussed elsewhere in this book.

There was more than a tinge of dualism in this approach: the bygone Showa era was held up as an icon, while the government stressed the need for a new beginning. A new beginning...or a coming of age? In some ways the hothouse conditions of the Showa boom had dulled the nation into a false sense of invulnerability. The harsher post-Showa environment has been a wake-up call to a less certain future, a future that has proved to be far more competitive, diverse, insecure and unpredictable than the preceding era. As in personal life, it is the classic and inevitable road to full maturity. But as we shall see in the course of our examination, Japan may not be adequately prepared to face these new challenges.

As for a day to remember the war, well, the end of World War II naturally evokes very different associations in Japan than it does in Western countries where it is celebrated for the victory it was. Although it arguably represented "liberation" for the Japanese people—from the bombs, the bloody battles, the rule of generals, and the lack of food—it is the overtones of defeat and destruction that dominate the nation's collective memory.

Most Japanese have tried hard all their lives to "forget" the shameful day the war ended, rather than commemorate it for whatever reason. Perhaps this explains the dearth of national war memorials in Japan, apart from the many monuments on Okinawa dedicated to the bloody battles fought there toward the end of the war, and a number of small, poignant memorials to the young kamikaze pilots, located in or near the bases from which they took off on their one-way journeys.

Of course, there is the Yasukuni Shrine in Tokyo, a perennial center of controversy because of its enshrinement of convicted war criminals, its narrowly patriotic interpretation of the war in the adjoining museum, and its cozy relations with the far right. The official war memorial at Chidorigafuchi, near Tokyo's Imperial Palace, is a secular monument to Japan's "unknown soldier" free from such taints, but its ceremonies are low key and it is still relatively unknown to the general public.

Rather than the end of the war, it is the war's greatest twin calamities, the destruction of Hiroshima and Nagasaki by atom bombs in August 1945, that are remembered each year, not with a national holiday but with solemn ceremonies. With an instant combined death toll of 160,000 that eventually rose to 300,000, it was by far the greatest single act of carnage against civilians of the war. Most historians, including many Japanese, agree that the bombs effectively ended the war, and thereby saved perhaps millions of lives that might have been lost if the conflict had led to a bloody invasion of the Japanese main islands. Others argue that the end would have come soon anyway, as Japan had run out of vital supplies. Either way, the atom bombings can in no way be compared in evil intent to the deliberately planned enormity of the holocaust, where in Auschwitz alone over a million Jews were systematically exterminated.

Yet the bitter fact remains that the Japanese were singled out as the first and only target of a nuclear device—not once, but twice in the span of three days. It is the second bomb, believed by many to have been "totally unnecessary," even more than the first, that many Japanese find impossible to forgive. In the minds of many, the atom bombing of their country outweighs any and all atrocities committed by Japanese troops in countries occupied by them. Such reasoning obviously is no consolation to the countries concerned, nor can one atrocity justify another. But the atom bombs certainly helped turn the Japanese into committed pacifists, which is why the proposed revision of the constitution to legitimize the existence of military forces has been meeting such opposition over the years.

Back to A-Class Status

It is possible to contend that—in the eyes of the international community, at least—Japan's new beginning took place long before the sixtieth anniversary of the Second World War. The greatest national events of post-war Showa were not only national but also global milestones: the 1964 Tokyo Olympics, the Expo 70 in Osaka, and the Sapporo Winter Olympics of 1972.

The 1964 Olympics changed the face of Tokyo and provided the impetus for the construction of the high-speed Shinkansen railway system. It has been called the "coming of age ceremony" of post-war Japan. No doubt it helped repair the country's wounded pride and confidence, and marked its return to the ranks of advanced, peaceful nations. In a country always concerned with how it is perceived in Western eyes, it was perhaps not strange for me to be asked repeatedly whether I thought the Olympics had restored Japan's position to the ranks of the world's "A-class nations." I readily assured my interlocutors that such was the case, although I never did find out who was in charge of the ranking.

There was one major Olympic shock for Japan: their failure to win a gold medal in judo, that quintessential Japanese sport that had become an Olympic sport in time for the Tokyo games. Anton Geesink, a tall Dutchman, walked away with that honor, reducing his Japanese adversaries to a state of utter incomprehension. But even this setback did not manage to spoil the party.

In keeping with the world exposition philosophy, Expo 70, held near Osaka, was a showcase for Japan's and the world's latest technologies as well as a stage for national cultural achievements. It was the first large-scale international fair held on Japanese soil, and during its six-month run attracted an astounding 65 million visitors, including half a million from overseas.

The Sapporo Winter Olympics were another milestone in Japan's impressive march toward full membership in the world's top club. Japan made a clean sweep of the medals in the normal hill ski jumping event—including their first Winter Olympic gold ever.

If Hiroshima and Nagasaki represent the nadir of Japan's modern history, the two Olympics and Expo 70 mark its zenith. Together they stand for Showa, as treasured examples of Japan's phenomenal achievements.

Chapter 3

Picture Postcard Showa

Remote villages—
Have the storms still to reach you
Deep in the mountains?

— SOUCHOU (1448–1532)

The poignant lyricism of Souchou's haiku cannot fail to touch the heartstrings of those who knew the Japan of the 1950s and 1960s. The time when most roads were still unpaved, the mountains were alive with the twitter of birds in their mixed forests, and rivers had banks where wildflowers grew and children chased butterflies.

For post-war Showa's early years bore little resemblance to the harried economic boom many associate with this era. Instead, they were relatively quiet and austere, a time when Japan's exactingly spare traditional values were central in everyday life.

The storms unleashed by the construction and reforestation lobbies characteristic of Showa's progress imperative were yet to come. Nature was unaware of the approaching assault on her hegemony: the fortification of shorelines and river banks, the damming of most rivers, the violation of her ancient landscape with roads and tunnels and concrete walls where once there were slopes that drained themselves. She did not know that many of her deciduous forests were to be cut to make way for uniform plantings of fast-growing conifers, to simplify forest maintenance (in a country covered by mountains on 70 percent of its surface) while at the same time satisfying the increasing demand for wood used in traditional house building. But the conifers would snuff out much wildlife and cause a pollen hazard for people all over the islands, a problem that would persist long after the market for timber would decline sharply due to the switch from wooden houses to multistory apartment buildings.

Traveling by Shinkansen bullet train from Tokyo to Fukuoka today, a distance of over 620 miles (1000 kilometers), the view of contiguous human habitation is seldom relieved by a burst of lush vegetation or a stretch of uninterrupted farmland. Zoning laws seem to be honored largely in the breach. Only the unassailable presence of mountains along the way guarantee the occasional caress for the eyes, with Mt. Fuji still reigning supreme, contemptuous of the urban sprawl lapping at its foothills.

The view of Mt. Fuji across Lake Kawaguchi, in Showa days enhanced by the graceful turrets of the old Fuji View Hotel, is now stabbed by the unfortunate concrete pile that has replaced it. The old Fuji View was one of my favorite destinations in the 1960s and 1970s. It had the ambience and style of a European mountain resort hotel, with a swimming pool, tennis courts, wide terraces, and lawns dotted with deck chairs and parasols. Inside there were spacious lounges and quiet corners for reading, writing and playing board games. Affluent families from Tokyo, both Japanese and Western, would spend part of their summer here. There is little left of that atmosphere in the present building, but then, the concept of a "resort hotel" itself seems to have vanished from these shores.

A recent stay at a hotel in the mountains beyond Nikko brought this home to me. The building itself and its lakeside location can hardly be faulted, but apart from a small lounge the hotel strangely offers none of the amenities of a resort hotel, even though it advertises itself as such. It even lacks a terrace, a ping-pong table or some lazy chairs under the trees. No chance of a relaxed resort life here, whatever the brochures claim. What the hotel does offer is plenty of deep bows whenever you exit from, or return to, its hallowed serenity.

In spite of late Showa's legacy of constant change, the history and love of the natural world that predated it can still be found throughout Japan. One particular marvel of the Japanese landscape is the way old buildings (temples, shrines, and the surviving farmhouses and feudal castles) blend with the natural attractions. Many of these structures have been preserved, shrines and temples in particular. Benefiting from favorable tax laws and the traditional support of their communities, they have, by and large, managed to maintain their time-honored appearance amid the hotchpotch of tasteless, forgettable buildings that have irretrievably replaced the old neighborhoods to suit human need—and greed.

Some old towns have done a splendid job in preserving traditional storehouses and residences. Most of Kyoto is, of course, a living museum of traditional building styles. Among other noteworthy surviving structures are Himeji's "White Heron" castle in Hyogo prefecture and Hasedera, a seventh-century temple near Nara, famed for its cherry blossoms and tree peonies. Kurashiki, a small town not far from Himeji, has carefully preserved its old storehouses known as *kura* from the days when it was an important rice-trading center. The kura, a solid, largely fireproof structure with thick, mud walls, was used for storing a trader's inventory or a wealthy family's treasures, which were not safe in the traditional wooden houses. Examples of the once ubiquitous kura are now increasingly hard to find.

In the more remote areas, there are still lovely sights to behold. The morning mists have not ceased rising from the Azusa River in the Japan Alps; the grand vista from near Nikko that includes the Kegon Falls and Lake Chuzenji has changed little, and the cherry blossoms of Mt. Yoshino continue to burst forth every spring in their four-stage splendor as they have for centuries, although the dirt roads taking you up were paved long ago.

The long, wide beach of Kujukurihama in Chiba prefecture is another story. On any summer day, you will find it packed with surfers and sun worshippers, but when I visited it in August of 1955 it was a lonely stretch of sand. The only time that the beach burst into action was when the fishing boats returned with their catch and half the village ran out to help haul in the nets. The happy shouts of the women—some topless—revealed as much their delight at seeing all those jumping fish as their joy at having their menfolk safely home. And I saw an old man gleefully take a bite out of a fish he plucked from the teeming net!

I have not been back to the Kofu area in decades, but I doubt if I would still find a horse and buggy waiting at the Shosenkyo Gorge entrance to take me around. As for the roaring whirlpools of the Naruto Strait between Awaji and Shikoku—they are still there, but they have lost their mystery now that a giant bridge spans the channel where once there were only seabirds and the ghosts of shipwrecked sailors.

But proof of Japan's age-old bond with nature is embodied by the expert gardeners who look after the grounds of temples, restaurants, city parks, and museum precincts, and the millions of Japanese who lovingly tend their private plots, often of minuscule size. There are also the nature reserves and the many volunteer organizations striving to protect, if belatedly, what is left of the country's natural bounty.

Together they attest to the stubborn spirit of responsible conservation and respect for growing things pitted against the juggernaut of massive public works and destructive private schemes. It is a spirit that is needed more than ever before.

Sweet Memories of Discomfort

The beauties of early Showa may not all have been lost in vain.

The paving of virtually every country road has blissfully ended the scourge of fine dust that blanketed every house along them. Summer traveling on such roads in the 1950s was a challenge. We used to quickly roll up the windows of our non-air-conditioned cars each time an oncoming or passing car enveloped us in a dense white cloud. What's more, the cross-rutted surfaces of some of these country lanes made traveling along them resemble riding an abacus, and broken springs was the frequent result.

When I Discovered Earplugs...

Tokyo, summer 1962. That barking dog! It tears the Sunday calm and the peace of the evenings to shreds with its incessant, high-pitched yapping and howling, right across the narrow road from my study. If only I had an air cooler in the room, I could turn it up high and drown out the noise. But I must keep the windows open for a whiff of a breeze in this unbearably hot and muggy weather. The poor mutt can't help it. Day and night it is tethered to a stake in the corner of the garden, right by the roadside, under a little sloping roof that gives it scant protection from the elements. Its short chain leash severely restricts its movements. It's cruel in the extreme and all the more remarkable as the dog's owner's son is a well-known veterinarian. My wife says we have no right to interfere—and no one else seems to be bothered by it. But it's been going on for weeks!

A week later. On my insistence, my wife finally crossed the street to complain. It wasn't an easy errand: the dog's owner, a rather reclusive lady of noble lineage, is the sister of our landlord. She was predictably defensive but in the end accepted my wife's suggestion to move the poor animal to the other side of the house, on a longer leash. Of course, keeping dogs in the house is not done in Japan.

Two weeks later. For a while, the barking did not stop, although it was more distant. Now it has ceased. Today my wife went over to express her appreciation. "I gave the dog away," said the lady grumpily. "It was too old to learn."

My sense of guilt is tempered by the hope that the dog is happier now. And by the balm of its departure to my frayed nerves.

Another annoyance during the summers of mid-Showa was the insects—mosquitoes, midges, and flies especially. They guaranteed an abundant bird life, but they surely were a nuisance. Nets and screens kept you reasonably protected against the mosquitoes, and there was always the green incense coil known as *katorisenko* to rely on, although its fumes gave you a hoarse throat. Small restaurants and watering holes made short shrift of flies with the help of spiral flypapers drooping stickily from the ceiling. They killed more than the flies, though—the sight of dozens of wriggling black things caught in the glue was enough to kill your appetite, too.

Strangely, though, even these memories of discomfort and routine suffering only feed the nostalgia for those bygone days. For with better roads came the tourists and the developers, and the sense of discovery and of, let's say, "the virtuousness of endurance" was lost forever. Wealth and technology have spread, but the storms of progress have left their indelible mark.

Chapter 4

Urban Vistas, Urban Life

The recent changes that have made Japan's countryside all but unrecognizable are nothing compared to what has happened to its cities. One never ceases to be amazed by the breathtaking dynamism and sheer exuberance of Japan's continuous urban rejuvenation. To a conservative European, the readiness with which old quarters are razed to make way for new schemes sometimes seems to border on recklessness, but Japan's urbanites take it all in their stride.

Of the fourteen different houses and apartments I lived in during my first twenty-four years in Japan—most of better than average quality—only three are still standing. Two—both in the Kobe area—were destroyed in the 1995 Great Hanshin Earthquake. All the others were demolished to make way for new structures as part of the relentless building boom that gripped the country in the 1960s and that has not let up since.

In the major cities, whole neighborhoods have succumbed to the wreckers' ball, to make room for office blocks, apartment complexes, shopping malls, and urban plazas, or to allow for the widening of thoroughfares. Although most of the demolished structures were arguably of low quality—built in a hurry in the aftermath of wartime bombings or natural disasters—the renewal fever also touched many intact, traditional neighborhoods and individual buildings of high architectural merit or relatively recent vintage.

Among the more noteworthy victims of compulsive redevelopment were the numerous Western-style buildings of Tokyo's Marunouchi business district, built in the late nineteenth and early twentieth centuries. Reflecting the evolving architectural tastes of Europe and the United States, from Victorian and Edwardian red brick to the columned classical structures beloved of the Chicago and New York financial establishment, collectively they provided a solid core to the city's changing appearance.

The twin catastrophes of the 1923 earthquake and the fire bombings of 1945 had razed much of the capital. The survival—reasonably unscathed—of the Marunouchi district was not only a boon but perhaps also a consolation to the shaken morale of post-war Japan. From 1954 to 1956, I worked in one of these low-rise "London-style" buildings, the Naka 8th Building. As our offices were on the raised ground floor, I do not recall if there was an elevator. There was certainly no air conditioning, except in the glass-enclosed office of my boss, who luxuriated in the cool breeze produced by an imported American window unit, while the rest of us sweated it out in the trenches. The area indeed had the feel of London's Lombard Street, on which it was modeled, and a lunchtime stroll along its wide, tree-lined streets never failed to revive our dusty spirits.

The tearing down of this venerable quarter, although superficially lamented, did not really encounter any serious protest, public or otherwise. It was no doubt seen as an unavoidable step in the larger march of Japan's progress—not to mention the salutary effect on the financial fortunes of the Mitsubishi group, which owned most of the land in the area. The demolition in 1968 of Frank Lloyd Wright's Tokyo landmark, the Imperial Hotel just outside Marunouchi, did attract vehement objections, but they came mostly from abroad—including a dramatic last-minute effort to save the building by Wright's widow—and proved ineffectual. The high commercial value of the site and reports of subsidence following the 1923 earthquake clinched the argument against conservation.

Among Wright's indirect legacy is the work of his associate, Antonin Raymond (1888–1976) who, after assisting Wright with the Imperial Hotel, started his own practice and designed a large number of noteworthy buildings and residences in Japan. From 1962 to 1972 my wife and I lived in one of Raymond's early 1930s houses. Its low ceilings, built-in furniture, and generous use of wood betrayed the Wright influence. Leaving this beloved house and garden, with its towering cedars, gorgeous rhododendrons, and Japanese iris pond, was heartbreaking to me, and I could hardly bear hearing, some years later, that the house was demolished in the 1970s to make room for two new ones. In the greedy gaze of the property developer, nothing is sacred.

But the loss of a beloved building is not out of the ordinary for those who have spent time in Japan in the past fifty years. In fact, many of my friends have had similar experiences, with some searching years later for an old address and finding not only the house gone but in some cases the street as well, the result of major rezoning of a city quarter.

One of the few major pre-war buildings in the capital is Tokyo Station, still one of Tokyo's main transportation hubs, its distinctive red-brick-and-stone facade and cupolas a stubborn holdout among the glass-and-steel behemoths crowding it from all sides. This pleases me and my fellow Dutchmen no end, as persistent rumor has it that its design—by Tatsuno Kingo—was inspired by

Amsterdam's Central Station. This is disputed, but the resemblance is undeniable, whatever the skeptics say.

As in the countryside, the 1950s and 1960s saw the paving of most city streets, and, of course, the repair of major thoroughfares badly damaged by the bombings. In the early 1950s, many streets in urban residential areas were still unpaved, as was, for example, the sloping approach to the Kiyomizu Temple in Kyoto.

Even my local railroad station in Kobe was surrounded by gravel—but then some of the trains passing through it were pulled by steam engines. I recall the nightly drone of those long-distance trains with mixed feelings. The train tracks were a scant ten yards (ten meters) away from my front door, so it was hard to get a good night's sleep. But the wailing whistles lent a plaintive touch to the winter nights, which somehow made up for the lost shut-eye.

The late 1950s and 1960s also saw a huge expansion in public housing known as *danchi*, with whole new towns arising along the many private railroads fanning out from the large cities. These apartment blocks were an improvement over the often poor quality of some of the post-war housing stock, but they were cramped and very basic. Gas heaters soon replaced charcoal fires, which produced lethal fumes, but the heaters formed a greater fire hazard and often proved deadly when the gas supply was interrupted, as frequently happened. The result was numerous deaths each year—including two of my friends, one an Englishman, the other American. Electric fires sometimes took the place of gas stoves, but they gave little heat and electricity was even more expensive than gas.

A niftier solution was found in Japan's traditional *hori-gotatsu*, a one-yard-square, half-a-yard deep depression in the tatami floor, with a low square table placed over it. You dangled your feet in the hole, which had a small electric heater hidden in it. (The earlier version used charcoal.) A quilt covered the assembled thighs to keep the heat trapped. The result was swollen feet and freezing backs—and a general reluctance to move. Some of the houses I lived in featured this facility. I loved it—for its coziness and warmth and the opportunity it offered to, well, really get to know your table partners.

The Showa Prosperity

The firebombing of 1945 had reduced large parts of Tokyo to ashes. Reconstruction, which began as soon as the rubble was cleared, was makeshift at first, aimed simply at providing shelter for the millions who had lost their homes. But as the Showa work ethic of late hours and no holidays caught on and the economy improved, so did the extent and quality of the building projects. By the time I arrived in Japan at the end of 1950, there were no ruins left to be seen, although much of the housing was still substandard, and most streets had empty lots where there had been houses or shops that were yet to be rebuilt.

The preparations for the 1964 Olympics triggered an unprecedented building boom in and around Tokyo. Thoroughfares were widened, elevated toll roads built, and at least half a dozen large new hotels added, including the Okura and the New Otani. And, of course, there was the auspicious introduction, shortly before the Games opened, of the first high-speed Shinkansen train service, linking Tokyo with Osaka. Riding in the driver's cabin on one of the inaugural runs of this state-of-the-art rapid transit system—courtesy of a young railway executive at whose wedding we had officiated—gave me a taste of Japan's unstoppable progress. It was a quintessential Showa experience.

What was especially wonderful about this period was the joy and optimism pervading the air, the widespread construction dust, noise, and inconvenience notwithstanding. All effort was directed at the same goal: to make the Games the greatest ever and show the world what Japan was capable of. Yet this ambitious agenda was refreshingly free from arrogance or boasting. Everyone seemed preoccupied with the task at hand, determined to do a perfect job, content to let the facts speak for themselves.

In the euphoria of the moment the larger picture was sometimes lost sight of. For example, the building of a network of elevated toll roads over existing streets and canals to alleviate the capital's traffic congestion was a thoroughly ill-conceived scheme. I was among the many who hated these concrete monstrosities, not in the least for the permanent gloom they cast over the streets below. The ultimate outrage was the construction of a viaduct right over the Nihonbashi, that historic bridge in central Tokyo from which all distances in the country were measured. It was like building a road over London's Hyde Park Corner or the Île de la Cité in Paris, right in front of the Notre Dame! What's more, the resulting smoother flow of traffic proved short-lived as the new roads attracted even more cars to the inner city.[1]

All this activity reflected a steady improvement in the standard of living. By the early 1960s, the success of Japan's economic policies was beginning to trickle through to the general population. Prime Minister Hayato Ikeda's emphasis on encouraging domestic consumption marked the beginning of Japan's consumer society and the rapid growth of its middle class. After years of frugal living during the latter part of the war and the austerity and twelve-hour workdays of the early post-war period, enjoying life was becoming respectable again.

Tokyo's Ginza district was turned into a "pedestrian heaven" by shutting the roads to cars on Sundays to encourage shopping. The large, fashionable department stores in the area in particular benefited from this arrangement, geared up as they were for customers of every purse. I can't forget the rooftop garden shop of my favorite store, the Takashimaya near Nihonbashji, where rare pet goldfish were swimming around in tanks with price tags pinned to their backs!

Young families' dreams of owning a modest My-Home and My-Car—buzz-words at the time for affordable products with financing provided that enabled the rising (lower) middle class to lift themselves above the bleak conditions that had prevailed thus far—were no longer impossible ambitions. The homemaker colleges were crammed with young women eager to learn dressmaking, flower arrangement, and the tea ceremony, and for those who could afford it, home air conditioning offered welcome relief from the oppressive summer heat.

Increasingly, people with savings began to forsake their traditional dwellings or low-quality post-war homes for newly designed and more comfortable houses that combined Japanese taste with a coveted semi-Western lifestyle. Designer apartment buildings also began to make an entry. One of the first to open in Tokyo had the ambitious name Novus Kingdom. My wife and I inspected it but found it to be a third-rate development built with cheap materials and without "class." We renamed it Bogus Kingdom. It would take several more years before quality of design and construction would find its way into Japan's real estate market.

All in all, urban life improved greatly during the Showa era, much faster than life in the countryside. The result was a steady migration to the cities, which is continuing to this day. Also ongoing is the shift from one-family or small apartment housing to high-rise towers with the consequent loss of neighborhood values and the accompanying social life.

The scope and breadth of urban renewal and expansion during Showa illustrates the determination of politicians and corporate leaders alike to lift the country out of its post-defeat gloom and place it squarely on the road to continued economic growth by any and all means available to them. Conservation of nature and historic buildings was a luxury that was not allowed to impede the march of progress. Raising living standards for the masses was the primary objective, not just as a laudable end in itself but also to ward off any attempt by left-wing political forces to seize power and turn the country into a socialist utopia. This objective—arguably Showa's chief accomplishment—was fully achieved.

In Old Kyoto's Bosom

Kyoto, June 24, 1986. Arrived last night and headed straight for Mr. and Mrs. T.'s traditional sukiya-style residence on Nijo-dori, set in spacious grounds next to the Matsushita property, and close to the Nomura residence, minutes from the Nanzenji Temple. We were warmly welcomed, and after tea in their Western-style reception room, were taken to the Warajiya for an eel-based dinner. It was delicious and very "Kyoto" in its rustic-elegant simplicity. Then back to the house for further conversation and to bed by ten.

Our room opened on to the splendid and well-maintained Japanese gardens, which looked poetic in the steady night rain. Our futons were laid out side by side, in front of the tokonoma, which contained a scroll depicting seasonal ayu fish and a small bizen pottery vase with a sprig of tiny white flowers from the garden.

This morning we woke to a lovely sight: five or six blue flag irises in full bloom, nestled between green shrubs across the pond and the stone bridge. We got dressed and joined Mr. T. for a walk to the beautiful Nanzenji temple, where my wife and I had acted as go-betweens at a friend's wedding in 1961. After that, we had breakfast, and left by ten o'clock.

Chapter 5

A Showa Phenomenon: the "Salaryman"

The natural world and the cities were not the only entities to experience fundamental change during the Showa era. Japan's economy was to surge massively in a charge led by a whole new breed of worker: the salaryman. Every society has its salaried workers, but Showa Japan had its "salarymen." The difference is vast. Hence the special term, coined in Japan. *Sarariman*, singular and plural.

In Europe or America the salaried person is someone of almost any age entering into a written or verbal employment contract that may be revoked by either party, and often is. The Showa-vintage Japanese salaryman on the other hand entered employment straight out of high school or college, for life, with one and the same employer—corporate, financial, or government. In exchange for his absolute loyalty, he could count on steadily increasing pay and position, permanent protection from dismissal, and most importantly, the social status of belonging to a prestigious organization.

In the West, employment usually (though less so now than before) involves little more than the formal working hours, five days a week. Outside these hours employees are their own masters. In Japan, the salaryman surrendered virtually all of his waking hours to his employer, seven days a week, twelve months a year. He surrendered his very soul.

Yet, this strange institution, a modern form of indenture, is now seen as an enduring and, yes, cherished symbol of the Showa era. For it was thanks to the exertions of the salaryman that Japan became a world power. And, of course, to the exertions of its engineers and bureaucrats and teachers and laborers and captains of industry, as well. But mostly because of its salarymen.

What was so good about this system?

Part of its success derived from the emphasis placed on collective effort, involving everyone from the CEO on down. Eschewing the Western-style master-servant relationship, the American "conflict model," and top-down directives, the Japanese working environment was—and still is, largely—characterized by *wa* and its illusion of equality. Wa is usually translated as "harmony," although it is more about ensuring order and maintaining the status quo. To this end, a semblance of classlessness based on a shared identity and the idea that all work was equally valued, was scrupulously cultivated.

In manufacturing companies, the president would don worker's overalls as he made his rounds, executives left their private offices unused in favor of a desk on the work floor, and senior managers made themselves available to officiate at employees' wedding ceremonies. As the bosses had to "work" Sundays entertaining bureaucrats and customers on the golf course, their underlings were equally expected to keep their mind focused on company business over the weekend.

Of course, such an environment left little room for individual identity, nor was such desired. Because he need not worry about losing his job, and was expected to identify himself wholly with his employer's objectives and company culture, the salaryman could usually afford to stop thinking about further personal improvement, except in the technical sense of honing the skills needed to maximize his usefulness to the organization. Loyalty and dedication to the organization's group spirit were more prized than the ability to argue logically or to develop ideas that were deemed "foreign" or too innovative. If he was diligent and did not let his personal character get in the way of the wa of the organization, his career would proceed smoothly. Other than for the top jobs, promotions were based on seniority rather than merit, and his salary—starting very low—would rise steadily.

Their Master's Voice

Tokyo, 1968. From my private office in the Mitsui Life Insurance Building, where the branch bank I run is an important tenant, I enjoy the daily spectacle of the Mitsui Life team of insurance salesmen, twenty or thirty strong, getting ready for the day's work. Shortly after nine o'clock they spill out of the inner offices, where they presumably received a briefing and their sales targets for the day, into the main hall. Here, a superior dispenses a final dose of hyped-up encouragement before telling them to hit the road, beginning a long day of calls on clients and prospects. As they burst through the doors out into the street, shouting warlike slogans and brandishing their fists in unison, they remind me of a baseball team streaming out of the locker rooms ready for battle. I imagine their adrenalin count hitting the ceiling but always wonder how long they can sustain their gung-ho spirit.

The Narrow Options of the Organization Man

From a Western perspective, the enforced uniformity of the Japanese salaryman made him a rather bland companion in social situations. Confronted with a pointed question or verbal challenge from me, he tended to laugh, or compliment me on my deficient Japanese. Or he might reply with a formulaic answer. Of course, at men-only drinking parties all pretence and self-restraint would crumble, but even then drunken teasing and inane games were more likely to take place than the exchange of confidences or any kind of meaningful discussion.

The system's strength, after all, lay in its closed nature and exclusivity. It was all for the company and the company for all. I could not help admiring it, because it worked so well—at least during the decades when the country was protected from foreign intrusions onto its home turf. But did I envy the salaryman's lot? Not in the least. I loved Japan, but I failed to identify with this abdication of control over one's own life.

What did the salarymen's wives think of their husbands' long working hours and frequent absences from home, to spend time on the golf course, in the nightclubs, or on company outings to the hot springs? They accepted them as the unavoidable consequences of a salaryman's career, and in any case they had their hands full bringing up the children, doing their share of neighborhood duties, and looking after live-in parents or—more likely—parents-in-law. The tight-knit social family structure left precious little opportunity for personal pursuits, let alone extramarital affairs. Nor, I am told, were most women even dreaming of romance.

Once the children had left home and the parents were deceased, they might take up a hobby, join a study group, help organize neighborhood events, or, if they could afford it, enjoy all-female lunch parties and trips to scenic spots. I suspect that the prevalence of women-only groups you encounter everywhere in Japan today—in restaurants and museums and on organized tours—has its roots in the Showa salaryman system. During late Showa, career and volunteering opportunities for women would rapidly open up, but the ingrained pattern of women and men living largely separate social lives is still mostly intact.

For all its constraints on individual freedom and the stark reality for the family of a mostly absent husband and father, the archetypal Showa salaryman has become for many older Japanese a symbol of lost stability. "Salaryman" once was among the most desirable of occupations, and middle-class young women vied with each other in finding a promising young salaryman for a husband. It was an institution that greatly helped in Japan's reconstruction and rapid growth—and the emergence of an affluent middle class.

Avoiding a Clash of Cultures

In the Japan branches of the bank I worked for, the staff were largely Japanese, but the management was expatriate Dutch. This presented a problem, as most of the Dutch managers had no clue about wa or group identity, and tended to treat the workers head on, as individuals. The solution commonly resorted to by foreign firms in Japan ever since the opening of Japan to trade and commerce in the late nineteenth century, was a Japanese *banto*, a senior clerk without executive powers but with great authority derived from the trust and confidence both management and workers placed in him.

The banto was both buffer and paterfamilias. He acted as a go-between for a staff and management that might not know how to deal most effectively with one another. He also helped the Dutch staff cope with the challenges of Japanese life and bailed them out when they got into a scrape.

At the same time, the banto had to have advanced business expertise, as he was the primary contact for the Japanese authorities, banks, and customers, and the arbiter in conflicts. As few Japanese visitors were comfortable with English or the foreign staff with Japanese, business meetings were usually conducted by the banto, or with him acting as interpreter. He often was an excellent business developer, frequently calling on Japanese companies to recommend the services of his employer. With the rise of a highly educated English-speaking workforce and Japan's increased prestige in the world, the bantos of foreign companies and banks were gradually replaced by regular Japanese executives with full powers of management and signing authority.

In my bank, we were lucky in having excellent, dedicated, long-serving bantos in both our Japan branches, who contributed greatly to the business growth and the motivation of our workforce during the early post-war decades. From the late 1960s onward they were in fact given executive status, comparable to their senior expatriate colleagues, and the term "banto" was no longer used.

At a recent reunion with former Japanese coworkers in Osaka—all hired over the years by the same former banto—his crucial role was affirmed. "The team spirit was excellent, largely thanks to him," was the verdict. "We are old men now, but we still meet. To remember those good times."

One thing my office had in common with Japanese employers was our annual company outings to the hot springs. They were a useful and pleasurable way to strengthen the bond between employees. It was in the communal tub and at the evening banquet that our mutual dependence was affirmed and any rough edges gently filed away with the help of sake and beer and silly sketches performed by the office talent. High and low hammed it up on these occasions. Our Osaka banto could be counted on to do his trademark belly-shuffle, balancing a jug of sake on his head as he crawled his way to the finish under the incessant strumming of the samisen and cheered on by his flushed underlings.

They were good, honest, memorable times indeed.

Chapter 6

Of Brawn and Drudgery: Japan's Manual Workers

The successes achieved in the Showa era would not have been possible without the sweat and total dedication of the country's farmers, fishermen, factory hands, mechanics, and other manual workers—the true weight-bearing pillars of the nation. As in other countries, their labors go mostly unsung, but in post-war Showa their contributions were increasingly valued and rewarded.

There was an historic precedent for this. Mindful that agricultural workers might be treated with contempt, the Tokugawa Shogunate—the feudalist dynasty that ruled Japan from 1600 to 1867—compensated the peasants for their inherently lowly status (and sometimes extreme poverty) by placing them high in the feudal class hierarchy, directly below the samurai, who were at the top of the heap. This did not allow them special privileges or a better life, but it did ensure them, at least nominally, more respect. By contrast, merchants—deemed wealthy and wily enough to take care of themselves no matter what—were placed at the bottom of the four-rung scale, below the artisans.

This instance of deft politics may have served the Tokugawa rulers more than it helped the peasants' plight. Yet it may well have instilled in the population a proper regard for manual labor in general and, thus, helped to keep Japan relatively free from the kind of severe class confrontations that plagued Europe during the nineteenth and twentieth centuries as a result of the social upheavals that accompanied the Industrial Revolution and the subsequent rise of Marxist ideology.

Wherever you go in the industrialized world, the essential nature of manual work, whether urban or rural, seems to have changed little over the past half-century. It is still and may always be largely a matter of "brawn and drudgery." But there are wide differences in each society's *attitude* to manual labor. In that respect, the painstaking advancement of the Showa work ethic with its emphasis on the positive, edifying aspects of labor is a remarkable achievement. It has become a permanent feature of Japanese society, and one of its greatest strengths.

Untarnished Kindness

Sagano, Kyoto, October 24, 1959. We arrived here by bus after an unforgettable visit to the Katsura Imperial Villa. Our first stop in Sagano was Suzumushidera, a small temple where they breed singing insects. Then it was lunchtime. Somewhere in a field, on the bank of a creek, we opened our lunch boxes: *nigiri* rice balls wrapped with seaweed and stuffed with pickled plums. Just as we tucked in, a country woman on a bike passed by. From a distance we saw her smile at us, and seeing us eating lunch, she waved a tea kettle. I shouted: "Thanks! But we have no cups!"

"Drink from the lid!" she shouted back. "I'm in the field up there. Drink as much as you want!" And she left the kettle by the roadside, for us to pick up.

Japan's rural population has long enjoyed the special attention and protection of the government, not least because the farm vote was crucial to keeping the ruling party in power. The party ensured the farmers' loyalty through a system of rice subsidies that guaranteed the rice growers an adequate income.

However, with the steady post-war migration of country dwellers to the cities—reducing the rural population from two-thirds of the total in 1945 to only one-quarter today—the importance of the farm vote would have become seriously eroded had it not been for the way the electoral system was organized after the Second World War. At that time, the rural vote was placed on an approximately equal footing with that of the urban population, and although some adjustments in the electoral districts were made over the years, they fell far short of a proper realignment. The result is that each rural vote today is worth about three urban votes, a situation that has greatly helped the Liberal Democratic Party stay in control of the government for the past fifty years—with the exception of one or two very brief interruptions.

Service First, Sleep Later

In the cities and the industrial belts, meanwhile, the Showa work ethic was honed during the decades of fast economic growth. Increasingly, constant activity and a search for perfection were expected from every worker (including most manual workers) at all times, and this is still the pattern today.

I doubt if there is another country in the world where, even today, deliverymen run to and from their vehicle, checkout workers at supermarkets call out the price of every one of your purchases as they rapidly ring up your bill, and building crews meticulously guide pedestrians away from the dust and danger of their site. In factories, too, an unfailing positive attitude and unrelenting striving to meet or exceed production goals and quality standards is the norm. The trains in Japan not only run on time, but they are also spanking clean inside and out, without a trace of graffiti and with even the windows washed and dried to perfection. Domestic and commercial rubbish collection is organized to a T, and city streets look like they are cleaned all the time.

The amount of sheer physical labor needed to consistently provide such a level of social and personal service, much of it performed during the night and early morning, taxes the imagination. No wonder that of all the peoples of the industrialized world, surveys say the Japanese—whether office workers or laborers—are the most sleep-deprived.[2] This may explain why half the passengers on trains and subways can be seen napping, at any time of the day.

What I find remarkable is that while wearing themselves out in the effort to please their customers and bosses, most Showa Japanese workers and tradesmen also seemed well aware of their vital place in the scheme of things. While practicing humility to all and sundry, they did expect—and usually still receive—due respect for their particular skills or physical exertions. Their closer adherence to standard speech and behavior than is the case among similar occupations in, say, London or Amsterdam has also helped to minimize class-bound attitudes. Along with historical precedent, this generally affords Japan's manual workers a higher social position than similar workers elsewhere.

The importance of the proper regard in which Japan has traditionally held its working classes can hardly be overemphasized. This respect has been reflected in the widespread realization of corporate management that employer and employee are in a relationship of mutual dependence, with generous working conditions being the quid pro quo for the expected workers' loyalty and the avoidance of strikes. Policies such as these may well have saved the country from the kind of critical labor shortages that have bedeviled Europe since the 1960s. The usual explanation for Western Europe's massive importation of foreign workers over the past forty years was the "unwillingness" of their own people to perform menial work in an increasingly affluent society. Apparently there has been no such hesitation among Japanese workers.

No doubt proper recognition of the manual workers' role in Japan's economy has been a major factor in motivating them, but perhaps equally important are the institutionalized sanctions for failure. Among some Japanese employers, especially those in areas such as transportation and industry, punishment for even relatively minor mistakes or lapses may include a combination of reprimand, withholding of pay, demotion or—most feared—compulsory reeducation featuring almost Maoist-style sessions of severe self-criticism. Scrupulous adherence to prescribed procedures and timetables is paramount in every organization. Things such as flexibility and "margin for error"—let alone judicious interpretation—hardly fit such a regime.

The constant search for perfection characteristic of Japanese society may well prove to be a crucial asset in an increasingly competitive world. But there is growing concern in Japan that *excessive* emphasis on perfection may also cause excessive stress and inhuman burdens on the labor force, thus creating new risks. A major train derailment in 2005 near Osaka, with over one hundred fatalities, and serious maintenance lapses in the same year at one of the leading airlines, were both caused by the extreme importance attached to punctuality, to the detriment of safety.

Sometimes fastidiousness comes at the expense of practical insight. When a trained construction worker agreed to help me drill some holes in my concrete wall and it turned out that he didn't know you have to stick in plugs before screws could be inserted, and when a gas mechanic who had tested the boiler was befuddled by the lack of water coming out of the tap but didn't think to check if someone had turned off the water valve (both recent personal experiences), well, then I want to shout: "how about thinking outside the box for a change!"

Town and Country, the Great Divide

Living in a metropolis like Tokyo or Osaka today one tends to forget what life in the country is like. Speeding through the landscape on the Shinkansen fails to give you a flavor, and getting out of the city by car is too much of an effort. So we stay in town, and head for a movie or a museum instead.

In the 1950s and 1960s a trip to the countryside may have been made tiresome by driving on largely unpaved roads or traveling on trains that were slow and filthy from the smoke of the steam locomotives. But such a trip was nonetheless easier then, when traffic was light, the cities smaller and therefore quicker to get out of, and the countryside itself more rural.

What made visits to the country memorable was not just the attractive scenery. It was the sharp contrast between city life and life in the provinces, with its endless manual labor: tilling the soil, bringing in the catch, steering boats through river rapids, running small village stores. Women serving demanding guests in country inns, hand-cutting soba noodles, winnowing grain or debarking felled trees. Men transporting lumber from the mountains. You could almost feel the fatigue of the workers as they soaked their tired limbs in the bathhouse or relaxed in their modest homes after a long day's labor.

The differences between city and country are, of course, not peculiar to Japan. But at least in my early Showa days, the contrast was much greater than in England or Holland, both physically and in terms of the prevailing mentality. For one thing, the countryside was largely spared the devastating wartime bombings. Centuries-old farm houses and time-worn village centers were still the norm, while the large cities, as we have noted, were substantially (re)built after the war.

Traditional housing and duties associated with the soil naturally influenced rural values and habits. Rural families typically comprised three generations under one roof who squatted and slept on tatami mats, wore country clothing—and the women kimono after work—and ate exclusively Japanese food. The women toiled on the rice paddies all their lives, their spines curving from the effort, until some of them walked, in their old age, with backs bent at a 90-degree angle, a piteous sight not at all uncommon during Showa.

Showa city dwellers, on the other hand, lived mostly in small, semi-Western-style apartments or row houses, increasingly used chairs and beds, and were used to a mixed Japanese, Chinese, and Western diet. Even laborers whose meals typically consisted of traditional Japanese rice, fish, and pickles, gradually came to change their habits, influenced by the wider choice on offer. These contrasts between town and country could not fail to have an impact on social values and political allegiances, with rural people being overwhelmingly conservative, while the urban population presented a more varied picture of lifestyle and opinion.

Today these contrasts are much less evident. Since late Showa, towns and villages up and down the country have modernized themselves, often losing their distinctive character in the process. Traditional wood-and-paper houses have been largely modernized or replaced by reinforced concrete or mixed-material structures and equipped with the latest gadgets. Fast transport into the big cities has turned many a once-rural community into a virtual suburb.

Showa's great divide between town and country has narrowed considerably. What has not been lost in the process is the importance and high quality of manual labor of every kind to the smooth functioning of Japanese society and the continued success of its economy.

Chapter 7

Authority Challenged

For all the concerted efforts of Japan's post-war political and industrial leaders to foster a sense of common purpose and national unity needed to improve the nation's fortunes and its citizens' living standards, they could not control the rising influence of socialist thinking and anti-American feeling during the 1950s. Mass demonstrations had been all but unknown in Japan, but when the US–Japan Security Treaty came up for renewal and revision in 1960, hundreds of thousands of protesters took to the streets to voice their opposition.

It was an unprecedented show of force by a usually docile electorate. The deafening chant of the large crowds of demonstrators still rings in my ears. *Washo! Washo!* it went, as the protesters wound their way through the capital, arms locked, undulating like giant snakes. The demonstrations, which had begun before the parliamentary vote on the treaty's renewal, continued after it passed, this time to protest the government's "highhanded" tactics in using its majority in the House of Representatives, the lower house of Japan's National Diet, to obtain approval, against the vehement will of the opposition and significant segments of the population. "They rammed it through" was the language used.

The new treaty was arguably more favorable to Japan than the one it replaced, but many still found it unacceptable, as it provided for the continued presence of American military bases on Japanese soil. This was seen by those opposed to it as violating Japan's pacifist constitution.

The protest movement was organized by a loose coalition of left-wing groups, including the Socialist and Communist parties, the major labor unions, and the radical student movement Zengakuren. While the latter's members were in the vanguard of the demonstrations and formed its most recognizable face, the protest involved a cross-section of the population, including large numbers of middle-class office workers and housewives.

The movement had a strong ideological element to it, for apart from the immediate goal of getting the treaty abrogated, the larger agenda of its organizers was to topple the entrenched, pro-American establishment and replace it with a socialist/communist coalition. Yet the participation of so many ordinary citizens—many of whom probably would normally vote for the ruling Liberal Democratic Party if they bothered to vote at all—was an indication of the growth of political engagement. It was the only time in Japan's post-war history that something resembling a fiery political spirit flourished, although it was driven more by blind passion than by fully informed debate and democratic process and, therefore, posed a serious danger to Japan's hard-won stability.

The protest was large and focused but in the end proved no match for the combined forces of government, big business, the rural areas, and the conservative middle class. Though threatening and intimidating, the demonstrators stopped short of serious violence. The *Washo!* chant was no war cry but a "Heave-ho!" yell borrowed from the rowdy shrine bearers of the rural harvest festivals. For their part, the police too held back on the use of force. They controlled the crowds mostly by closing ranks with the shields of their riot gear and some use of water cannon. There was only one fatality, and an accidental one at that.

The Diet vote was not reversed, and the ruling elite stayed in power. But Prime Minister Nobusuke Kishi resigned over the confrontation, yielding his place to a prominent member of his cabinet, Hayato Ikeda. The new government quickly shifted its priorities to the spreading of wealth, and the protest movement fizzled out.

The way Ikeda went about this was by announcing an "Income Doubling Plan," the principal objective of which was to double incomes, both national (in terms of gross national product) and personal, as measured by consumption. It raised the hopes of the masses for an affluent future, and it had the hoped-for effect of getting the people's minds off the treaty.

The protest's failure did not surprise me. Throughout the crisis, I never doubted that Japan's deep-rooted conservatism would win the day. The possibility of Japan turning communist seemed too far-fetched to lie awake over. But I did bemoan the speed with which the budding involvement of students and ordinary citizens in the political process collapsed after this one major defeat. The electorate showed less and less interest in national affairs and, lulled by material comforts, slowly sank into a state of complacency from which it has yet to be roused.

The challenge to authority of 1960, a daring, disturbing, but nonetheless potentially promising Showa event, ended before it had a chance to alter the terms of the democratic process. Its legacy is passive acceptance of the status quo rather than a realization of the vital importance of sustained political engagement.

History Has No Sell-By Date

Nishinomiya, near Osaka, July 1959. My friend Ysbrand Rogge, who has left the bank and is now a professional cinematographer, has come to stay with us for a while. He has filmed the Tokyo protest demonstrations from every angle and wants to combine this record with other footage into a documentary about "the old and the new Japan." Looking at the scenes of the traditional snake-dancing demonstrators and episodes of the autumn harvest shrine festivals known as *matsuri*, we are struck by the similarity of the crowds' movements and their identical chant of *Washo! Washo!* So the film's title will be *Washo!*, and I am to write the scenario and do the narration.

The heat and rudimentary technical facilities at my house make the work hard, but while I am at the bank Ysbrand somehow manages to complete the editing. During the weekend, I record the commentary. Soon the film is finished. It is twenty-five minutes long.

A year later: Ysbrand writes from Amsterdam that the film has been shown on television and that copies have been purchased by two museums.

Forty-six years later (2005): NHK television (Nippon Hoso Kyokai, Japan's public broadcasting company, similar to the BBC or PBS) includes scenes from *Washo!*, together with the narration, in a documentary about post-war Japan.

Chapter 8

The Foreign Element

For a better comprehension of the importance of Showa, it is necessary to consider the role of foreigners, especially Westerners, in this crucial period of Japan's history. Not only will such examination be interesting from a Western perspective ("how great was our influence?") but far more relevantly, understanding the gradual shift in Japanese attitudes to outsiders reveals much about the nature of the Showa mindset, and the differences between Showa and its successor era, Heisei.

For centuries, Japan has pursued a highly selective immigration policy. Japan has often been called essentially xenophobic, and although that characterization is harsh, it is not without foundation. The distrust of foreigners goes back centuries.

A Historical Perspective

Japan has a long history of isolationism. As an island nation, it probably had relatively little close contact with its immediate neighbors during the early centuries of the first millennium, but from around the middle of the sixth century AD. the influence of China became pervasive, mainly as the source of Buddhism and as a model for the organization of the Japanese state. The transmission of Chinese culture lasted a few centuries, until in the course of the ninth century Japan began to reassert its own cultural and spiritual independence, a process that was accelerated by China's political decline under the T'ang dynasty.

Ever since, Japan has essentially minded its own business, with a central government centered around an imperial court that was challenged from time to time by domestic warlords, but never seriously threatened by hostile forces from abroad. Only the Mongols under Kublai Khan attempted to subjugate Japan, but their joint Chinese-Korean invasion force of 150,000 men, the greatest armada ever until that time, failed spectacularly when their fleet was destroyed by a giant typhoon. The Japanese called it the *kamikaze,* the "Divine Wind," which they believed protected the lands of the gods from foreign usurpers.

This seminal experience may well have set the country upon its permanent course of closely guarded isolationism, which reached its height in the seventeenth century. Convinced of the danger of being colonized by Western powers, and of the related threat of Christian (Roman Catholic) missionary activity, the Shogun Tokugawa Iemitsu enforced a policy of isolation known as *sakoku* between 1636 and 1641. He banned both the Christian faith and all intercourse and trade with the outside world on pain of death. After expelling the Spaniards in 1624, he drove out the Portuguese in 1638. To prove that he was serious, he ordered the execution of two Portuguese envoys when they visited Japan later that year to try to negotiate a resumption of ties.

Ships were refused entry even for bunkering or shelter from heavy weather, and sailors unlucky enough to be shipwrecked on Japan's rocky coast were often put to death. The fortunate ones were required to renounce their own country and prevented from ever leaving Japan again. The brightest and boldest ended up as councilors to local lords or even—like Will Adams, the English pilot of the Dutch ship *De Liefde*, and Jan Joosten, one of the ship's sailors—to the Shogun himself.

There were two exceptions to the policy of exclusion. Chinese merchant vessels were allowed to enter the harbor of Nagasaki for purposes of trading, albeit under severe restrictions. Likewise the Dutch were permitted to continue trading, on condition that they moved their settlement (a warehouse and living quarters), established in 1609 on the island of Hirado, to Dejima, a small artificial island in the harbor of Nagasaki. There a changing complement of expatriate merchants, subject to constant supervision and complex rules, carried on a gradually diminishing trade, while keeping the Japanese leaders informed about developments in Western politics and science. They would prove to be a vital window on the world, and a crucial factor in Japan's eventual modernization.

The policy of isolation continued for more than two centuries. The arrival of Commodore Perry's US naval expedition in 1853, demanding that Japan open its ports to foreign ships, finally forced the Shogunate to permit a crack in its sakoku policy, although it still took some years before it was officially abandoned. That occurred, after a protracted struggle between rival Japanese political forces, when the Tokugawa shogun formally surrendered authority to rule the country to the fifteen-year-old emperor Meiji in 1867.

The Meiji reformers, many of whom had been secretly schooled in the ways of the West by scholars and scientists attached to the Dutch trading post in Nagasaki, placed top priority on catching up with the West in the shortest possible time to stave off colonization by Western powers. This change in direction triggered an outward change in the attitude to Europeans and Americans, whose help was needed to realize the ambitious plans. Foreign residents were now welcome although confined to certain sections of a small number of cities.

But eventually this positive relationship with the outside world crumbled once more. The militarist regime that ruled Japan from the early 1930s to 1945 did a thorough job of fanning hatred of Westerners all over again. They also showed contempt for most Asian peoples whose land they occupied, committing frightful atrocities and behaving in every way like a conquering army. (Current revisionist claims that the Japanese were not invaders but liberators are not shared by the countries concerned or, indeed, by many Japanese.)

Japan's surrender in 1945 at the end of the Second World War brought an abrupt change in Japanese treatment of Americans and Europeans. Foreign occupation was accepted as the bitter but inevitable consequence of defeat, and rather than resisting it on principle, most Japanese were keen to make the best of the situation and show a friendly face to the conqueror. Defeat was not digested but swallowed whole.[3]

The residual mistrust of and resistance to anything foreign—including ideas and things that had not passed through a fine Japanese sieve—did not change fundamentally as a result of the tactical adjustments. With the end of the Occupation in 1952 came a reversion to the previous tight controls on immigration, merchandise imports, and foreign investment, mostly, and understandably, aimed at preventing a wholesale takeover of the Japanese economy by foreign business. The economy was effectively closed to new foreign involvement, and the resident (nonmilitary) Western community remained accordingly small.

Controlled Discomfort—Polite Respect

Until the late 1960s or so, the only foreigners living in Japan (apart from Chinese and Korean permanent residents) were a few thousand Western expatriates working for foreign trading companies, banks, and the embassies, and a number of missionaries and teachers of English. There were very few foreign-owned manufacturing companies, and the resident foreign banks were largely barred from doing business directly with Japanese companies and individuals. Foreign banks' lending to corporate Japan—essential to the country's economic growth—was done mostly through the local banks.

Given these circumstances, there was little incentive for foreigners to study the Japanese language or attempt to integrate into Japanese society, even after war-bruised feelings had run their course and mutual respect was restored. Another discouraging factor was the Japanese tendency to treat even long-staying Western expatriates as visitors rather than residents, and at least until the mid-1970s, social relations between these resident Westerners and Japanese tended to be quite formal.

Foreigners' invitations to home parties or private dinners were seldom reciprocated. (It is fair to add here that home entertaining did not come into vogue in Japan until quite recently.) Educated Japanese with an internationalist bend who freely associated with Westerners were seen as mavericks, and were usually not in positions of power. Those who were, and dared to flaunt their predilection, were rare indeed, and not devoid of courage and foresight.

Western bankers and businessmen in Japan were treated to lavish dinners at restaurants and plied with gifts. Their lack of command of Japanese was seldom a problem, as their Japanese hosts welcomed the opportunity to practice their hard-won knowledge of English. Besides, foreigners were widely believed to be incapable of mastering the language or understanding the Japanese psyche. Japan was for the Japanese.

Westerners' outsider status in their society has traditionally suited the Japanese ruling classes, as it formed a protective shield against unwelcome influences (and inquisitiveness) and the need to adjust laws and customs to accommodate diverse minorities. Of course, every nation and most individuals display some degree of instinctive rejection of aliens. As an island nation Japan, like Britain, has been even less accommodating to the presence of outsiders than maritime nations such as Portugal or the Netherlands, or countries with many land borders like France.

Japan's almost total ban in the seventeenth century on any form of intercourse with the outside world was perhaps the ultimate example of institutionalized xenophobia, though, as we have seen, it was arguably inspired more by fear of conquest through Christianization than by racism. Even after it ended, a degree of suspicion and discomfort about outsiders persisted almost until the end of Showa. It is rare now, and where it still does occur, it is mild compared to the racial slurs and outright violence Japanese and other Asians sometimes have to endure abroad, even in the West.

In fact, if sublimation of hostile instincts is one measure of civilized behavior, then the way the vast majority of Japanese during Showa handled their feelings about foreign, especially Western, elements in their midst is indeed most civilized. At times this must have been difficult, especially during the Occupation, when victorious American troops renamed Tokyo's thoroughfares. They nailed signs like "X Avenue" and "15th Street" onto lamp posts, and arrogant foreign businessmen sometimes refused to pay their bus or train fares. And what about the English banker's wife I knew in the 1950s, who had the fine hardwood pillars of their Japanese house near Kobe painted in bright colors, and the age-old moss scraped off the rocks in their exquisite garden? She was by no means the only one showing ignorance of or contempt for Japanese aesthetics in those unhappy years.

But resentment seldom boiled over into active hostility. My own experience of over half a century of living in or visiting Japan bears this out. Apart from some early post-war taunts by scruffy youngsters, and the occasional drunk shouting obscenities at me, I have seldom encountered any serious sign of hostility. Quite the contrary. Japanese from all walks of life and in all parts of the country have been unfailingly courteous and often helpful to me, whether they knew me or not. And the times that I have been favored with generous hospitality are too numerous to recount.

Admittedly, I had the advantage of a "respectable" occupation, acceptable manners, and Caucasian looks. I am not sure if I would have fared as well had my skin color been a few shades darker or my comportment less accommodating.

The lengths to which Japanese hosts will go to return a favor is illustrated by the following, perhaps trivial, anecdote. In the late 1970s, Japan's ambassador to The Hague paid a formal visit to the Caribbean island of Curaçao, which formed part of the Kingdom of the Netherlands. I worked there at the time, and my wife and I treated the ambassadorial couple to an informal tropical dinner. They liked my favorite cocktail, piña colada, a rum, coconut, and pineapple juice mixture. On our next visit to Holland, the ambassador organized a dinner party in our honor. He had taken the trouble to import a crateful of tinned piña colada as a special welcome to us. (To my embarrassment, we lost our way driving over to their residence in the wooded suburb of Wassenaar. This was unforgivable, as the ambassador knew that I had grown up in that very neighborhood! By the time we arrived, the cocktail hour was over and we had to go straight in to dinner. The evening never quite recovered from my faux pas.)

A Question of Origin

Contrasting with Japan's accommodating, if self-conscious, attitude toward Westerners during the Showa period was its barely concealed lack of respect for its own neighbors, which has not completely disappeared since, despite the growing economic and political clout of most of Asia, China in particular, and Japan's enormous economic stake in the region.

Even so, the number of foreign Asians in Japan, especially Koreans and Chinese, has long exceeded and still vastly exceeds the Western presence. Of the approximately 2,011,000 registered aliens in Japan in 2005, around 75 percent were ethnic Asians, mostly Koreans and Chinese. But these are overwhelmingly the descendents of laborers brought over, often forcibly, before and during the Second World War to work in Japan's mines and factories to alleviate the manpower shortage caused by the wartime mobilization. Their status has always been low, and most have not succeeded in obtaining Japanese citizenship—or declined to accept it when the opportunity arose, for fear of losing their identity, while not being accepted as equals by native Japanese.

A separate sizable group of residents are immigrants from South America, 376,000 in 2005, predominantly the descendants of Japanese who emigrated to Brazil in the early twentieth century and again in the immediate post-war period. Because of Japan's economic prosperity, these second and third generation Japanese settlers started returning to their ancestral land in the 1980s, where they were readily welcomed. But when it turned out they spoke no Japanese and were strangers to Japanese customs and values, their presence became a problem. In most cases, they have found employment as workers in industry, but they often need special assistance in education and social adjustment.

As for China, the smoldering disdain certain Japanese apparently still feel for that country surfaced in May 2005, when Tokyo's governor, Shintaro Ishihara, publicly referred to China as "shina," a now-taboo term used during Japan's occupation of the country. His remark added fuel to the fire of already strained relations between the two countries in the wake of former Prime Minister Junichiro Koizumi's annual visits to Tokyo's Yasukuni Shrine, which honors Japan's war dead, including those executed after the war as "war criminals."[4] It was not the first time that the governor had courted controversy. Back in 2002 he warned that *sangokujin*, a derogatory reference to immigrants from China, Korea, and Taiwan, were likely to commit crimes in the aftermath of an earthquake.[5]

Some aging Japanese apparently cannot forget Japan's glory days, when it considered itself a superior race and dominated large parts of Asia. Last year I was taken aback by the way a minor, elderly immigration clerk snarled at a young Korean woman who politely asked for a certain application form, and then turned to hand me the very same form with an ingratiating smile. The Japanese government's repeated denials that Japan's wartime military was responsible for the recruitment of mainly Korean (and, in Indonesia, Dutch) "comfort women" (a euphemism for sex slaves) to serve their soldiers, has further complicated Japan's relations with its Asian neighbors.[6]

However, the roots of this lingering haughty attitude toward Asians can be traced back much further than their last war—perhaps to the momentous decision made by the Meiji reformers of the nineteenth century for Japan to stop thinking of itself as an Asian nation and instead "emulate the West" by becoming a colonial power. The educational reformer Yukichi Fukuzawa, founder of Keio University in Tokyo, formalized the concept in his *datsu-a ron* ("break away from Asia") thesis.

For all that, the appreciation of all things Western both during Showa and today has generally been concerned more with appearances than fundamentals. Thus, it is highly selective and noncommittal, and seldom touches the deeper layers of public morality and private values. Deftly and often uncomfortably balancing between opposing worlds Japan stands as a country apart.

Chapter 9

Religions and Traditions

It may be helpful to consider the role of religion and traditions in Japan's march forward during the Showa era. The pre-war and wartime deification of the emperor as a descendant of the Shinto sun goddess, Amaterasu-omikami, left the impression among some post-war foreign observers that despite the emperor's public rejection in 1945 of the myth of his divinity, in their hearts many Japanese still worshipped him.

Whether that was true or not there is no way of knowing. At least in my own experience, though, there was not much evidence of Japanese religiosity during Showa, let alone an emperor cult, the occasional shouts by far-right fanatics notwithstanding. In fact, to me and many Westerners along with me, the Showa Japanese did not seem a particularly religious people, if religiousness is measured by such outward signs as (1) paying regular visits to a place of worship to listen to sermons, (2) adherence to one sect or denomination to the exclusion of all others, (3) following a set of moral precepts prescribed by a specific religious organization, (4) and being intolerant or suspicious of those following other religions. The vast majority of Japanese did not, and do not today, display any of these traits.

I found this secular nature of Japanese society especially attractive when I began living here in the early 1950s. The rarity of a missionary zeal among Japanese Buddhist and Shinto organizations and of public display of cloying, sentimental religiosity or holier-than-thou attitudes so typical of some forms of Christianity, was a relief. No less attractive was the apparent ease with which most Japanese seemed to accept both Buddhism and Shinto, and even—as at some schools and weddings—Christianity in their lives, as if they were equal or interchangeable. (The exception is Japan's avowed Christians: most of them would not go near a temple or shrine.)

Happily Coexisting Faiths

How could this be? Did not Shinto and Buddhism compete for adherents in Japanese society, the way Christian faiths did in the rest of the world? What was the function of religion during the Showa era?

Buddhism was first introduced from China in the sixth century, and it achieved almost total penetration of Japan. Yet it never really replaced the native animistic traditions of Shinto. In a sense it complemented them, with the two religions coexisting both in space and in the mind of the population. To this day, you can find small Shinto shrines within the compounds of Buddhist temples, as well as in private homes. Many Japanese consider themselves followers of both Shinto and Buddhism.

It has always been my impression that the spiritual nature, temperament, and aesthetic sensitivity of many Japanese are closer to Shinto than to Buddhism, let alone Christianity, which in any case represents only a few percent of the population. In my own contacts over the decades, I seldom met a Japanese ready to unequivocally acknowledge the existence of one supreme being. Even many traditional Buddhists (in other words, almost everybody) seemed to be more comfortable with the notion that there are "spirits" everywhere: one's ancestors, historic warriors, mythological figures, deceased pets—the list is endless. Even inanimate entities like rocks and rivers may have spirits worth venerating. The failure of Christianity to gain more than a toehold in Japan after centuries of missionary work can perhaps in part be explained by this deep-seated hesitancy to accept one all-powerful God at the expense of a world filled with gods and spirits.

Another factor in Christianity's small presence in Japan may well be the long-standing popular perception that Christian values are essentially un-Japanese. After all, their ethical foundations are completely different: Christian morality draws from religious dogma, sermons, and readings of sacred texts, while Japanese morality seems to issue primarily from group responsibilities, social convention, and peer pressure.

In spite of its amorphous nature, Japan's spirituality has had lasting effect on day-to-day life, an effect that was certainly evident in post-war Showa. The preoccupations with newness and cleanliness and bathing rituals, and the minimalist lines and spaces of Japanese architecture, all hark back to Shinto, as do the harvest festivals up and down the country. Many weddings are still solemnized in spare ceremonies conducted in Shinto tradition, though church weddings have gained in popularity, for their "romantic mood" rather than their vestigial religious implications, which are usually ignored. Funerals, on the other hand, have always been the province of the Buddhist temples, with their tradition of providing family tombs and their dark, gloomy interiors, which form a suitable backdrop for the solemn chants of sutra texts and the sounding of deep gongs. In contrast, Shinto considers death to be a form of "pollution" and Shinto's funeral services must therefore be held outside the shrine's premises.

Perhaps it is not too rash to say that to most Japanese "religion" is more a matter of tradition than confession or personal quest. The rites at temples are hard to follow. The sutras, whether read or chanted, are unintelligible to the layperson. Most visitors to temples do not expect sermons but content themselves with clapping their hands, to attract the attention of the spirits believed to be hovering about—or more likely out of habit. Throwing a coin down the grating and buying an amulet for good luck complete the ritual. At Shinto shrines the routine is pretty much the same.

The fuzzy religious borders stem in part from the general lack of proprietary zeal of Japan's traditional religions, at least in the spiritual sense. Apart from some modern cults that require active belief in and application of their doctrines, most temples and shrines do not expect their followers to demonstrate their faith other than by making donations and using the available services: funerals and memorial services at the Buddhist temples, marriage rites at the Shinto shrines. Believers in need of comfort or divine intervention do, of course, come to pray, but the kind of duties typical of the Catholic parish priest or the Protestant minister—offering succor and moral guidance—are not a regular feature of a Buddhist or Shinto priest's activities.

Japan's True Religion

Granted, some religious sects in Japan, whether Buddhist or Shinto in origin, do proselytize vigorously and provide moral guidance to their followers. And so do certain Christian groups, some of which stoop to using offensive high-decibel loudspeakers to urge city-center shoppers to repent and join the flock. But mainstream Japan, undeniably secular, seems largely oblivious to these efforts. "Repent?" seems to be their response, "Of what?"

I realize that I am entering slippery territory here, and I shall refrain from going beyond the observation, based on long personal exposure to Japanese society, that for most Japanese it is not staying on good terms with one's personal god figure that preoccupies their mind but maintaining correct relations with their social environment. What needs to be avoided at all costs is not "sinning against God"—a poorly understood concept in this culture—but breaching vital social codes. The shame associated with violating social mores can have consequences as severe as those guilty of trespassing against the Christian God, if not more so, since they are played out in the public sphere. But if you keep your nose clean and observe the social proprieties, anxiety can be held at bay and life's harmony preserved. Shame is a social matter, not a personal or religious one.

In short, the vast majority of Showa Japanese were doubtless more preoccupied with maintaining correct social relations than in nurturing their relationship with the infinite, and this is still largely true today. In the view of my wife (who was brought up in a traditional, if relatively cosmopolitan, Japanese milieu) "social ethics" constitute the true religion of the Japanese, an assessment I support. Its impact on the success story that was Showa can hardly be overstated: acting as motivation and common bond among the people of Japan, it was the driving force behind many of the era's greatest accomplishments.

The Aesthetic Power of Zen

Let us examine briefly the position of Zen Buddhism in the scheme of things. For well over a century, Zen has fascinated Western visitors mostly for its spare aesthetics and emphasis on bypassing logic in seeking spiritual enlightenment. Zen's austere sense of beauty, often referred to as *shibui,* still permeated Japanese life during the mid-Showa period, the 1950s through the mid-1970s.

As noted earlier in this chapter, for the spiritually inclined in Japan, quiet contemplation of the wonders of nature and a sense of communion with all living things and, perhaps, with the spirits of dead loved ones, has often been more helpful to one's inner well-being than an understanding and acceptance of the tenets of established religion.

The serious practitioner of Zen Buddhism went much further. He sought spiritual truth by meditating on irrational riddles, with the objective of penetrating directly into the essence of being and thus achieving *satori* (becoming enlightened). Few reached their objective, but the austere surroundings in which they lived and observed their strict discipline defined not only their spiritual identity but also their tastes and manners, and their aesthetic sensibility.

A Zen Experience

Sojiji Zen Temple, Yokohama, 13–14 April, 1963. I was invited to stay the night in the monks' sleeping quarters, and join the morning activities. This is a brief record of the experience.

3 AM—Wake-up gong—got up immediately with all the other monks—used *tosu* (toilet) and splashed water on my face, then rushed barefoot through long cold corridors to the Zendo meditation hall to grab any open place (they are a few places short, to encourage prompt arrival; when the hall is full you sit on the veranda, a point against you). I arrive seconds late, ending up on the veranda with two or three other slackers.

We perform *zazen* (sitting meditation) for forty-five minutes sitting stock still in half-lotus or tailor's squat, concentrating the mind on one, preferably nonsensical subject, for no longer than eighteen minutes at a time, which I was told was considered the maximum attention span.

3:18—I shifted. A sadistic monk holding a *kyosaku* (flat stick) notices and slowly shuffles over to me with the obvious intention to hit me hard on the shoulder. He does. Ouch! I'm supposed to bow in gratitude. I do.

3:45—End of meditation; my legs are horribly painful.

5:15—To Hokodo hall for morning service; it lasts forty-five minutes, followed by a thirty-minute sermon.

7:00—Zen questioning (*mondo*); it is for monks only, so I can goof off. I walk around to restore circulation in my legs and to refill my head with familiar trivia.

7:30—Breakfast in Zendo (rice gruel with *umeboshi*, pickled plum). We eat fast without speaking and clean our dishes with hot water passed around in a kettle. We then drink the dishwater.

A truly memorable experience. I am still unenlightened.

As is well known, Zen has had an enormous, perhaps disproportionate, influence on Japanese culture. Landscape gardening, architecture, the Noh theater, and even *bushido,* the spirit of loyalty and sacrifice that defined the moral code of the samurai, all owe a tremendous debt to Zen, as do calligraphy, ink painting, and the deceptively rustic pottery and implements used in the tearoom. It impressed me deeply, and for the better part of two years I commuted regularly during weekends to Kyoto's Tofukuji Temple to absorb some of its spirit.

I felt especially attracted to Zen's *shibui* aesthetic. The word comes from *shibu*, the astringent juice of the persimmon. Its adjective, *shibui,* embodies the nature of traditional Japanese taste: rough but refined, restrained yet elegant, austere. The noun form, *shibumi,* implies a deep spiritual quality as well—an aesthetic made into an ideal of feeling and behavior that was typical of the literati but in a broader sense stood for the ideals of the educated classes as a whole. During Showa, some Japanese companies sent their young executive trainees to Zen temples for a week or so of meditation, presumably to learn how to concentrate the mind on matters corporate.

Shifting Values

Today, the great temples and their gardens—Zen or otherwise—are as beautiful and well tended as they were forty or fifty years ago. But tourists—masses of them—have largely replaced the priests and acolytes, and entrance fees are levied where once the welcome was free and more personal. Somewhere in the course of Japan's march to economic greatness, Zen's influence declined to the point where it has become part of history.

To a large extent, the same can be said of the rural harvest and shrine festivals and such events as Kyoto's annual ceremonial processions and performances evoking its rich history and the arts of the geisha. Superficially, these events differ little today from the way they were half a century ago. But they now seem to cater more to tour groups and television cameras than to their own communities. And inevitably there is an increasing disconnect between the images they project and the reality of the actual, greatly modernized lifestyle of their participants.

On the domestic level, too, age-old traditions have been falling by the wayside. Among the rituals that I remember well and that now seem to be almost extinct are the annual pounding of the *mochi* rice cakes in time for New Year's, the replacement of *fusuma* (indoor paper-and-wood partitions) by light bamboo blinds in summer, the moon-viewing rite in September, the periodical replacement of tatami mats, and the throwing of beans on *Setsubun*, February 3, the old lunar New Year's Eve, to chase out the evil spirits of the past year—not as a silly caper by a gaggle of TV starlets but seriously, out of conviction.

The hollowing out of religion and ancient customs, a feature of achieved economic wealth everywhere, seems particularly deep in Japan, because its cultural palette was so rich to start with, and the pace of change has been so fast. The decline of the countryside as a consequence of mass migration to the cities and the sharp drop in the birthrate has driven further nails into the coffin of rural tradition.

These far-reaching shifts have created further challenges to post-Showa Japan's society. With the loss of the moral authority of religion and the comforts of tradition, other sources of strength have to be relied on—values like community spirit, individual self-confidence, and national pride. The former is still reasonably intact in post-Showa Japan. But the fostering of personality is not high on anyone's agenda. As for national pride—that is, by most measurements, surprisingly weak. Recent governments have been working on its restoration, as we will discuss later in this book.

Chapter **10**

Arts, Crafts, Culture, and Fashion

As we observed in the previous chapter, traditional Japanese artistic taste was permeated by the austere shibui sense of beauty. A related and arguably even more profound aesthetic is what in Japan is known as *mono no aware*—a concept that is better described than translated. It refers to the perception of the transience of life and of all things, and the feeling of sweet sadness that accompanies it. Mono no aware has inspired Japan's stylized, esoteric Noh musical theater and some of Japan's enduring literary masterpieces, beginning with *The Tale of Genji,* the eleventh-century novel about life at the Kyoto imperial court.[7] Both reflect to quintessential Japanese sensibility, not completely dead even now, to the unspoken, the emotional, the quietly perceived.

Yet paradoxically, neither the austerity of shibui nor the melancholy of mono no aware stood in the way of the use of bright colors and bold design. Quite the contrary. The gorgeous costumes of the Noh and Kabuki theater and the striking patterns and hues of many styles of kimono are proof of an exuberant streak in the otherwise restrained national character. The same could be said of some of the grander room screens and door paintings. Both in conception and in execution they were a far cry from the reserved comportment of the people wearing them and moving among them.

Could it be that vicarious display was the necessary compensation for the repressed behavior required by traditional Japanese society? An intriguing thought, the plausibility of which I will gladly leave to more qualified minds to ponder.

One might well ask which of these two extremes represents the "true" *traditional* Japanese spirit. The answer must of course be: both, although not in equal measure. I for one always felt attracted to the shibui tastes of the literati, which also seemed to represent the values of the educated classes in general. To me, it was in this refined, quiet, unassertive aesthetic (which at the same time represented their guiding ethic) that the essential nature of Japan's culture was to be found.

Women can have their Kabuki, I thought, and the merchants their bunraku puppet theater; my soul needs deep tea bowls and shady bamboo groves and books printed on hand-made *washi* paper. Let the popular singers belt out their *kayokyoku* (pop song) tearjerkers, for me it's the throaty chant of the Zen monks, or the basso *utai* chorus on a Noh stage. Shibumi was my big discovery, sometime during mid-Showa. I thought it was forever. It was not a *brand*, but it should have been. A comprehensive life-brand.

But it lost out to other brands—the super brands, mostly. Not literally, of course; they are different concepts. But as wealth spread and semi-Western styles of living became the norm rather than the exception (as they had been in Showa), shibui slowly came to stand for fogeyish, unfashionable, dull—at least in the eyes of the trendy brigade. I used to be complimented on my shibui neckties. Now they would be called drab.

Traditional Arts Adapted to Changing Tastes

Showa visitors to Japan inevitably and rightfully gushed about the country's rich traditions in arts and crafts, and many of them ended up taking some course or other in *ikebana* flower arrangement, tea ceremony, or pottery making, or tried their hand at haiku or brush calligraphy. International esteem for Japan's cultural heritage increased greatly during Showa, and it has continued to grow since.

Yet the drift away from tradition in Japanese daily life that marked the Showa prosperity has not spared the arts. More precisely, although many of the ancient arts were still practiced with great skill and dedication—as indeed they are to-day—their *intrinsic* connection with everyday life became increasingly tenuous. For example, calligraphy, a universal means of written communication only a few decades ago, was shoved aside by ball point pens and computers, although it survives as an elective art for its own sake. Refined artistic pastimes such as the tea ceremony and the savoring of incense traditionally require squatting on tatami mats, which have been steadily disappearing from Japanese urban living.

Once a Craftsman...

Tokyo, 1964. As my wife has stopped wearing kimonos, she has been asking around for a jeweler to convert some of her obi-dome silver clasps into brooches or pendants.

"Ah," said our local electrician, "I know just the man. Satomi-san, he lives in the neighborhood, eking out a living by making little pornographic contraptions in silver and gold for the rich. You know, they do naughty stuff when you open them, ha-ha. But he's a real craftsman, who has seen better times."

My wife decided to give it a try. She took an elaborate clasp of layered chrysanthemum design which her mother had worn when she graduated from high school over to Satomi's workshop.

When the man's wife saw it she exclaimed "I know this piece! My husband made it, when was it, in the late 1920s? You know, in those days we could survive for two whole months from an order like that!"

My wife, struck by the coincidence, ended up ordering a matching chrysanthemum ring for herself and cufflinks for me. Satomi executed them with the same exquisite eye for detail he had used in the earlier piece. He had lost none of his skill.

Even ikebana, that most quintessentially Japanese art, showed evidence of struggling. Where once flowers, grasses, and branches were the only materials used in the creations of the Ikenobo School—the standard bearer of classical, formal ikebana since the fifteenth century—by the end of Showa one was hard put to find an arrangement that did not prominently feature plastics, metal wire, and other inorganic elements. "Just flowers" was apparently no longer done in trendy flower circles.

A more charitable view would be to welcome this break with the rigid rules and requirements of more traditional kinds of ikebana as proof that even the most ancient of arts is not above modernizing. Perhaps. But ikebana evolved in the surroundings of low-slung, wooden houses. The flowers—small arrangements to suit the alcoves in which they were placed—were to be viewed from a low, squatting position. It was an intimate, quiet process. The guiding philosophy was one of respect for all living things, which dictated the cutting of a minimum number of flowers.

The modernization process has continued during the two decades since the end of Showa. Nowadays, the mixed-material creations, placed on tables, are often large, meant for offices or public spaces. The arrangements' components are sometimes daubed with paint and broken or twisted into completely unnatural forms. The change represents the drastic shift in overall living patterns, from *wafu* to *yofu*—from Japanese to Western style—that has been such a conspicuous feature of the Showa era and beyond.

Part Two
The Breathless Eighties:
From Boom to Bust

The excesses of Japan's golden years were in a sense a reaction to the long years of austerity and self-control that preceded them. They were a celebration of the nation's newfound place in the ranks of the most prosperous and successful of the world's leading nations.

It could be argued, when looking for the causes of the bubble, that post-war frugality, dictated by the realities of the time, had been stretched far beyond necessity. The ruling elite made sure that traditional discipline and docility stayed in place, to keep the workforce from spending their hard-earned savings long after the need for such self-restraint had evaporated. When external market pressures and pent-up demand finally forced a policy change, the spontaneous reaction was a wild shopping and investment spree—both corporate and personal. The know-how to tell good investments from bad had not been acquired in the protective environment of the post-war economy, not even by the nation's bankers and portfolio managers.

In Japan the 1980s are usually referred to as the decade of the bubble economy, for its classic hallmarks of excess and overheating. The economy grew at breakneck speed, Japan's exports conquered the world, and "Japan as Number One" grew from an American writer's catchphrase into a bold national ambition.[1] Toward the end of the decade the bubble became pronounced as assets (stocks and real estate, especially) became excessively overpriced; it finally burst, with a disastrous drop in share and property values.

While the whole of post-war Showa, right up to Emperor Hirohito's death in 1989, is commonly viewed as Japan's Golden Age, the economic bubble of Showa's last decade or so deserves separate treatment because the country's achievements and international prestige arguably reached their zenith during this period. The hubris and wild speculation that eventually defeated sound judgment and ended in crisis is worth exploring.

There seems to be no agreement on the length of Japan's asset bubble. Most sources locate it from around 1986 to 1990. Mark Thornton, a noted American economist, says it began in the early 1970s. There can be no disagreement on when it peaked: at the end of 1989, coinciding very closely with the death of Emperor Hirohito and the end of the Showa era.

Although the boom-to-bust cycle had profound consequences for many individuals, companies, and the nation as a whole, the pre-bust euphoria of free spending, luxurious living, and looking forward to an impossibly bright future, is not easily forgotten. Perhaps it has a place in the Showa nostalgia, alongside the more sentimental memories of the austere times that preceded it. And the era of the bubble did after all bring with it changes widely believed to be for the better, such as a greater diversity in Japanese society, a greatly expanded choice of international art and cultural manifestations of every kind, and more cosmopolitan options in food and fashions.

Chapter 11

Investing the Bubble Way

While the most dramatic phase of asset price inflation did indeed occur toward the end of the decade, there is ample evidence that it all began in the early 1970s. I remember it well: the rampant spending on entertainment, the rising market for luxury cognacs and whiskeys, the speculation in land. I was among the countless thousands duped by the property hustlers. It started with a respectable investment in a modest residential lot somewhere in a new Kobe suburb, which I managed to unload within a year at double the price. But my next move still makes me cringe at the recollection.

The year was 1972. Enticed by seductive brochures and salesmen's sweet talk I persuaded my wife into accompanying me on a long car trip into an obscure mountainous corner of Fukushima prefecture, about 150 miles (250 kilometers) northeast of Tokyo, to view some "highly desirable" building lots for the "ideal weekend home." To my manipulated mind, it seemed a sensible way to reinvest the proceeds of that fortuitous Kobe sale. In those pre-motorway days, it took us five hours to get to the site, but we were greeted by happy banners and a welcome reception where scores of city dwellers like us were being indoctrinated in the virtues of investing in land, here, in this beautiful but isolated backwater. Soon we were trudging up the dirt tracks of the hilly subdivisions, eagerly following the smiling salesmen around in search of the best buy. "Prices are still low here, but they are sure to rise!"

When we finally settled on the ideal plot, it had just been snapped up by someone else. We ended up buying one of the leftovers, an awkward half-acre lot for the bargain price of 10 million yen—about $100,000 at the time. But at least we had acquired a stake in Japan's invincible future.

And that was just the *beginning* of the bubble.

Don't ask me what the plot is worth today. Probably only a fraction of what I paid for it, if I could find a buyer. Which is unlikely: in that neck of the woods alone, there are today over five hundred other proud owners trying to part with their wise bubble investments.

The Investment Heard 'Round the World

Private citizens flush with the results of decades worth of hard work were not the only ones who spent big. During the mid-1980s, Japanese corporate property investors increasingly turned their attention to overseas markets, chiefly the United States, with California as their first target. In 1986 Shuwa Investments acquired Arco Plaza—a twin-tower, fifty-five-story office and retail complex in Los Angeles—for $620 million. Total Japanese property investments in the United States that year alone were estimated at $6 billion, some of it at highly inflated prices.[2]

By far the most spectacular acquisition was Mitsubishi Group's purchase, in 1989, of a 51 percent interest in Rockefeller Group Inc., owners of Rockefeller Center in New York, which the *New York Times* dubbed "the Hope diamond of the world property market." The following year Mitsubishi increased its stake to $1.4 billion for an 80 percent ownership. The deal was controversial, not only because the Japanese were beginning to be seen as disturbing the market by paying any price for whatever they set their sights on but also for the symbolism of seeing one of America's supreme urban icons slip into foreign hands. I was just leaving New York at the time, after a stint of eight years, and I remember one American muttering darkly to me "Is this their revenge for Hiroshima?"

Senator Joseph Lieberman of Connecticut put it more delicately. "This year," he was quoted as saying, "when they turn on the lights of that Christmas tree in Rockefeller Center, we Americans are going to have to come to grips with the reality that this great national celebration is actually occurring on Japanese property." Comments like these caused surprise in Japan at the time, but I suppose the Japanese might have reacted similarly if, say, the capital's iconic Tokyo Tower had moved into American hands.

By no means were all Japan's overseas investments of a commercial nature. Beginning in this period of explosive growth, its foreign aid to developing countries was consistently among the highest of all donor countries, as were its contributions to the United Nations (UN) and other international institutions. In addition, both government and private sources donated generously to numerous foreign cultural and humanitarian projects. This activity continued well after the bubble had burst; witness, for example, the opening in 1999 of a large new wing on the Van Gogh Museum in Amsterdam, made possible by a gift from the Yasuda Fire & Marine Insurance Company through the Japan Foundation.

Location, Location, and Never Mind the Price

It is not surprising that the overheated economic climate led the property market in Japan to go berserk in the late 1980s. There is no other word for it, as once again my own experience bears out. My wife had inherited her mother's well-located two-bedroom, 1,367 square foot (127 square meter) apartment in Tokyo's Minato Ward originally bought in 1971 for 27 million yen ($75,000 at the then prevailing rate). In 1989 she received an offer for it of 800 million yen (over $6 million). She did not trust the buyer and in any case did not want to sell, as she was using the apartment actively and would have to buy a replacement property at a similar insane price. But two identical apartments in the same building in fact changed hands for 900 million yen a piece!

The previous year I had arranged a loan of 200 million yen against collateral of the very same property, in order to take advantage of the wide interest rate differentials between the yen and the dollar. In previous years even small personal bank loans were almost impossible to obtain, as the government told the banks to refrain from most consumer lending other than residential mortgages. This was a holdover from the days when all available financial resources were to be employed first and foremost for the development of trade and industry. With the anything-goes mood that characterized the bubble, these restrictions were finally lifted.

So this time around the application was waved through with a minimum of hassle, based solely on the presumed market value of the apartment, which the bank appraised at 300 million yen! (We repaid the loan within a matter of months when exchange rates started turning against us.) Today, the apartment is worth no more than *one-tenth* of the rejected peak-bubble offer.

The most telling proof of the extreme overheating of the property market was the estimate at the height of the bubble that the grounds of the Imperial Palace in Tokyo, smaller than Disneyland, were worth more than the entire state of California.

The reckoning soon followed with the collapse of the markets. The Japanese bubble would go down in history as comparable to the Tulip Mania in seventeenth century Holland and the South Sea Bubble of the early eighteenth century. Immense paper fortunes were wiped out overnight, and the banks, those dumb banks that had failed to use their heads and loaned money indiscriminately, were in deep, deep trouble.

The Arrogance of Success

How did all this come about?

From the late 1970s onward, a boundless sense of triumph suffused the country, a direct consequence of the booming economy at home and the apparent wavering of American and European self-assurance. At last Japanese technological and commercial savvy were beating the Americans at their own game. The era of Americans lecturing the Japanese on how to behave was over, as the Japanese ambassador to Washington at the time made clear in articles written for the US media. "Learn from *us*" was the essence of his message.

And Americans listened. As far back as March 1970, Herman Kahn, a political strategist and cofounder in 1961 of the Hudson Institute think tank in upstate New York (now situated in Washington, DC), had already written a major article in *Time* magazine entitled "Toward the Japanese Century," followed in 1973 by an influential book, *The Emerging Japanese Superstate.* But it was another book, the seminal *Japan as Number One: Lessons for America*, published in 1979 by Harvard professor and eminent Japanese studies guru Ezra Vogel, that became the model for a decade of books and university courses extolling the superior virtues of the Japanese system of production, management, and labor relations to Western audiences. The book was a bestseller in both the United States and Japan. American and some Japanese management consultants did a thriving business warning Western business that the future belonged to Japan unless we changed our ways.

In Japan this sudden adulation of the Japanese way met with initial bemusement that quickly turned into belief. Belief, that is, in what they regarded as undoubtedly a correct prediction by such eminent men as Kahn and Vogel. Belief, therefore, in the apparently unstoppable advance of their industrial juggernaut and, incredible as it may sound, the *defeat* of the revered American giant.

How Not to Interview a Bureaucrat

September, 1995. I led a delegation of about twenty graduate students from Erasmus University in Rotterdam on a tour of Japanese companies and ministries. The students were a surprisingly mature and urbane group, tall, well dressed, and in excellent command of English. This was the high point of their one-year research project entitled "Japan, distressed financial markets at a turning point." The group broke up into two or three smaller groups, each with a different focus. The visits to banks and corporate bastions were fine—not terribly informative on the whole, but we were welcomed and treated to lunch, and there was mutual respect and touches of humor.

But the visit to the Ministry of International Trade and Industry (MITI), attended by seven or eight of the students, was different. We were seated at the long end of a huge oval-shaped arrangement of tables. The three MITI officials occupied the center of the opposite side of the oval. Off to the far end, on the officials' side of the oval but barely so, sat an interpreter, a woman. As it turned out, her services were hardly drawn upon as the senior official, who was also the spokesman, understood our English perfectly well and his replies, in Japanese, were so poorly rendered into English by the interpreter that I—and sometimes the unsmiling official—had to help out.

From the start the officials' attitude was stern, almost hostile. They obviously resented this Dutch group's prying into Japan's financial affairs, and their answers were cursory and unhelpful. In a word, these bureaucrats were an arrogant bunch, and the rather casual—though not impolite—manner in which my young Dutch charges posed their questions may not have helped. They should have been more deferential.

There was a noticeable increase in the swagger of Japanese businessmen, politicians, and bureaucrats during the late seventies and throughout the eighties. It wasn't just the profligacy; it was the *attitude* that grew in its wake that riled many observers. As far back as 1975, an aristocratic European banker who had lived in Japan for many years vented his feelings to me. Witness this note in my journal:

My friend L. is hoping for a left-wing takeover in Japan. He expects they will break up the big combines, which will be a good thing. "The hoarding, the profiteering, the land speculation and the ignoring of workers' health and living conditions, the reckless spending on the Ginza [Tokyo's most elegant shopping quarter], the lavish gift giving—it all demands redress. Perhaps it is from spite, but upstarts from Mitsubishi and the like are living it up with chauffeured limousines and five-star brandy, while we tighten our belts. The arrogance is intolerable." And this from a patrician gentleman known for his modesty.

American open-market conditions tempted some Japanese businesses into what Americans considered unfair trading practices. The huge and growing car imports allegedly at prices set below those for the domestic Japanese market were a major and well-publicized target, but Japanese banks, too, on occasion managed to upset their domestic rivals.

The Charge of the Money Men

Toward the end of the 1980s, I was chairing the Institute of Foreign Bankers (IFB) in the United States, which represented all 240 foreign banks operating in the States at the time. I received complaints from the Federal Reserve Bank in Washington that Japanese banks were suddenly and aggressively offering jumbo bank loans to leading US corporations at below-market rates of interest. The complaints, they said, originated from US banks, who considered the Japanese assault a form of disruptive "financial dumping," referring to the intermittent 1960s and 1970s US charges that Japanese manufacturers were selling merchandise in US markets at below-cost prices. I verified this with our own American customers, some of whom admitted gleefully that they had accepted the "Japanese money" but added they had no intention of starting a regular banking relationship with Japanese banks. Nor, it seems, were the Japanese banks necessarily looking for long-term relationships with American companies. All they were interested in was to make a quick profit on large, short-term dollar loans to excellent borrowers at rates that—however low—still left them a small profit, as they funded the loans mostly from the interbank market. In that sense it wasn't really "dumping," just cut-throat lending.

One might argue that in America—the mother of all free markets—such competitive moves should have been welcomed, not condemned. But this could hardly be called free and fair competition: *all* fifteen-odd major Japanese banks active in the States at the time simultaneously entered the market with their bargain-basement mega-loan offers, apparently acting on some directive or "green light" from above. When the head of the Foreign Department of the Bank of Japan, whom I knew well, visited New York, I brought the matter to his attention, and he agreed to reign in the banks, which apparently is what happened, as the complaints ceased.

In other ways, too, the attitude of Japanese banks active in the US market during this period was sometimes more exploitative than participative. Although they were all members of the IFB, they rarely showed any interest in helping run it. Once, in New York, right in the middle of a large, high-profile IFB dinner, a friend of mine representing one of the large Japanese banks came up to the dais where I was sitting flanked by five or six members of the Institute's board. His face flushed, this senior banker vented his indignation at not seeing any Japanese on the dais. "We should be there! We are members! You should recognize the importance of Japan!" he hissed.

Trying to avoid a scene I took him aside and explained that presence on the board and, therefore, on the platform was not determined by status, but by merit, that is, the ideas and time one was able to contribute—the degree of active involvement. Why, my own bank, still new on the American scene, was hardly a giant, but that had not precluded me from getting elected to the chair. By contrast, none of the Japanese bankers had shown much interest in the Institute, whose main purpose was to protect the interests of *all* foreign banks in the United States.

Later, my friend apologized for his intemperate outburst. He admitted that he had not realized how organizations like ours functioned. He thought that size alone mattered. It was a classic case of a hierarchical as opposed to a functional approach, a cultural difference that often bedeviled Japanese-Western intercourse.

A characterization of what was going on was delivered by Christopher Wood, a journalist who covered Japan for about twenty years. He wrote that Japan "became so arrogant in the late 1980s because it really believed it was immune from the natural laws of the marketplace. This really was one of the most astonishing acts of mass delusion ever, and future historians...will marvel at it."[3]

Chapter **12**
Bubble Excesses

Expatriate bankers and businessmen like me, used to the more sober social relations of the sixties and seventies, were aghast at the corporate spending power displayed during the bubble years.

Take the lavish receptions at Tokyo's top hotels. The introduction of a new CEO or simply the start of the New Year were adequate excuses for inviting a few hundred business relations to a glittering affair, sometimes featuring top-class hostesses and always an abundance of alcohol and sumptuous food.

Waiters in traditional Japanese *happi* coats cracked open large barrels of sake in one corner, and Hiroshima oysters and long-legged king crab from Hokkaido in another. Succulent cuts of costly Kobe beef sizzled on the grill, and the fish at the sushi bar were the freshest and most delectable available. For those with a sweet tooth, the dessert offerings ran the gamut from delicate petit-fours to cherries jubilee and crêpes Suzette cooked before your eyes. And there usually was a consignment of juicy musk melon, which in Japan for some reason vies with caviar in priciness.

These parties were clearly more about eating and drinking than conversation. Yet, to be seen frequenting functions of this level was a mark of importance in its own right. For a while in the early seventies, when my bank was lending heavily to Japan's booming capital-hungry industry, I hovered precariously on some of Tokyo's corporate guest lists, sometimes dropping in at two or three receptions before heading for home. I tried to feign indifference when on emerging from these affairs I heard the doorman instantly call for "Mr. B's automobile!" over the public address system without having to be prompted. I never ceased being amazed at such prodigious professional memory.

By the mid-1980s, first-class receptions could easily cost 40,000 yen and frequently much more a head, or $100,000 and up for a party of 300, including the cost of a substantial take-home gift on leaving.

The Price of Getting Hitched...and of Hitting a Ball

Wedding banquets, too, reached new peaks of opulence. Ten million yen ($70,000) was just about the minimum you had to budget for a respectable middle-class affair at the Okura or the Imperial Hotel, stretching over several hours with breaks of champagne sorbet and live entertainment between courses and three dress changes by the bride. These occasions were as much a test of stamina for the 50 to 150 guests as they were challenges to the financial muscle of the bride's father, who usually had to foot the bill.

Increasingly during the 1980s, hotels and restaurants built would-be Christian chapels on their premises to accommodate the trendy Western-style wedding ceremonies that were replacing traditional Shinto rituals. And honeymoons were, of course, taken abroad, with Hawaii and Australia the favored destinations of the 90 percent of newlyweds who took their honeymoon trips outside Japan during the late 1980s.

Even funeral costs soared. As late as 1997, eight years after the end of the bubble, the average cost of a Japanese funeral was tens of thousands of dollars, even in remote Hokkaido.[4]

Another area of extravagance was the world of executive golf. In a country where golf had always been the corporate sport-cum-entertainment par excellence, both for the top of the house and for the aspiring young executive, private golf club memberships had long been a coveted item. Now, with demand skyrocketing and suitable sites within traveling distance from the city centers in short supply, prices for these memberships went through the roof as they became an object of unrestrained speculation. At the peak of the bubble, transferable memberships in the most prestigious golf clubs in the greater Tokyo area could cost up to 400 million yen ($3.5 million). Picture our excitement, therefore, when my wife found among some dusty family papers the share certificate of her late father's pre-war membership in a fashionable Nagoya golf club. But our dream of acquiring a sumptuous villa on the Riviera with the cashed-in proceeds of the precious share quickly evaporated when the club informed us that those particular certificates had been declared null and void after the war.

By the end of the eighties there were approximately 1,700 golf courses in Japan, fifty times the number there was in the mid-1950s. Environmental lobbies protested vehemently against this rampant destruction of nature and its attendant hazards of deforestation and air and water pollution caused by the vast amounts of pesticides and other toxic chemicals used in their maintenance.

Yet the runaway property and stock prices did not lead to serious inflation of daily living expenses generally. Even so, some unscrupulous characters tried to take advantage of the prevailing mood by charging exorbitant fees for services rendered to those they thought could afford it. In some circles, this unsavory side of the bubble mentality persisted well into the 1990s. Around the turn of the millennium a friend of mine told me that she had uncomplainingly paid the rising medical and dental bills of her family over the years, until one day—after serious bridgework—she was presented with a bill of 20 million yen, almost $200,000. *Then* she complained. Without blushing, the dentist reduced the bill to 3 million yen, $30,000.

Art for the Sake of—What?

An altogether different way in which some Japanese companies and individuals chose to flaunt their newfound wealth was by investment in Western art.

Perhaps following the lead of the great American art collectors of the nineteenth and early twentieth centuries, Japanese individuals and corporations used bubble conditions to invest heavily in fine art, often at seriously inflated prices. A new record was set for a van Gogh painting when in 1987 a Japanese investor paid $40 million for *Sunflowers*. Three years later another van Gogh, *Portrait of Dr. Gachet*, went for an astounding $83 million,[5] again to a Japanese buyer, who also bought a Renoir for $78 million. Hundreds of other paintings were snapped up by Japanese investors during this period, and not always with due regard for quality.

Some of these investments in art were made with profits realized in the booming real estate and stock markets, but most of the paintings were acquired with the help of bank loans secured by property that, as the bubble burst, proved to be disastrously overvalued. As a result, much of this art ended up in bank vaults as collateral security, instead of in museums or on the walls of private residences or corporate boardrooms for which they had been intended.

Chapter 13

Sex and the Japanese City

Bubble-era excesses were not only economic in nature. Another feature of those heady years was the rapid acceleration of a trend that was already well under way: the replacement of the geisha by the bar or nightclub hostess.

The late-Showa executive's habit of dropping in at a favorite watering hole after work with a colleague or two usually had an ulterior motive barely disguised by claims of preferring the place's "atmosphere" or choice of top-brand whiskeys. What really drove him back there time and again was a particular hostess—some well-groomed beauty wearing top-brand outfits and catering to his every whim and desire. She was to him what the geisha would have been in mid-Showa, only more so. For not only did she look more natural than the classic geisha with her white-powdered face and heavy wig, but she also was free to flaunt her figure and her legs, which with her geisha predecessor had been hidden beneath layers of kimono. This new consciousness of one's own body and the interest in fashions to express it grew rapidly among young women in general during the boom. It was the antithesis of the self-effacing shyness that had been considered proper in leaner times.

Few aspects of Japanese culture have intrigued Westerners more than the institution of the geisha. Its sheer exoticism—of dress, makeup, comportment, and lifestyle—may account for some of this interest. But no doubt it is the geisha's erotic "function" that has captured the imagination of generations of Western men—and women. The geisha was an *accepted* extramarital outlet for the successful married man. Accepted—because she lived in a world that was safely separate from society proper, a twilight world with its own strict codes of behavior, which laid no claim to her customers' other lives. Accepted, too, because the true geisha is no whore but an *artiste* accomplished at dance or witty conversation, not available for casual affairs but only, at a price, as a steady mistress.

Everyman's dream, one might think—if you could ignore the cost of gaining access to a favorite geisha's sexual favors and the often-heartbreaking stories of how the girls ended up as geishas in the first place—sold by penniless parents into a life of bondage.

The irony is that as Western enthrallment with the darker side of the geisha phenomenon grew during the eighties and beyond (culminating in Arthur Golden's bestselling 1997 novel *Memoirs of a Geisha* and its Hollywood treatment of 2005), the geisha tradition as such was already long past its heyday and had lost its poignant allure. No longer were girls sold into servitude, with their release from it dependent on a successful financial settlement between their owners and the courting customer. The geisha had become a career woman, who *chose* to be a geisha and could leave the profession any time she felt so inclined. Some modern geisha even boast a university degree.

Behind the Screens of Decorum...

Part of the geisha's demise was due to the businessmen's (and bureaucrats') growing preference for less complicated, more transient forms of pleasure, perhaps more like those offered by the licensed red-light districts of old, which disappeared when prostitution was outlawed in 1956. The sex trade had naturally found ways around the ban, which often turned out to be sleazier than what they replaced.

Dubious massage parlors thrived, as did the "Turkish" baths where the customer's coat hung on a peg obscured an open view through the mandatory window of the private rooms, facilitating the pursuit of any banned activity. (The sordid reputation of these de facto brothels would later prompt the Turkish embassy to launch a successful campaign against the use of the word "Turkish" in this seedy context.) Another innovation was the "love hotels" with their mirrored rooms, hourly rates, and pleasure-enhancing equipment, patronized alike by young couples and older men who had scored in a bar or nightclub.

The bubble years saw an explosion in more sophisticated employer-sanctioned and paid-for erotic enjoyment, accounted for as corporate entertainment and served up in the elegant (or steamy) surroundings of bars, nightclubs, and private rooms of posh Japanese restaurants with well-dressed hostesses in attendance. The staggering bills were presented on little scraps of paper without breakdown and approved without a murmur. No self-respecting executive wanted to leave an impression of pettiness by asking for specification.

There was no question of actual sex being purveyed in these establishments, although there were racy reports of occasional louche parties where delectable slices of raw fish were served on the naked bodies of winsome girls. The nightclubs often did serve as handy venues for making your own arrangements, which were usually a cinch for a regular customer. And you never needed to travel far from the nightspots of Ginza, Shimbashi, or Akasaka to find one of those ubiquitous love hotels to consummate your night out on the town. Afterwards, hundreds of taxis were waiting to take you home, at twice or three times the meter fare billed to your company, to your suburban home and the waiting wife.

Or if you wanted to take your date out to an upscale *ryotei* restaurant, it was not too difficult to find one featuring private tatami rooms for couples, where you could ask for "unhurried service," to allow for intimacy between courses.

But for the top executive with ample income and a generous expense account, it was the elegant young hostess in one of the more exclusive clubs that he would, sooner or later, set his sights on. If he played his cards well—persuading not only the girl but the club's madam too—he might succeed in making her his exclusive mistress, a coup that usually involved a serious financial commitment, like setting her up in a bar or business of her own. Such outlays were seldom a problem for the boom-era businessman.

While the old-style geisha, a generation or so back, typically was unintellectual but excelled in some form of traditional dance or music, the high-class hostess was a contemporary, well-educated woman who knew her world fashion brands, followed the world news, and could be savvy in business. The replacement of the geisha by the nightclub hostess was yet another illustration of the demise of Showa values.

Goings-On at the Spas

My outsider status and my own employer's rather puritanical standards generally shielded me from exposure to these interesting possibilities, but I do recall one notable exception. It concerned a small group outing by air to a Kyushu hot spring at the invitation of a steelmaker in appreciation of a five-year loan we had made to help their plant expansion. It was a mixed group of bankers and businessmen, foreign and Japanese. After we checked in at the mountain inn a banquet was served up in a large tatami room, where local "hot spring geishas"—a notch or two below the classy urban geisha—kept us plied with sake, whiskey and risqué banter.

It seemed all good innocent fun until the banquet turned into a bacchanal. It didn't take long before some of the men began to fondle the geishas, soon pairing off with them and disappearing to their rooms. The rapid breakdown in decorum frankly astonished me, but not to be outdone, I myself ended up in the bathtub with a buxom lass whose main attribute was her ability to keep smiling happily through every stage of the proceedings. The experience was more homely than erotic (the food had been humdrum, too), and I rather regretted having wasted the weekend. But what bothered me more was the compromising nature of the event: the patently unwise intrusion of sexual favors into an otherwise perfectly upright bank-customer relationship.

But this questionable fling proved a mere peccadillo when compared to a *fortissimo* variation on the theme that was growing in popularity around the same time: corporate sex tours to foreign destinations. At first Taiwan, with its residual familiarity with Japanese men and language, was the main port of call, desirable for the ready availability of women at the Peitou hot spring resort and elsewhere. After Japan officially recognized Communist China in 1972—simultaneously withdrawing their recognition of Taiwan's Nationalist government as the legitimate representative of all China—direct flights to Taiwan were suspended, and the gentlemen from Japan set their sights on Thai, Filipino, and South Korean women instead. The trade boomed, triggering protests and demonstrations from human rights activists at each location, but the practice persisted and flourished throughout the eighties and beyond.

As one commentator put it in 1993: "The heart of the problem is that sex tours have become part of accepted business practice. Corporations now use sex just like alcohol to serve clients and to socialize with colleagues."[6]

It could be argued that Japanese businessmen were (and are) not alone in pursuing illicit pleasures in a corporate context. Other Asian countries are also known to frequently mix sex and business, and major scandals in the United States and Europe are often tainted by sexual favors offered and accepted by parties to questionable transactions. What makes the Japanese variety different is its collectivity. A rather startling example of this inclination occurred in September 2003, in Zhuhai, China, when local authorities shut down a five-star hotel where nearly 500 girls were allegedly serving around 400 Japanese men aged 16 to 37 on an organized sex tour.[7]

As in so many other respects, those Japanese men interested in cross-border sex apparently prefer the group to the individual foray. The popular, idiosyncratic comedian and film director Beat Takeshi expressed this Japanese proclivity for collective endeavor brilliantly with his famous *senryu* (humorous haiku):

Akashingo/minna de watareba/kowakunai
(The light is red—but/if we all cross together/it won't be scary)

An extreme instance of the ongoing interest in group activity was delivered to my laptop as I was writing these words. The Japanese version of my personal Web site, which focuses on twenty-first century Japanese society, was suddenly invaded by an avalanche of porn, through the Links option. One of the images showed a large hall full of naked fornicating couples, more than a hundred of them. They were all obviously Japanese, and real people, not computer-generated clones. For a moment I wondered how the show would end, but I suppressed my curiosity and called my webmaster. He instantly cleaned up the site.

For many years before Japan's economic boom in the eighties, some of the nouveau riche and yakuza gangsters had been keen on acquiring a European or American mistress to enhance their status. Once, on a visit to Kyoto in the late seventies, I happened to meet an attractive young French woman at a bus stop. While waiting for the bus we struck up a conversation, and I soon got the impression that she was deeply troubled, and in need of help or advice. I ended up spending part of the day with her, gradually ferreting out the nature of her problem.

She was the mistress of a petty Japanese gangster, the derailed son of a rich businessman, who had charmed her in Paris, where he studied at the Sorbonne, and persuaded her to come back to Japan with him. Once there he had soon fallen in with the wrong crowd and gotten involved with extortion schemes and loan sharking. When she objected to these activities and turned cold on him, his attitude to her rapidly changed. He kept showing her off to his friends, but at the same time put her under surveillance and threatened violence if she dared to bolt. He kept her on a short leash and the little money he gave her was barely enough to manage an occasional afternoon in town.

While sympathizing with her plight, I also felt she could escape from her predicament by appealing to the French consulate or asking for help from her family in France, but she was too scared to run away. Besides, she had actually come to like Japan and did not want to return to France. I took her back to her street in a taxi and never saw her again.

I asked the taxi to recommend a simple inn for the night, and he took me to a cheap place, where I was given a bare tatami room next door to what turned out to be a noisy bunch of yakuza. It sounded like an underling was being severely scolded for dereliction of duty: he had failed to keep tabs on somebody. At one point the boss turned violent, the heavy thud of a body repeatedly hitting the flimsy wall accompanied by yelling and screaming. I sat up straight, ready to throw my duvet over any intruder that crashed through the thin paper door of my room, which was rattling in its frame. At last the ruckus ended, and I could catch a few hours' sleep. I have always suspected that it was the French mistress the punk had lost sight of, although the coincidence seemed hardly credible.

The Kyoto gangster was not alone in indulging his taste for exotic female beauty. Young white women were also much in demand at Tokyo's nightspots. Many of these girls—often overstaying their tourist visas—made good money flattering their Japanese expense-account customers in basic Japanese and making sure that they ordered nothing less than five-star whiskey and cognac and, for themselves, fancy cocktails sprinkled with gold-leaf confetti.

Yet all of these prurient pursuits took place behind a well-maintained screen of public decorum. Kissing in public continued to be frowned upon. Women never bared anything more seductive than a lower leg or a shapely neck. Cleavage was concealed, and eyes cast down. There was not a nude to be seen in advertising or on movie posters. Even the raciest magazines observed the prohibition against the depiction of genitals. Imported glossies like *Playboy* and *Hustler* were censored for lurid images, and the offending parts blotted out with squares of black, bureaucratic ink. Explicit scenes in films and videos were hidden from innocent eyes by "mosaic" patterns that obscured the action, which had the side effect of enhancing their power to arouse.

I remember an early breach of this puritanical regime. It occurred in 1969 with the opening of the Akasaka Tokyu Hotel in one of Tokyo's upmarket entertainment districts, not far from the Crown Prince's palace. There, at the entrance of its second-floor casual restaurant, I was greeted by a larger-than-life-size nude photograph of the luscious Mie Hama—the chief Bond girl in the 1967 James Bond film *You Only Live Twice*. The actress was depicted in a reclining, horizontal position, and the photo was backlit for extra effect. This daring deviation from respectability caused a predictable stir, but perhaps less so than had, a year or so earlier, the *Playboy* centerfold displaying the intimate charms of Hama and other Japanese actresses from the same film. It was not the nudity as such that caused the controversy—it was the fact that *Japanese* girls, actresses no less, had allowed their naked bodies to be displayed like that, and in a foreign magazine to boot. That was scandalous.

As it turned out, these mild offences against public decency did not open the floodgates. Censorship laws remained firmly in place, and by and large, society's long-held preference for keeping a clean front while turning a blind eye to what happened indoors, prevailed. At the stylish Tokyo bathhouse where some of the Bond film's risqué scenes were filmed it was "business as usual" when I visited a year or so after the release of the film. It seemed hardly the better—or worse—for the publicity it received.

The profligacy of Showa's bubble years did not erase the deeply rooted distinction between one's public persona and what one did in private. The Victorians would have felt at home here.

Chapter **14**

The Emergence of Subcultures

B ut for all that, the extravagant ways of the bubble years were mostly confined to the class of corporate executives with generous expense accounts, and to those politicians and bureaucrats closely connected to them. Personal wealth was of course growing, and there were some highly successful entrepreneurs, but right until the end of the bubble, executive compensation remained relatively modest. Ironically, fabulous fortunes on the American scale were not really amassed until *after* the bubble had burst, and the arrival of the market economy began to gnaw away at prudent standards of income distribution.

By the end of the 1980s, Japan could boast of a huge middle class, an average income that was among the highest in the world, and an equally high level of personal savings. What was still lacking was leisure time. Mid-Showa levels of commitment were still common, with people working all hours and not having outside social lives.

The rise of the *otaku* generation of alienated young people who shunned conventional society and fled into self-absorption, perhaps the most striking social phenomenon of the 1980s, may be considered a reaction to this. Initially compulsively focused on computer games, these nerdy characters gradually took up other interests: comic books, pop music, collecting toys or trivia about film stars and girl singers—whatever caught their obsessive minds. Many wore outlandish—or deceptively plain—clothing and accessories. Their particular object of desire was less important than their "mode of being," the common thread of asocial behavior that bound them together.

The otaku phenomenon gave birth to other subcultures. The extravagantly named *shin-jinrui* ("new human species") differed from the otaku in that they were more empty-headed, emphasizing outward appearance over any kind of inner pretension. They were typically born between 1958 and 1967. Their brand-oriented consumerism and trendy way of life formed the inspiration for Yasuo Tanaka's 1980 bestselling novel, *Nantonaku Kurisutaru* (*Somehow, Crystal*), which is often regarded as the ultimate expression of the hedonistic subcultures of the day. Despite its flimsy plot it sold over a million copies, on account of its real aim: to be an insider's guide to a superficial lifestyle. Here every would-be snob could find in its over 400 footnotes the names and addresses of Tokyo's "in" shops, restaurants, clubs, and other sources of a joyful consumer existence.[8]

The otaku, shinjinrui, and similar youth-culture manifestations of the 1980s and beyond were largely made possible by the exertions of the previous generation. The enormous pool of savings accumulated during the decades of fast economic growth was mostly left untouched by those who created it and who now could only watch with indulgence—or exasperation—as their offspring flaunted the family riches in ways that would have been unacceptable in their own time.

A More Diverse Society

The emergence of the information society and the spread of the computer gave a major boost to the development of alternative lifestyles. If effective interpersonal communication was never the strong suit of many Japanese men, the increasing preoccupation with the cyber-world only aggravated the deficiency. At a major Japan exhibition at London's Victoria and Albert Museum in 1991, the architect Toyo Ito summed up the trend in these words, which were projected on the wall of a large empty hall:

> People are turning into androids, getting a stronger sense of intimacy from communication through machines and images than they do from face-to-face communication. Our lives and circumstances become more artificial by the day. We are losing the capacity to express emotions in a living, active way and we look forward to a state of peaceful, information-saturated bliss, a nirvana wrapped in white noise.[9]

In the intervening decade and a half, Ito's vision appears to have been at least partly fulfilled: witness the growing problem of computer game and internet addiction, and the millions of social dropouts, ranging from the various categories of freelance workers and otaku nerds, to the solitary *hikikomori* ("hidden bat"). What all of these men and (to a much lesser extent) women have in common is that they have placed themselves outside society's mainstream, either by refusing to accept or being unable to find regular employment or, more seriously, by holing up in their parents' houses to lead a totally reclusive life.

The first category—the freelancers and nerds—is today by far the largest, estimated at between three and four million, compared to half a million in 1982 and over one million in 1992. It encompasses a wide range of individuals. Some simply abhor the "bondage" of traditional employment, preferring instead to survive on part-time jobs. They are known as "freeters" and include those who tried but were unsuccessful in landing a regular job. Others, known as NEETs (Not in Employment, Education, or Training), are jobless for long periods of time, though not necessarily averse to working. Both freeters and NEETs live frugal lives, but they are seldom impoverished, often living off their parents or in shared accommodation. They are a new breed, a tribe of urban drifters and searchers, victims of the disintegration of society, both city-bred and migrants from the countryside, and unsure of what to do with their lives.

The second group are the hikikomori, the "hidden bats," young hermits in the middle of throbbing urban life, holed up in their rooms, some already for over a decade. They are between their late teens and late thirties or early forties, living with parents sickened and embarrassed by their offspring's alienation but indulging them and unwilling to knock sense into them. The mothers can't bring themselves to stop feeding them, even if it means placing the meal at the bottom of the stairs for the recluse to fetch when no one is around—for hikikomori usually do not eat with their families. Their number has been growing alarmingly and may be as high as a million.

Theories about the cause of this epidemic of social withdrawal vary, but most sources now agree that the phenomenon is a social one, not a mental-health disorder. Many see it as a form of extreme, passive resistance against social codes demanding the kind of unquestioning dedication to career and country that was the rule in the high-growth post-war decades, but in the eyes of many young people has become an anachronism. I believe the educational system and certain salient aspects of traditional upbringing may be equally to blame. Schools, and even universities, still place high value on rote learning. They rarely encourage vigorous debate and the development of critical faculties, emphasizing instead the duty to accept leadership ("fit in") and solidarity with one's group. Many of the hikikomori that do respond to probing into their motives are reported as complaining of a traditional Japanese truism, that now as before the "nail that sticks out gets hammered down." To be different is to suffer.

Balancing this largely unproductive segment of current Japanese society is a post-Showa phenomenon: the proliferation of artists, designers, writers, freelance journalists, consultants, and the like. Their talents and drive allow them to lead a kind of life that was virtually unheard of twenty or thirty years ago: that of the independent creative professional or intellectual, whether man or woman. Thanks largely to their efforts, life in the large cities today is a lot livelier than it was in the staid days of Showa.

And thanks, too, to a whole new generation of youngsters who have found their own way of rejecting establishment values, not by hiding themselves but by flaunting their feathers as they parade down Tokyo's trendy Omotesando—a long, tree-shaded avenue lined with fashion stores and café's—in outlandish, absurdist, but seldom expensive outfits. If nothing else, they give lie to the still lingering notion that the Japanese are a race of grim salarymen and obedient women.

Chapter **15**

The Advent of Mass Travel

From the early seventies, after the liberalization of overseas travel restrictions by the Japanese government in 1965, foreign group travel began to develop, with the emphasis on Europe and America. During the bubble, it grew exponentially, with private travel in particular taking off. The high-growth era had emboldened many Japanese of all age groups to set off on their own, though group travel remained the preferred choice of mainly older Japanese.

A brief historical overview may be of interest here. In the course of the late 1960s and into the 1970s, orderly Japanese groups of mostly women and retired couples herded around by tour leaders, holding up a flag and dispensing a stream of explanations and admonitions to their flock, became a staple feature of the world's popular tourist spots. Their shopping habits gave a foretaste of the voracious Japanese appetite for luxury goods that was to mark the 1980s and 1990s.

Private tourism of working-age and retired couples followed in the eighties, in step with the increase in leisure time and the growth of linguistic and travel savvy in the ever more prosperous middle classes. And then there were the new breeds of travelers: the backpacking, adventurous student, and the single woman, traveling alone. In fact, Japanese individuals or couples have become a common sight in the world's top tourist spots. They often are smartly dressed and well groomed, the young women exhibiting their often unusual fashion sense without a trace of shyness.

What a contrast to the seventies, when individual foreign holiday travel was still highly unusual. No wonder my offer, in 1970, to take my wife's mother and her best friend, Kyoko-san, along on a world tour met with incredulous delight. Kyoko-san packed her kimonos and acquired a conspicuously thick wad of American Express dollar traveler's checks from her local bank. As we were soon to discover, she needed only the slightest excuse to unleash these magical monetary instruments on unwary local merchants.

While we checked in at a Vienna hotel, Kyoko-san went temporarily missing. We found her back at a fruit stall outside trying to make herself understood to the vendor, waving her "*toraburu chikku,*" as she called them, making the words sound like "trouble chick." When treating us to tea in an Amsterdam café she was puzzled why the shop declined to accept a trouble chick in payment, having been persuaded by her bank back home that travelers' checks were almighty.

Kyoko-san was a widow in her late sixties. She lived in a spacious suburban house with a large garden. She was an accomplished calligrapher and, like my mother-in-law, a traditional painter of considerable merit. She had never been abroad. Her delightful naivety and the way she pronounced English was a cause of constant amusement to us, as was her habit to have her picture taken in front of every famous monument or museum, without necessarily feeling the urge to explore its meaning or interior. "*Moo mita!*" ("I've already seen it!") she would announce with a broad grin, though she would of course follow us if we did want to go in.

Although the vintage Kyoko-san–type traveler had become rare, most foreign travel still followed the well-trodden itineraries during the boom, whether in groups or not. Twenty years on, this pattern still holds. A New York travel coordinator recently said that "Japanese people don't like to go online and plan their own trips." They want to go where others go.[10]

But even the most famous destinations sometimes pose unexpected challenges to the Japanese visitor. Sheltered as most urban Japanese are from many of life's rough edges in their own society, Japanese people are sometimes shocked by the "primitive" conditions encountered in the West where they least expect them. A telling example is the "Paris syndrome," the name given by the media to the severe emotional letdown experienced by some visitors, mostly young Japanese, when they find that that epitome of romantic elegance in reality is a city of blunt manners, rude waiters, and dirty streets, with the absence of the refinements and the polite, if stereotyped, greetings that are the norm in Japan. In some cases psychiatrists need to come to their aid to help them through the crisis.[11]

By and large, though, overseas travel has clearly proved a boon to Japanese society, especially during the years of the bubble economy. It not only greatly broadened the personal horizons of tens of millions of Japanese, but it also whetted the travelers' appetite for foreign goods and foods, which increasingly translated into the opening of the home market to hitherto unavailable merchandise. The Japanese palate grew cosmopolitan. There was an explosion of French and Italian restaurants, of bread shops and patisseries, of ice cream parlors and coffee chains.

The internationalization of the hospitality industry has pervaded the domestic market as well. Most Japanese now prefer a modern hotel to a Japanese-style inn, even in traditional towns where one would expect authenticity.

In Search of the Genuine Thing...

Takayama, Gifu prefecture, January 2005. We came here to immerse ourselves in the authentic atmosphere of this picturesque old town in the mountains of central Japan. A friend recommended a new hotel "with Japanese features" sitting in spacious grounds among verdant hills at the town's edge. We booked a room.

The hotel does have a Japanese restaurant with a garden featuring a pond, steppingstones, and lanterns—but it's fully indoors, on the sixth floor, with low ceilings. The French restaurant and fancy bar are mock-European as purveyed by American interior designers. They come complete with fake books and a fake open fire that is all orange light without even the glow of electric heat, let alone a real log fire that would grace the public spaces of a mountain hotel anywhere in Europe or even America.

The windows of the bedrooms don't open. Here we are in the mountains, eager for a taste of rural Japan and to breathe its fresh air, and all we get is a phony interior and filtered air mixed with the chemical fumes of newly laid carpets.

But the hotel is full, and the traditional ryokan inns in town are struggling.

Chapter 16

The Rise of Culinary Chic

The bubble conditions stimulated the Japanese palate like nothing that went before it as food entrepreneurs, both Japanese and foreign, took full advantage of the rapidly rising consumer power, contributing greatly to the expansion of Japan's culinary horizons.

Until the mid-seventies, the choice of fresh food in the stores had been largely limited to domestically grown produce, some of which—such as giant strawberries and flawless muscat grapes and fine Kobe beef—were so expensive that they were bought only as gift items or served in expense-account restaurants. But now the average citizen could benefit from the opening of Japan's borders to imports and have access to Malaysian mangoes and French beans and American sirloin steaks at reasonable prices.

Domestic producers fought back with cheaper and improved products. Affordable greenhouse strawberries became a winter staple, apples were grown larger and without blemishes, outsourced beef from Japanese wagyu cattle raised in Australia undercut the authentic domestic product.

The upheaval in food tastes and marketing rang the death knell for many a mom-and-pop grocery and greengrocer as supermarket chains and convenience stores—almost unknown before the 1970s—invaded every neighborhood.

Western-Style Restaurants, Showa Style

As for eating out, mid-Showa—the fifties and sixties—of course offered a wide choice of Japanese eateries for every pocket, but there was a dearth of genuine Western-type restaurants, even in the large cities. In Kobe, there was Ivan's steak house up on Tor Road, the dining room of the Oriental Hotel, and very little else. Tokyo was hardly better equipped. In the early sixties, we had perhaps half a dozen decent Western eateries, including a Russian restaurant, Volga; a few commendable French and Italian bistros; and for businessmen the posh but uninspiring Tokyo Kaikan.

When Japanese families wanted to eat European *in style* the obvious places to go were the grand hotel dining rooms, with their fine linen and well-spaced seating, where you could count on a limited menu of regulation French dishes like coq au vin or steak chateaubriand, served in hushed surroundings by silent waiters drilled in the art of removing the mock-silver dish covers resembling Prussian helmets simultaneously at a precisely choreographed moment. But even these outwardly authentic establishments made concessions to local taste, as when you were asked if you wanted bread or rice with your main course, or when the salad you ordered turned out to be a bland wedge of iceberg lettuce on a flat plate, a few drops of dressing dripping from the sides, instead of a happily tossed creation in a bowl.

The opening in 1970 of a fine Czech restaurant in Tokyo's Roppongi area was, therefore, a welcome event to both expatriates and Japanese diners. It had been a major draw at the 1970 Osaka Expo, where the red star crowning the adjacent Soviet pavilion was reflected in its windows, an unsubtle reminder of its vassal status. But after the fair closed, the restaurant managed to relocate from Osaka, complete with chefs and waiters and Bohemian crystal ware, to permanent premises in the capital. The food was good, but what I remember more vividly is the skill of one of the older waiters in playing the glass harp, a collection of drinking glasses partially filled with water. It delighted young and old alike.

But these places were beyond the means of most Japanese. For the ordinary citizen with an interest in European or American-type food, there were the *yoshokuya*, the "Western-food houses." They were not exactly what the name implies, being the result of early Japanese exposure—from the last quarter of the nineteenth century—to European and American home cooking. The simpler and more affordable yoshokuya limited themselves to items like beef stew, omelets, and potato croquettes, with the more upmarket diners offering deep-fried breaded oysters, pan-fried pork with soy sauce and ginger, and hamburger steak with a demiglace sauce—all adapted to Japanese taste and served with rice.

In the early 1970s the yoshokuya got company in the shape of the American hamburger and fried chicken chains. The first McDonald's joint was opened at Tokyo's most prestigious address: the ground floor of the Mitsukoshi Department Store at the Ginza 4-chome crossing, the Tokyo equivalent of New York's Bergdorf Goodman or Harrods in London. Of course, it was a mismatch, and it didn't last—not at that location, that is. But McDonald's expanded fast throughout Japan and today boasts over 3,500 outlets, second only to the United States. Other similar chains, both foreign and Japanese, have also made deep inroads.

In fact, from mid-Showa onward Western-style restaurants for every pocket have been proliferating to the point where virtually every one of the world's major and minor cuisines is now represented. Yet the yoshokuya still survives, too, a nostalgic reminder of simpler times.

The Arrival of World-Class Cuisine

So while the middle classes saw their living standards rise steadily during the bubble years and could graduate from the yoshokuya to an ever-widening variety of international dining, it was the rich that had the biggest hand in making Tokyo what it is today, a sophisticated metropolis with an almost infinite choice of excellent restaurants of every description and every conceivable food culture.

Formerly, corporate entertaining at restaurants had been the motor that drove the hospitality sector, but it stuck largely to Japanese restaurants and lacked cosmopolitan allure. That all changed from the mid-1970s onward. Elegant, nouveau riche couples, affluent groups of women, and expense-account executives with a taste for Western food filled every new upscale French and Italian restaurant that opened its doors. Tokyo's traditional hotel dining rooms were upstaged by posh newcomers: l'Osier in 1973, followed in time by the likes of Wolfgang Puck, Gordon Ramsay, Alain Ducasse, Pierre Gagnaire, and—to top them all—Joel Robuchon and his fabulous *chateau gastronomique* in Ebisu, four miles (just over six kilometers) from Tokyo's main business center.

Actually most of these celebrated chefs did not open their Tokyo branches until long *after* the bubble burst, when property prices had returned to affordable levels, and the moneyed elite proved to be largely unaffected by the economic malaise. Before and during the bubble years, it was mostly the Japanese themselves who had opened up the market for Western-style dining with hundreds of bistros and serious restaurants in every large city of Japan. True to form, they had usually learned their trade in Europe, as apprentices to renowned chefs.

With European food came the wine, and here too market penetration gathered steam in the 1980s, following the sharp reduction in excise duties on alcoholic beverages, which in the 1960s were still over 300 percent. The domestic sake industry, threatened by the increasing coupling of wine with Japanese food, tried to protect their turf by emphasizing long history and the local equivalent of terroir.

The rising sophistication of Japanese diners posed new challenges to would-be hosts in America and Europe. No longer was a good steak joint or a quaint ethnic eatery an adequate venue for extending hospitality to important visitors from Japan—if it ever was. Nothing short of two- or three-starred French restaurants seemed appropriate. Once during the mid-1980s in New York, I was asked to entertain the head of the Japanese Red Cross, an aristocratic gentleman, scion of one of Japan's ancient families, and his equally noble wife. I booked a table for four at the Lutèce, then one of New York's finest restaurants. From the start the conversation would not flow. My guests seemed uncomfortable in the rather casual, cramped bar where we had our pre-dinner drinks. At the table, the exquisite cuisine failed to outweigh the crowded conditions and the noisy groups of businessmen around us. As my wife and I tried to put a brave face on the situation, I realized that a private room at a hotel or a more dignified, formal restaurant would have been a more appropriate choice. I should have remembered that for the more traditional Japanese, a dignified setting was more important than the quality of the food.

As for hotels, some foreign chains had been operating in the Japanese market since 1980s or earlier, but like the restaurants, the top-brand hostelries didn't start arriving until after the turn of the millennium. By now, some of the world's most famous names, such as the Ritz-Carlton, the Four Seasons, and the Peninsula, have added their glitter to the increasingly sophisticated Japanese market.

Given the rising availability of fine Western restaurants, it should come as no surprise that elegant Japanese-style dining declined during the boom years, a trend that has escalated since. Yet Japanese food is still the default choice for most Japanese. But what they go for now is easy-access eateries with tasteful designer interiors and counters or tables. Among these the *izakaya*—convivial drinking places offering eclectic Japanese food served on small plates, tapas-style—enjoy enormous popularity. Modern Japanese like informality. And they don't much like having to remove their shoes and squat on tatami mats.

The category of Japanese restaurants that has suffered most from the shift in lifestyle during and after the bubble is the exclusive *ryotei*, high-class, expensive eating establishments that were patronized by politicians and top businessmen. They were virtual membership clubs, some going back to the days of the Tokugawa Shogunate (1603–1867), reserved for a regular clientele that prized discretion above all else. According to the *New York Times*, there were 524 ryotei in Tokyo in 1977, but "demands for greater transparency and accountability with public funds have steadily grown, and as a result [by 2001] their number had dwindled to 82."[12] And, no doubt, because the younger generation of diners suffered from leg cramps from the long hours of squatting.

A unique kind of Japanese restaurant—some of which function as ryotei, but are mostly less pretentious—is the *fugu-ryoriya*, which specializes in *fugu*, variously translated as globefish, swellfish, or pufferfish. The latter name is derived from its habit of puffing itself up into a spiky ball when threatened. Its flesh is considered a delicacy whose allure is heightened by a hidden danger: the admittedly infinitesimal chance of falling victim to its deadly poison. Specially trained chefs know how to remove the poisonous parts, and today eating fugu is considered quite safe. But Japanese lore abounds in *fugu* horror stories, some also involving the death, by suicide, of the responsible chef. In the early 1970s, an American friend of mine was hit by serious fugu poisoning in a Tokyo restaurant recommended by a prominent Japanese acquaintance. My friend survived—just. I asked him if he had told his acquaintance. "No way," he answered. "Imagine what he might do to himself if he knew!"

But the decline in high-end Japanese eating should not be laid at the door of such rare misfortunes. Rather, it is the consequence of a general shift in lifestyle and a tightening of belts after the collapse of the bubble.

Tearooms, Bars, and Cafés

Along with the proliferation of Western-style eateries, the latter Showa years also saw an explosive growth in various types of cafés to facilitate casual meetings away from home or the office. The oldest type, going back at least to early Showa and still going strong, was the *kissaten*—a comfortable tearoom or coffee shop serving cakes and ice cream concoctions along with a choice of teas and coffees and used by salesmen and housewives alike. In the late 1970s came the café bar, a meeting place more suited to couples and ladies. The café bar was cozier and darker than the traditional *kissaten* tearoom, served alcoholic drinks, and breathed a more adult, nightclub-like atmosphere. It was a boon to working women and dating couples, who were not welcome at men-only nightclubs and bars, with their usual complement of hostesses.

A parallel development was the appearance of coffee chains, starting with the native Doutor group in 1971. They grew fast, especially during the bubble years. Starbucks didn't arrive until 1996 but now boasts well over one thousand outlets, similar to Doutor. As in other parts of the world, this new type of café proved a great hit with office workers for grabbing a quick breakfast on the way to the office or a snack for lunch.

Not that drinking coffee was a new discovery for the Japanese: as in Europe, coffee had long been a beverage of choice for the student/scholar and the discerning aesthete. There is a record of Toyotomi Hideyoshi, the sixteenth-century unifier of Japan, regularly drinking coffee, no doubt obtained from Portuguese or Spanish missionaries. And I well remember the atmospheric owner-run coffee shops of the 1950s and 60s, with their woody interiors and aroma of good coffee brewing slowly in a glass percolator over a Bunsen flame. But the chains brought coffee to the masses, and put the small coffee bars on the defensive.

"Would You Like a Child with Your Coffee?"

I can't resist the temptation to retell an old café anecdote of mine, told earlier in my book *The Magatama Doodle*. The year was 1995. I had just visited a sanctuary in a village east of Tokyo dedicated to Sakura-no-Sogo, a village headman, who in the seventeenth century had committed the capital crime of protesting directly to the Shogun against widespread famine and oppressive taxation by the local lord. Although the protest was justified and the injustice remedied, the headman, his wife, and his four children were put to death in accordance with the law. This shocking story, well known to the Japanese, shook me up, and I felt a need for strong coffee.

I found a small café, and as I was the only customer, I struck up a conversation with the elderly lady running it. When she heard I had no children, she offered me one of her grandchildren. I thought she was joking, but she seemed dead serious. "My daughter won't mind," she assured me. "She complains that three kids is one too many." I knew that adoptions had been the traditional way to counter childlessness and ensure the continuation of the family line, but I thought the practice had lapsed. In any case, I politely declined the lady's kind offer. Her coffee was excellent, though, and so was the thick slice of buttered toast—the only snack she was able to offer me for lunch.

In food terms, the bubble brought diversity and abundance in its wake, a development that benefited all layers of society. The middle class had greatly expanded in the mid- and late-Showa years, the result of spectacular economic success and sustained government policies aimed at spreading its fruits. This large middle class—of which everyone but the lowest laborer by now counted themselves a member—enjoyed the declining prices and increasing choice, which did not necessarily translate into better quality or healthier eating. For many, home-cooked meals made way for a huge array of instant noodles and prepackaged meals ready for the microwave.

Bread, until then hardly a popular staple, took the country by storm, with bread boutiques that offered a colorful selection of rolls and buns popping up everywhere. But the bread was all white and refined, and usually sweetened, as it is to this day. Reared as I was in a culture of whole-wheat and rye breads, I still find it hard to understand this "girlish" taste of the Japanese consumer. Fortunately, for those who persevere, the real thing can usually be found somewhere in today's Japan.

With the bubble, rose the power of the demanding consumer. They welcomed the opportunities to indulge in luxuries and personal favorites that met their aspirations. Aspirations that they felt they had been suppressing for far too long.

Japanese Cuisine Goes Global

Western culinary penetration of Japan during the 1980s was matched by a thrust in the opposite direction. At the time I was living in New York, a city then already well endowed with Japanese restaurants, some catering to Japanese expense-account executives, others of the neighborhood variety, patronized by Japanese and Americans alike. My wife and I frequented one such eatery, on 2nd Avenue, not far from where we lived.

It was a counter-type wateringhole, with exquisite cooking of the *omakase* type—meaning you basically left everything to the chef. What he or she came up with depended on mood and what had been available at the market that morning. The dainty or hearty dishes would be placed in front of you over the course of an hour or two, suitably spaced to allow for drinking and digestion, and perhaps getting to know your neighbor at the counter.

On one such visit my neighbor turned out to be a curator at the Metropolitan Museum of Art. "Specializing in Japanese art, of course?" I ventured, as I watched her savoring an intricate sea-urchin creation. "No, no, seventeenth-century Dutch paintings," she answered, adding "I've never been to Japan." My cherished notion that exquisite Japanese cooking was the preserve of the cognoscenti, those who had lived in Japan—who could *understand* its cuisine in its cultural context—was shown up that night for what it was: thoroughly dated.

For by the 1980s, at least in New York and other world capitals, refined Japanese food was way past the "interesting" stage. It had become a cuisine of choice among the discerning elite, with a repertoire that had widened beyond the standard noodles, tempura, and sushi to embrace even the delicate possibilities of the multicourse *kaiseki*, that most refined form of Japanese seasonal cooking.

In food terms the bubble years had narrowed the culture gap between Japan and the West. Did that symbolize a general trend toward harmony in Japan's relations with the outside world? Unfortunately not. The mood in Japan had grown too blinkered for that.

Chapter **17**

The Bubble Bursts

Japan's bubble finally came to an end in 1989, when the stock market collapsed, shedding a third of its value almost instantly and 75 percent eventually. Real estate prices held up for another year or so before telescoping similarly.

I have often wondered what caused a nation known for its austerity, risk avoidance, and consensual decision making to become as wild and hubristic as Japan did during the bubble years. How its tradition of prudence could almost overnight turn into a happy romp, with scant concern for soundness and sustainability. Was the heady belief many held in Japan's newly minted superiority supported by cool analysis? Definitive answers to questions like these will remain elusive, but I will venture a thought or two in an attempt to illuminate the forces that were at work here.

Throughout its post-war history Japan had been prone to extreme shifts in popular mood in response to changes in economic conditions or the effect of other countries' actions. President Nixon's decision in August 1971 to impose a 10 percent surcharge on imports caused profound shock in Japan, the more so as it was accompanied by a decision to end the convertibility of the dollar into gold, the longstanding (though largely symbolic) right of (foreign) owners of dollars to demand from the United States Treasury gold in exchange for their holdings, at a predetermined price of $35 per ounce. The sharp rises in the price of crude oil of 1973 and 1979 also set off the alarm bells—not simply for the expected negative impact on Japan's (and the world's) short-term economic prospects, but because it caused the Japanese public to abruptly lose faith in their very future.

Take the situation as I found it in 1975, on a visit from London. The oil crisis of 1973 had triggered a worldwide recession, and the mood among Japanese businessmen and bankers had turned particularly defeatist. "We are sustaining heavy losses," I was told by the president of Okuma Corporation, a well-known Nagoya machine tool maker. "I'm pessimistic. We Japanese are a pathetic race. I see no way out. There are hard years ahead." (The company survived and thrived.)

Other businessmen were equally gloomy. But resident Americans and Europeans saw the slowdown merely as a passing phenomenon and were upbeat in their assessment of Japan's long-term viability.

And of course the foreigners were right. Japan recovered with a vengeance, not least because the sharply higher oil prices triggered a strong foreign demand for small cars, a field in which Japan excelled. Yet after the 1980s bubble burst proved itself to be permanent, gloom and doom once again took over. This is what I overheard an older Japanese man say to his younger companion in the Tokyo Station Art Gallery. They were standing in front of a large painting depicting Napoleon's surrender at Waterloo. "We are in the same position. Japan had its moment of greatness, like Napoleon, but it's all over. This is our Waterloo."

What all this shows is that the typical Japanese reaction to a new, unexpected situation tends to be emotional rather than rational. A change in fortunes is taken at face value, with cheers or tears, but with little analysis. The result is a roller-coaster journey of public sentiment, through the dales and over the peaks of economic performance, from despair to euphoria and back again. This is the opposite of what we in the West are traditionally told about the inscrutability of the Asian character. The mask is deceptive, a mere social convention in a culture that condemns the *display* of emotions but not their inner nurturing and—paradoxically—the occasional intemperate outburst of pent-up frustration.

In the final analysis, the responsibility for the Japanese bubble and its bursting must be laid at the door of the political establishment of the day: the politicians, the bureaucrats, the central bank—the latter's task being to act as the government's agent for establishing monetary policy—who lacked the vision and the competence to guide Japan through its conversion from a closed to an open economy and a more diverse society. But the commercial bankers and the foreign management gurus must share the blame: the bankers for failing to see that their mindless lending zeal fuelled the speculative frenzy and could only lead to disaster (the recent subprime loan crisis in the United States seems an eerie echo...); and the American experts for not understanding that the "Japanese way" might not work in an open economy.

Part Three

The Magellan Decade:
A Post-Bubble X-Ray

Japan's transition from the well-controlled growth and prosperity of Showa to the uncharted waters of "unruly Heisei" resembled the early mariners' passage from the relative calm of the Southern Pacific through the treacherous Strait of Magellan into the stormy Atlantic. Like those intrepid sailors, Japan's leaders needed every skill to survive the journey.

The severe crash of the property and stock markets that occurred between late 1989 and the early 1990s was the greatest economic calamity to befall Japan since the end of the Second World War. As we have seen, there had been serious jolts before: the oil crises of 1973 and 1979, and the twin "Nixon shocks" of 1971, the first the announcement of his diplomatic overture to Maoist China, the second the abandonment of the dollar's gold standard and the imposition of a 10 percent import tax. But their effect had turned out to be short-lived, and the harm done to Japan's growth and diplomatic position entirely manageable.

This time round it was different. Very different. Abruptly, and totally unexpectedly, Japan found itself face to face with the consequences of its own reckless behavior. As the initial disbelief made way for despondency, the fabulous Showa years suddenly seemed unreal, a mirage. The wealth and glory so painstakingly accumulated now seemed cast upon the scrap heap of history. And to its shame, Japan's crisis was played out in the full glare of a globalized market economy eagerly anticipating the resulting bargains. The depression was deep and painful. It would take Japan over a decade to sort itself out—after a fashion.

This part of the book is an eclectic examination of that brief but momentous transition period, which I will call Japan's "Magellan decade." We will look at what I believe have been the main components of the tumultuous legacy of the bust: the end of the tradition of lifelong employment; an emerging trend toward individualism at the expense of the group culture; the continued rise of subcultures in the wake of loosening social strictures; the explosion of high fashion and indulgence of every type as the middle class shrank and new wealth contrasted with increasing poverty; and a creeping identity crisis, both national and personal.

The simultaneous occurrence of these diverse but loosely connected social phenomena—part confluence, part clash—make the decade of transition one of immense importance in Japan's recent history. Our discussion will be largely unstructured, in keeping with the character of the time, but it will set the stage for Part Four, in which we will cast our eye forward to Japan's "unfinished business."

Chapter **18**

The Morning After

Of my four visits to Japan in the 1990s, the last one left the strongest impression. That was in 1999—a decade after the end of Showa and the bursting of the bubble—and I found a nation I hardly recognized. What struck me was the blank look on many people's faces in the street, and on others the look of consumptive pleasures indulged in cheap bars and places like the *pachinko* pinball machine parlors found everywhere. There was a palpable sense of desolation, of dreams lost, even hopelessness.

Television shows tried to bring relief, but their exaggerated cheerfulness and childish programming only emphasized the void. For there was no hiding the stark facts: the continuing recession, layoffs and hiring stops, suicides, aimlessness among the young. Even drug culture, long virtually unknown in Japan, seemed on the increase.

The good news, from a foreign perspective, was that the crash hadn't dragged the rest of the world along with it. Japan had managed to keep major bankruptcies to a minimum, thus preventing a ripple effect to other markets. Rather than let the undeserving, mismanaged banks and companies go under, Japan's leaders had opted for the harsh medicine of restructuring, mergers, and takeovers. Also, the huge pool of individual savings, the largest in the world, helped cushion the effects of recession.

But industrial overcapacity continued to be a major headache as consumer demand was held back by shrunken incomes and worries about the future. Export markets, always a vital outlet for Japan's industry, became crucial in the face of stagnated domestic demand. And so did the need not to let the yen get too strong. (Two years earlier an MITI official had told me that 120 yen to the dollar was the "best rate" for Japan: a stronger yen would hamper exports, a weaker one invite criticism from foreign trade partners, and cause price inflation at home. The rate had stayed close to the 120 mark since then, but by the end of 1999 the yen had strengthened to about 103, impeding exports.)

The Effects of Deflation and Downsizing

But it wasn't inflation that proved the problem, it was the opposite. After decades of mostly moderate consumer price rises Japan had its first experience with deflation, a steady and prolonged drop in prices due to overcapacity, slack consumer demand, and the arrival on its home market, from the mid-1970s onward, of cheaper, foreign-made products. The lower retail prices were of obvious benefit to the consumer, but their cruel companion was a drop in incomes and job security as employers tightened their belts and resorted to hitherto unheard-of layoffs.

This latter development had a particularly dramatic impact on a culture that prized the reciprocal loyalty of employer and employee above all: companies did not exist to enrich shareholders but to maintain market share and provide permanent employment to their workers. This lifelong bond was stronger than any law; it was rooted in a moral commitment that was wholly mutual. Labor unions—which were "company unions" rather than organized by trade—were only there to refine the details of wage agreements and employment conditions, not to confront management with harsh demands. The maintenance of *wa*, harmony, was the highest good, to which all other considerations had to yield—even the level of the company's profitability.

But when the early to mid-1990s witnessed year after year of stagnant sales and plummeting profits, coupled with the collapse in asset values, the alarm bells finally went off. The unthinkable happened: company after company went into *risutora* ("restructuring"), referring to widespread corporate reorganization involving expense cutting through layoffs, early retirement schemes, and other means. These drastic measures suggested that profitability had become the chief corporate preoccupation rather than market share or maintaining employment.

For some the shame of being laid off was unbearable, and the media was full of stories of mostly older salarymen leaving home in the morning clasping their briefcases, pretending to be off to the office but in reality facing a day on park benches and in coffee shops until it was time to go home again. Others, unable to face life and financial hardship after losing their jobs, chose the ultimate escape from their misery. They bought a one-way ticket for the train to Aokigahara, a dense forest on the slopes of Mt. Fuji, to end their lives in solitude. In 1998 seventy-three bodies were found hanging in these woods, and in 2002 the number was seventy-eight.

These human tragedies were the apparently inevitable cost of even a partial overhaul of Japanese society in the wake of the bubble's collapse. They pointed to the extent and nature of the corporate restructuring that was taking place, and flew in the face of the fashionable claims in the Western press that nothing was being done to get to the bottom of the crisis and strengthen Japan's position in the age of globalization. True, some companies were slow to react to the challenges, and the banks in particular at first seemed at a loss how to handle the massive bad-loan portfolios that had resulted from a decade of mindless lending against heavily overvalued assets. The entrenched culture of hierarchy over merit, of usefulness measured by up to twelve-hour workdays rather than efficiency, needed time to be examined and modernized. The task was a huge and daunting one, especially since there was no immediate agreement on what was to be done.

The End of Lifelong Commitment

If there was one quest that had occupied the thoughts and behavior of ambitious young Japanese men and their families since the end of the Second World War, it was to find permanent, lifelong employment with a major corporation. The security and prestige attached to carrying a business card with a name like Mitsubishi or Sumitomo or Toyota can hardly be exaggerated, and Japan's economic success must in no small measure be credited to the stability and mutual loyalty this system produced in all echelons of the labor force.

All through Showa, the top employers were not interested in hiring men of any age who had worked elsewhere first, as if experience gained in others' service had somehow soiled or damaged them. Once hired, the new employee, fresh out of college—or, for the lower jobs, high school—was safe for life, a member of an elite, virtually guaranteed steady promotion and an income at least adequate for maintaining a comfortable living standard. Even after formal retirement (between age 50 and 55, except for top executives to whom no age limit applied) he was usually taken care of with some sinecure, to enable him to supplement his modest pension.

Entrance-level employment with the top companies needed to be secured in the student's senior year—graduation being assumed—or at the latest during the hiring season the year after, on a second try. Those who failed the selection processes of the most prestigious employers were up for grabs by the lower rungs of the business world, or they could strike out on their own or join a family business if there was one.

But the collapse of the bubble fatally undermined the system, and company after company abandoned the employment guarantee in favor of more flexible policies that included layoffs and promotions on merit.[1] The harsh awakening from the bubble-and-bust debacle had also opened their eyes to the need to transcend traditional preferences for home-grown staff, uncontaminated by foreign schooling or employment by competitors. Reluctantly at first, then more willingly, companies started hiring the likes of Harvard MBAs, and in the end even some of their board-rooms welcomed non-Japanese professional executives—all part of their quest to retool themselves for the changed environment.

Whether out of choice or necessity, the changed environment also created a new mood among recent graduates. Many now claimed they were not really interested in Showa-style lifelong employment with one company, expressing a preference for full labor mobility instead. Most seemed to be much more relaxed than their fathers had been about finding employment, and taking a gap year or two backpacking in Australia or trekking across Asia before settling down to some kind of work gained in popularity. The dwindling ratio of applicants to vacancies, even in the top companies, was another indicator that times had changed.

The shaky financial position of the banks—once among the most desirable employers—and some of the large corporations also undermined the old consen-sus that outside the bureaucracy, academia, and the professions, a corporate career with one employer was the only respectable way to go through life. Moving from one employer to another was long frowned upon and even taken as a possible sign of some undisclosed "problem." But suddenly, head hunters were doing a thriving business in Japan, as changing jobs no longer carried a stigma. Indeed it became the new mark of success. A professor at Tokyo's Hitotsubashi University told me that "nowadays it's those who advance their career by changing employers that are admired, with the traditionalists who stick to one employer seen as losers."

Implicit in this trend was a growing assertiveness and personal ambition, traits that were discouraged—not to say condemned—in the hierarchical model. Although youthful middle managers and assistant professors might still listen politely when their superior—in his mid-fifties or older—lectured them on the virtues of loyalty and patience, their docility became increasingly misleading. Many no doubt began to nurture their own thoughts about this "fossil mentality" (as they called it), while preparing themselves emotionally to jump ship at the first knock of opportunity.

For a while, I suspected that the apparent shift in attitude to lifetime employ-ment was little more than a bow to the inevitable. Permanent jobs have become harder to come by; that's a fact, and it's useless to moan about it—that sort of thinking. But at least among young people the change in priorities seemed genu-ine. A number of university students I spoke to in recent years confirmed this. I quote some of the reasons they gave me: "Any job will do, even if it's temporary or menial. Something else will turn up after that. We live in an open labor market now, and if necessary we'll go abroad for a while. There's always work, somewhere. Besides, to be out of work is no longer 'embarrassing' or 'shameful,' nor potentially calamitous." With this last remark they were referring to parents they could rely on for money, and to their belief that in a pinch they could always find some part-time work to tide them over.

This confident attitude could turn out to be a good thing if the newfound disdain for a traditional salaryman's life fosters true independence and self-reliance. But although many of the unemployed (and usually unmarried) under-forty generation of college graduates claim to live the life of perennial adult student or "freeter" (odd-jobs casual worker) from *choice*, more often than not they are simply drifting. They either are content to live a hand-to-mouth existence, or as mentioned above depend on the support of understanding or supine parents. The kind of parents it should be added who, in the hardworking decades of the 1950s through the 1970s, built up a sizable nest egg in the unquestioning, vacationless service of Japan Inc.

By the end of the Magellan decade, the monolith of Japan's elite as we knew it appeared to have split in two groups: the traditionalists and the liberals. The traditionalists were still seeking the security and prestige of a major corporate name and eagerly lined up for the demanding interviews and examinations they needed to pass to secure a coveted position (though they might well change jobs later on). The liberals were a motley and growing group of restless searchers, mold-breakers and ambitious young men and women at one extreme, and unfocused, self-indulgent dreamers at the other.

Were they the new individualists who would determine Japan's future?

Chapter 19

Individualism—Ah, You Mean Selfishness?

There is little doubt that Japan's vaunted group ethic started creaking in its hinges after the bust. For all its impressive successes during the Showa boom, the collapse of the bubble economy rendered it suspect overnight. The search for alternatives was on.

The shift in focus and early indications of changes in corporate governance created the perception in the West that "individualism" was taking hold in Japan. This development was seen as salutary, as many of Japan's supposed ills were ascribed to its longstanding emphasis on group identity and its attendant lack of social diversity, open competition, and personal accountability.

This Western—especially American—reading of what was going on in Japan was not without an element of *schadenfreude*, notably among those in government and industry who had been severely critical of the blind adulation of the "Japanese way" during the 1970s and 1980s. It didn't take long after the plunge of Japanese asset values and revelations about the depth of the financial crisis before thoroughly American concepts of free markets, pragmatic thinking, and hard-nosed competitiveness were dusted off and placed back on their old US pedestal, and America once again donned its mantle of superiority. Japan was "encouraged" to "reform" its systems to conform to "accepted" free-market standards.

So did they occur, the fundamental changes that Western observers and politicians, in their wisdom, urged upon Japan if it was to survive the Magellan passage? Or were they in the offing? Any such systemic reform surely would have to be accompanied by a shift away from the ingrained group culture that Western critics claimed stifled political opposition, thereby perpetuating rule by the colluding forces of government, bureaucrats, and big business bosses, without any meaningful role for the elected parliament.

There was little evidence of a formal shift. Yet something was going on. Not only was corporate Japan finding its own approach to the crisis, selectively adopting elements of Western-style management, but there was also a growing grassroots curiosity about the *idea* of individualism, and a wish among some of the younger generation to break away from the well-trodden path of their parents and grandparents and do something on their own.

Skepticism about Individualism

Yet most of the many people I discussed this subject with, including students, showed considerable ambivalence about the need for individualism. The prevailing opinion was that the collaborative approach had proved its worth and should not be jettisoned. Some even advanced it as the prime reason for being proud of Japan, others as their nation's main distinguishing feature and source of success.

Four graduate students at the prestigious Kyoto University, although fiercely debating the subject in front of me, came to a similar conclusion. They argued that individualism is a Western concept that is poorly understood in Japan. They equated it with egoism and excessive personal freedom, and they feared that having too many options in life might lessen, not increase, the pleasure of being free. Besides, one of them added, the Japanese don't accept the morality of bearing personal responsibility for one's actions, so they can't grasp the real sense of individualism, or the need for it. The result of this lack of understanding is a distortion of its true meaning.

Given these doubts, even among budding intellectuals, I decided to explore the topic further, this time with older academics and businessmen.

How to Stop "Killing the Self"

A prominent law professor in Tokyo saw no need for the promotion of Western-style individualism. "Members of the ruling bureaucratic elite—those that have passed the state examinations for public officials—decide for themselves what to do and say. Their lives, both professionally and privately, are determined by their own will." And even in group situations, he added, there is always a leader. "Those who complain about the lack of individualism do not belong to the elite."

A Tokyo professor of international relations noted that, although Western-style individualism was not right for Japan, it was highly desirable for Japanese to be more emphatic in living their own lives, for their own sake, not for the sake of parents or society. "At the same time we should be collaborative and respect harmony in dealing with others."

A senior executive of one of Japan's largest advertising and marketing groups observed that individualism had been a dirty word in Japan, as it is diametrically opposed to the objective of killing the ego—the *ko*—which had been the central tenet of Japanese education and social behavior for centuries. Thus, introducing the Western concept of true individualism was a hard task and bound to cause misunderstanding. He agreed that, so far, individualism had been largely equated with egoism and selfish indulgence in personal pursuits. It was not realized that true individualism implies the ability to judge the appropriateness of one's actions in the social context, and to assume full personal responsibility for those actions. "Japanese are used to being protected by the community," he said. "Therefore, without a firm commitment from the government to a change of culture from group to individual through education, change would not come."

Clearly, what all these voices were agreed on was that the most appropriate and desirable way forward was a kind of mixed system: not a complete abandonment of Japan's group approach to problem solving and policy formation but a new social value system in which the worth of the individual and respect for his or her rights *as an individual* are balanced against or combined with the traditional search for harmony (wa).

Toward More Diversity, Japanese-Style

In fact, change along these lines, consciously or otherwise, was already being pursued during the turbulent post-bubble decade. The professor of international relations quoted above told me later that among the under forties, both men and women, the old docility was fading fast. They had learned to think for themselves, and many were losing patience with the old order. The real power, he added, was with the middle layers, not with the top, because they were more flexible in their approach to problem solving and no longer in awe of their superiors, who were too old to change.

With traditionalists and progressives now grappling for supremacy, now searching for a workable synthesis, Japanese society during the Magellan decade was in a state of turbulence. And that in itself constituted real change from the uniformity of Showa's societal model. In my opinion this questioning and remolding of time-honored ways was the most profound and potentially far-reaching consequence of the collapse of the Showa economy.

But even the new nonconformists were seldom "individualistic" in the Western sense, with its connotation of being assertive, combative, self-confident, and intellectualized. They did not constitute a radical element in the political sense. In fact they were mostly apolitical. What they did display was greater *individuality* compared to their elders. Their ideas and initiatives, fermented in the crosscurrents of home-grown and imported values, found their own form and expression, neither traditionally Japanese, nor the product of westernization.

I came away with a sense that, if properly organized and given a political ideal by vigorous leadership, these millions of men and women in their twenties and thirties could, in time, help reshape Japanese society to ready it for greater internal diversity and a more global role.

Chapter 20

The Myth of the Lost Decade

In spite of the movement away from lifelong employment and traditional ideas of group orientation, the assertion in some Western media that Japan had no choice but to adjust its corporate management culture on the American or European model was always suspect. In time-honored Japanese fashion, every available option was examined, every opinion listened to. The process took time, often excruciatingly so. But in the end, in most cases, solutions emerged, and they were Japanese solutions for Japanese problems. They involved mergers and takeovers (some by foreign buyers), corporate restructuring, changes in compensation and promotion systems, outsourcing, and yes, layoffs. But the need to be humane and preserve the integrity of the organization as much as possible was generally not lost sight of.

As we have seen, changing jobs began to lose its previous stigma as did working for foreign companies. Nissan and Sony and other big-name corporations even appointed Western executives to help sort themselves out. Yet the resulting structures and the dominant corporate behavior were still identifiably *Japanese*. My good friend the late Dr. James Abegglen, a well-known management consultant and foremost scholar of Japanese management practice, described the restructuring process in the *kaisha* (Japanese companies) this way in his book *Twenty-first Century Japanese Management:* "...culture still controls. It is fascinating to see that the major changes in kaisha have been in the finance area, the least personal, least 'human' part of the total company complex. Where people matter, adaptive change has occurred but within very clear cultural constraints."[2]

The notion, much bandied about in Western and Japanese writings, that the 1990s were Japan's "lost decade," is simplistic and inaccurate. What was "lost" was rapid growth, that holy grail of robust economic performance, and this failure was apparently equated, by some clever labeler, with a cessation of economic, technological, and financial development. With paralysis.

This take on the post-bubble decade does not accord with the facts. Growth did slow down to a crawl. From 1991 to 1999, real gross domestic product (GDP) grew at an average of about 1.5 percent, compared to 4 percent during the 1980s, and, for a time, public and corporate confidence was severely shaken. But not the will and the ability to meet the changed circumstances. After some initial hesitation Japan's managers got busy reshaping their companies. Not all were in need of surgery, though; in information technology and car designing, to mention just two vital areas, companies held their own throughout the 1990s and beyond. Meanwhile, construction of high-rise buildings, fancy retail outlets, and grand urban plazas hardly ever stopped throughout the Magellan decade, not as pork barrel schemes but in recognition of shifting demand patterns: continued migration to the cities and the burgeoning of the affluent consumer sector even as the economy as a whole faltered.

Which is not to say that the end of the bubble economy did not saddle Japan with serious problems and cause large segments of the population financial and emotional hardship. It did, and as we will see later, these things would continue to tax the minds of politicians, bureaucrats, academics, and community leaders to come up with the right solutions for years to come. As if this wasn't enough, Japan was severely shaken in the bust's aftermath by a bizarre act of mass murder without equal in its history.

A Brush with Disaster

Although the Magellan decade brought fundamental—if slow—change to Japan, the nation's inherent faith in the goodness and correctness of its way of life did not seem to change similarly. The overwhelming majority of Japanese remained essentially decent and trusting, intent upon maintaining decorum and correct social relations.

Why then did this orderly society suddenly suffer two vicious attacks by an obscure, domestic religious cult, potentially on the scale of the 9/11 outrage in the United States? As these extraordinary events occurred right in the middle of the tumultuous post-bubble decade, discussing it here is, I believe, appropriate, all the more so as it revealed certain aspects of the Japanese national character that are relevant to our analysis. What exactly happened?

During the early 1990s, the Aum Shinrikyo, then a still little-known "Buddhist sect" under the leadership of a self-appointed guru, Shoko Asahara, began to attract attention for its apocalyptic predictions and belief in the need to cleanse the "corrupt world." It attracted thousands of followers in Japan and abroad. The cult's beliefs turned fatally perverse when they started manufacturing sarin nerve gas and other lethal chemicals for use against "humanity." In 1994 and 1995, they actually unleashed their weapons, first in a kind of tryout in the city of Mat-sumoto with three deaths, then on the Tokyo subway system during rush hour. The gas, released from punctured plastic bags left on trains and station platforms, resulted in 12 deaths and over 5,500 afflicted, many with appalling injuries.

In retrospect the attack in Tokyo should be ranked among the most heinous attempts in modern times to destroy civilized society by fanatics employing state-of-the-art technology. Investigations brought to light that the relatively low death toll was caused by impurities in the sarin gas, without which the number of deaths would likely have been in the hundreds if not thousands.

The attack in Japan was in a class of its own in that it was not the work of for-eign terrorists inspired by hatred of "infidels" occupying their land or threatening their people and their religious beliefs. Aum was not threatened; on the contrary, they were protected by laws guaranteeing freedom of religion and assembly. Yet they wanted to destroy Japan from within to obey their leader's deluded predic-tion that the year 1996 would witness the "sinking of Japan," an "evil landmass devoured...by the waves," from which would "rise a race of 'superhumans'": Asahara and his followers.[3] The most chilling aspect of the Aum episode is that Asahara's star recruits, his inner circle of scientists, managers, financial experts, and media-savvy types, mostly university graduates, were drawn from the cream of middle-class Japan, and were indistinguishable from the typical salarymen and academics one encounters at Japan's corporate offices and campuses.

The shock caused by the Aum attack was profound. It totally dominated the Japanese media for weeks on end. Yet, as in the case of the bloody deeds of the Sekigun-ha (the Japan branch of West Germany's Red Army Faction) in the early 1970s, some of the perpetrators were not without their ardent admirers. One Aum member in particular, Fumihiro Joyu, the telegenic spokesman for the cult, was adored by some young women for his "slender figure and irresistible beauty," even after the full scope of the cult's crimes became known.

But leaving these mindless fans aside, the Aum episode did not appear to ruf-fle the equanimity of the population at large for long. People in the big cities did become more vigilant after what happened, but once the media had exhausted the story, life returned to normal, and incisive analysis of how a peaceful nation could spawn such evil was not attempted, at least not in the public arena.

If the 9/11 attacks on America's own soil, perpetrated by outsiders, destroyed that country's "innocence," no such effect could be ascribed to the sinister and lethal assault on Japanese society *from within* by the Aum conspirators. The Japa-nese Diet refused to ban the cult. Aum still exists as a religious sect and contin-ues to seek members under its new name, Aleph. It has renounced violence and apologized for its past deeds, but continues to follow Asahara's spiritual teachings. It supposedly has been purged of its criminal elements, some of whom have been found guilty and executed. Others, including the uncommunicative Asahara, have been sentenced to death and are awaiting execution.

The organized conspiracy by a band of well-educated, self-appointed couriers of divine judgment, with its doomsday agenda of wholesale extermination of fellow citizens, was apparently dismissed as an aberration, not even requiring the eradication of the faith that produced it.

So what are we to make of this? A rather obvious inference would be that by their remarkable ability to quickly turn from total preoccupation with calamity to total disinterest, the Japanese reveal that they are moved more by emotions than by reasoning. Another is that a nation as highly civilized and polished as Japan is also highly vulnerable to abuse and danger. At the very least, the experience proved that, far from being the harmonious society it usually believes itself to be, it is as internally fraught as the next one. Recognizing that fact, I felt, could help it successfully navigate its turbulent transition from Showa to Heisei.

The Aum affair did have one lasting effect: the disappearance of rubbish bins from rail stations as a precautionary measure. But the stations are as spotlessly clean as ever; passengers dutifully take their waste home with them.

Putting on a Brave Face

Tokyo, 2002. A first-time visitor to Japan today may be forgiven for failing to find a nation in disarray, a declining society, a demoralized population. For over a decade persistent (Western) media reports have suggested that Japan's society is in the grip of self-doubt with its financial sector on the verge of collapse and unemployment and resulting suicides soaring, reports that are not wide of the mark.

But the casual visitor sees no evidence of any of this. What he or she encounters instead is a fully functioning, apparently affluent, high-tech nation with spotlessly clean streets, state-of-the-art architecture, superb public transportation, and everywhere well-dressed citizens living their lives in peace and security.

Our visitor is confused. Could all those clever writers have utterly missed noticing the country's abiding strengths, expending their energies instead on the aberrant, the transitory, the sensational? Or do those reporters know something that is hidden to the untrained foreign eye? Is Japan's reputed malady an insidious one, something obscurely psychological, a gradual failure of will, the death of talent under an outward sheen of well-being?

Of course, on this first trip to Japan our innocent visitor does not stray far from the city's glamor spots and is, therefore, spared the sight of hundreds if not thousands of homeless camping in certain designated parks and passageways. But even there they might seem to be little cause for distress, because Japan's *houmuresu* live in neat tents or cardboard boxes, leave their shoes outside, regularly wash their clothes and bodies in public lavatories, seldom beg, do not use drugs, and can often be seen reading books or newspapers, some even in the English language. The unacceptable face of this orderly society is, thus, transmogrified into something that is at worst an unattractive and embarrassing blemish, and at best an admirable example of self-discipline and pride in adversity. I couldn't think of any Western parallel.

But it's not only the homeless that will escape the stranger's eye. He or she will fail to notice the bust's broader legacy too: rising poverty, ruined careers, youngsters adrift, fired office workers hanging out in cheap cafés. For this society minds its manners even when it's down on its luck. It is an admirable trait, but one that may easily confound the uninitiated outsider.

Chapter **21**

A Question of Identity

Do you understand Japan?

I have often been asked this question. Or another one: "What do foreigners think about Japanese identity and culture?" These are extraordinary questions, probing as they do outsiders' understanding of Japan's essential nature—its national character.

In most of the West we rarely confront foreigners with questions like this, perhaps because we are not preoccupied with worry about what outsiders think of us. Or because our very diversity precludes any notion of some kind of national common denominator. On the whole our personal and national identity seem to be rooted firmly enough for us not to lose sleep over how we look to others.

An exception is Germany, which, like Japan, had to come to terms with defeat and still wonders how it is perceived in the world. Unlike Japan, Germany's identity is further complicated by the ordeal of reunification with the communist half of the nation. Some other European nations are also struggling to varying degrees with doubts about their national identity, resulting from heavy, perhaps excessive immigration, which challenges established social values.

For the Japanese, the trauma of the bubble's collapse brought many individuals face to face with their true nature. If in the booming 1970s and 1980s they had glossed over longstanding uncertainties about their identity, the harsh realities of the Magellan decade revived them with a vengeance.

Japan's existential doubts differ from those of European countries in that they are neither the result of their lost war, nor caused by challenges from immigrant communities, which in any case are minuscule, compared to European minorities. Instead, they appear to result chiefly from the perception that Japan is alone in the world, somewhere between Asia and the West, but part of neither, a view that is rooted in their leaders' conscious decision in the late nineteenth century to "leave Asia" and join the West.

"Do you understand Japan?"—the question we began this chapter with—gains an additional layer of meaning if one realizes that the Japanese word for "understand" (*wakaru*) often carries the connotation of "appreciate" or "accept." It took me years to grasp this subtle aspect of Japanese negotiation: that "understanding" the other's position while respectfully disagreeing with it is not an option. One Japanese intellectual even went so far as to assert to me that "we Japanese cannot see other people's point of view." I have often found this to be true in my own experience.

The Japanese "loneliness" and sensitivity to outsiders' opinions may be traced to a fragile sense of personal and national identity. The lack of personal identity, goes this argument, must be related to the suppression of personality and individual character, going all the way back to the class-based police state of the Tokugawa era. And on a national level, the dualism of Japan's long-running attempt to assimilate the "best of the West" without surrendering its essential Japanese nature is the primary suspect for a weak sense of national identity.

But this argument unearths a deeper issue to be considered: the very nature of identity in Japan contrasts with Western understandings of this word. *Webster* defines it as "the distinguishing character or personality of an individual: individuality." In Japan, on the other hand, it more typically refers to one's place in society as determined by one's relationship to family, school, career, and country. The difference in emphasis is telling: the lone wolf versus the social animal.

I have my own pet definition of "identity," which I will reveal here for what it is worth. I believe one's identity can be broken down into four components:

- **Nature and background**: Place and circumstances of birth, inherited character, parents, nationality at birth

- **Nurture**: Upbringing and early education

- **Social status**: Work, hierarchal position, educational achievement, family, group affiliations

- **Personality**: Developed character, convictions held, interests, imagination, perception of how one relates to one's country's history and place in the world

One's identity is the sum total of these four elements.

In both the West and the East, the first two are beyond the control of the individual. The different perceptions of identity then arise from the next elements: social status and personality. In the West, these components are largely a result of one's own efforts, and therefore nonstatic. But in mid-Showa Japan and to a large extent still today, the development of the personality, the fourth element, was restrained by social control and career strictures and overshadowed by one's social status, which in turn was heavily influenced by one's background and nurture.

What's more, for most Japanese, career path and social status were exceptionally stable factors when compared to the more volatile conditions in Western society.

Thus defined, in Showa Japan identity typically derived more from objective facts, such as one's place in the social hierarchy, than from any subjective factors such as distinctive intellect or personality. Career paths were determined early and followed conscientiously, in an environment where conspicuous personal achievement was not encouraged, other than in terms of meeting the goals set by one's superiors. These conditions had little bearing on one's personal identity, which was in effect a function of one's given place in the hierarchy.

If this analysis is correct, it may help explain the extraordinary reliance Japanese place on their *meishi*, or "name-card," aka business card. The name-cards are exchanged at the very start of a meeting. They provide instant identification and establish one's identity in the eyes of the other. Without meishi no fruitful discussion can be held.

It has become clear to me, as I am asked again and again if I understand Japan, that the motivation behind this question may very well be the questioner's own uncertainty about how to perceive his or her nation. To my mind, the weakness of the "fourth element"—the formation of personal opinions, individual beliefs, and convictions—goes a long way toward explaining why the Japanese people are preoccupied with how they and their nation are perceived by others.

Of course, the Japanese group orientation has an impact on this issue, too. Their understanding of their personal identity is closely linked with social hierarchy and the opinions and behavior of the people around them, so their *national* identity might be built in the very same way: according to the opinions and behavior of other nations.

It should come as no surprise, then, that the severe challenges to group culture, family structures, and lifetime employment of the post-bubble decade revived the question of Japanese identity, both personal and national.

Japaneseness: Does It Exist?

The uncertainty about Japan's national identity is rooted in the past. Ever since the Meiji Era (1868–1912) Japan's leaders emphasized the existence of a special, almost divine "Japaneseness" that helped the country's rise from its feudal seclusion to the position of world power and master of Asia. This belief in a unique and superior Japan suffered two severe blows during the past century: military defeat at the hands of America and the collapse of the economic bubble around 1989. That unique something—whatever it was—had proved wanting in the face of powerful forces arrayed against it, be they superior armies, geopolitics, or globalization. Not only its practical value but the very notion of Japaneseness came into question.

In fact, Koichi Iwabuchi, a Japanese sociologist, argues that the idea of Japaneseness was no more than a cultural construct, fashioned in response to Western stereotyping in the late nineteenth century of Japan as an exotic, inscrutable society, fundamentally different from the European "other."[4] Instead of refuting this stereotype, Japan's leaders at the time embraced and reinforced it, and used it to inspire its people to unified effort. While in the midst of a Herculean attempt to emulate the Western powers militarily, technically, and economically, the Meiji reformers also laid the basis for Japan's view of its own uniqueness. Iwabuchi wrote:

[The] emphasis on "Japaneseness" has been crucial as a means of mobilizing the people. This strategic "Japaneseness" is something which maximizes national interests and minimizes individualism, consisting of traits such as loyalty to or devotion for the country.

This deliberate strategy to stress the inherently "different" nature of the Japanese race has yielded two profound results. It laid the basis for the emergence, in the 1930s, of a genre of nonfiction literature known as *nihonjinron*, literally "theories about the Japanese," and, crucially, it helped shape the character and attitudes of generations of Japanese by fostering, through nihonjinron and other means, the concept of a unique, and by implication, superior, Japaneseness.[5] It is probably not too rash to say that Japan's identity—its self-image—ever since the latter part of the nineteenth century was derived to a large extent from the West's conception of it, and from the justification and strengthening of this self-image through what came to be known as nihonjinron.

Interest in nihonjinron has waxed and waned over the decades, but it has never been far away. Its authors include both Westerners and Japanese, both independent academics looking for root causes and writers using it to advance a specific agenda. In the mid-1980s a virulent form of nihonjinron emerged, inspired by Japan's formidable economic power and America's difficulties in dealing with it. It reached a pinnacle with the publication, in 1989, of a highly controversial and popular book, *NO to ieru nihon* (*The Japan That Can Say NO*). The book was written by right-wing politician and later Tokyo governor Shintaro Ishihara and Sony chairman Akio Morita. (Its 1991 English version did not include Morita's essays, for reasons that were not disclosed). While not typical of the genre, it does stress the great talents of the Japanese people, with Ishihara aggressively demanding that America treat Japan with the respect it deserves. It argues that Japan, based on its history, accomplishments, technology, and economic power, deserves full recognition as a world leader alongside America.[6]

The book was a symptom of Japan's overconfidence at the height of the bubble, as discussed in Chapter 11. It is doubtful, though, if it reflected the mood among the general public, which did not turn noticeably anti-American or anti-Western. The bubble "arrogance" was largely confined to proud, successful, and nationalistic figures among the business and political elite.

Off with Those Labels!

The problem with nihonjinron and its historical link to the formation of Japan's identity is that "national identity" is, of course, impossible to define precisely and, therefore, does not really stand up to close scrutiny. Even in a society as relatively homogeneous as Japan with one national language, regional, class, and individual differences can be as great as anywhere. If we try to define Japaneseness in terms of what unites the Japanese, the well-worn clichés we must needs rely on—like "the Japanese are a highly disciplined race" or "the cleanest people in the world" do not hold up.

For example, during the Meiji period, Western visitors to Japan commented on the "undisciplined habits" of Japanese workers. My early experiences in the 1950s with public littering, vomiting in trains, and urinating in public places could have justified me in calling the Japanese a disgusting people. And some of the respondents to the survey I conducted in the course of my research for this book used the term zurui (cunning, scheming) in reference to their own race—quite a contrast to the competing view that the Japanese place a high value on honor. Labels are so easy to apply, and they tend to stick, even after they are found to be not—or no longer—warranted.

The establishment-cultivated notion that Japan's unique group culture and superior social and moral values ensured the ultimate success of whatever it chose to undertake, served as the central tenet of pre-war education, and did so again from the 1960s onward, although in a different way, as it was now embedded in post-war democratic principles. No doubt it concentrated people's minds and thus helped Japan achieve its fast economic growth in the post-war decades. But it took the place of self-reliance and critical thinking. It relieved its workers—right up to senior managers—from the responsibility of setting their own priorities in life. It effectively turned Japan into a nanny state.

The collapse of the bubble rudely removed this security and pulled the rug from under the very concept of Japaneseness. What had been regarded by broad swathes of Japanese society as a distinctive, inalienable, Japanese national character turned out to be the people's unquestioning willingness to abide by a set of rules long ago instilled by astute rulers to help them rule. As those rules had proven to be no longer effective, the concept of Japaneseness, the foundation of Japan's identity, lost its footing.

In Search of Self

In this new, uncharted era, not only national identity is in question. As group and family structures in Japan have always been exceptionally strong, the discontinuity we have explored on many levels of society over the past few decades cannot but have hurt the sense of personal identity of many Japanese.

The generation gap, not unknown in the West, has been particularly yawning in Japan. Values such as frugality, sobriety, loyalty, obedience, formal good manners, and chastity (for women), which informed every aspect of their parents' and grandparents' lives, today are better known by their antonyms to the under-forty generation. The complaint "you don't understand me" leveled at fathers and mothers by teenagers everywhere has a particularly cutting quality in Japan. The sight of workaholic fathers and accommodating mothers, coupled with the influence of rampant commercialism, sexual license, and exposure to novel if still half-baked notions of individualism, have turned a whole generation away from what might have been role models for their own lives. Their rebellion has created unbridgeable chasms in many families.

During the post-war reconstruction and rapid economic growth periods, stretching from the late 1940s to the late 1980s, every Japanese salary-worker knew what was expected of him—yes him, for women were seldom employed in other than subservient functions and were expected to quit when they married or before they turned thirty. (Like in all Japanese banks, women's pay scales in the Japan branches of the bank I worked for in the 1950s and 1960s ended at age thirty!). Rebuilding the country and then challenging America's position as the number one economy in the world were clear, quantifiable goals that left little room for doubt or worry among the rank and file. With the bursting of the bubble and the maturing of Japan into a low-growth economy riddled with problems of adjustment and globalization, the country's leaders have been hard put to find new slogans to inspire the workforce, slogans that might help these lost individuals define themselves and find a greater purpose in life.

Chapter 22

Personal Priorities in Life

When I lived in Japan in the 1950s and 1960s, the word "lifestyle"—first used by Austrian psychiatrist Alfred Adler in 1939—was seldom heard, as indeed it was in Europe, until it came into vogue there in the early 1960s.[7]

Perhaps this is appropriate, as the common way of life in mid-twentieth-century Japan was hardly complex or affluent enough to require such a word. The routine at the time for men was essentially one of work-eat-sleep. Office workers worked late hours. Their suits were invariably dark, their shirts white, their cars black—if they could afford one. If they had a kind employer they might get a few days' vacation once a year, to spend in a company-owned mountain lodge with their family. Executives and aspiring managers got their relaxation by spending nights out on the town and Sundays on the golf course, but even then they were entertaining clients or bureaucrats. It was a men's society: the wives took care of the house and the kids. Foreign vacations—a privilege reserved for the retired with savings—were available only in the form of JalPak Tours, which provided round-the-clock security and nanny-like care.

This honest life of hard work and small pleasures changed from the mid-1970s onward, and by the end of the bubble decade of the 1980s, everybody under forty seemed to have found some kind of cool, even extravagant, lifestyle determined by one's particular tastes in fashion, cosmetics, cars, computer games, food, music, holiday destinations, and sex, not necessarily in that order.

How did the extended recession of the 1990s affect this just-emerged way of life? Those most directly hit by the bust obviously had to tighten their belts, some severely so. The ranks of the poor swelled, and the middle class shrunk. But some fared well even after the bubble as shifting economic realities created opportunities in sectors such as information technology (IT), communications, finance, and banking, as well as in retailing and catering.

The fashion business continued to thrive, even as the recession played itself out, the newly rich picking up the slack left by the squeezed middle class. Company types were still wearing suits and ties, but Prime Minister Koizumi introduced the *cool-biz* look—short-sleeved shirts without jacket or tie—for the summer months, to enhance informality and comfort and save on air conditioning.

The young, sexy crowd that had been parading down Tokyo's Omotesando and Takeshitadori in their eight-inch heels, pink afros, and outlandish getups during the bubble went on doing so. And the throngs of look-alike, itsy-bitsy schoolgirls did not stop cluttering the streets of Shibuya by the thousands, with their white school socks, identical vocabulary and pinky-pearl mini-mobile-phones, making you wonder if cloning had already become a fact of Japanese life.

But this hedonistic, freewheeling and often silly way of life was largely confined to a small urban minority. Ordinary Japanese were still comparatively conventional in their living habits. As the economy stumbled, work and balancing the budget once again became the top priority for the vast majority of Japanese, whatever their age.

Even so, the under-forty generation judged their own habits and lifestyle to be very different from their parents', partly because of dissimilar eating and sleeping habits but also because of divergent values and priorities in life and the loss of employment security. Some comments I heard from people in this age group illustrate the differences they see between their lifestyles and their parents': "My parents live in a routine, I don't." "Their priority is society, mine is myself." "They are too preoccupied with 'balance' in life." "They are diligent, while I'm easy-going."

Nonetheless, some younger people did express their appreciation for the greater freedom made possible by their parents' exertions. And despite the generational gap, the same people considered relations with their parents to be generally satisfactory.

What's Most Important in Your Life?

This is a question I asked in several ways in the course of my survey. I knew that this kind of probing was fairly uncommon in Japan, and that in any case I could hope for little more than routine answers. I expected a lot of "my work" or "happiness" kind of replies, and maybe some revelations of impossible dreams from the young.

What I was not prepared for was the heavy emphasis among adults and students alike on travel and getting to know the world, a preference that reflects both a degree of escapism and a lack of focused ambition. Even among university students travel has a higher priority than intellectual pursuits and education! For most, preparation for a career or profession apparently was not the primary objective. Students showed unusual interest in "discovering myself and realizing my dreams."

Emperor Hirohito, posthumously known in Japan as Emperor Showa, makes his annual birthday appearance on April 29th, 1960, in the public grounds of the Tokyo Imperial Palace. *(Photo by Ysbrand Rogge.)*

Emperor Hirohito's annual birthday appearance in 1960. Left to right: Prince Hitachi, Crown Prince (now Emperor) Akihito, Emperor Hirohito, Empress Nagako, and Crown Princess Michiko. *(Photo by Ysbrand Rogge.)*

The signs of Japan's growing affluence provide a stark contrast to this war veteran begging in front of the old Nichigeki theater in 1960. Note the war-themed movie poster in the background. *(Photo by Ysbrand Rogge.)*

Women returning home on the train after a hard day's work in 1958, before air condition-ing became common. One is eating a self-prepared meal brought from home. *(Photo by Ysbrand Rogge.)*

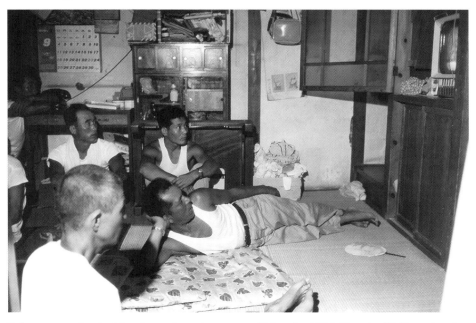

Laborers watch television in a private home near Tokyo in 1959. Regular TV broadcasting began in 1953 and rapidly became popular. Note the paper fan on the floor; even today these fans are used alongside electric fans and air conditioning. *(Photo by Ysbrand Rogge.)*

In 1960, bowing was part of everyday classroom routine in this primary school near Tokyo. *(Photo by Ysbrand Rogge.)*

A cigarette shop in Togakushi village, Nagano prefecture, in 1960. Simple stores like this with open fronts and squatting shop owners now belong to the past, swept away by affluence and modernization.

Demonstrators in happi coats carry an effigy of Prime Minister Kishi during the anti–US-Japan Security Treaty riots in Tokyo in 1960. *(Photo by Ysbrand Rogge.)*

Boys dressed in traditional costume for a theater performance in 1958.

A street in the Marunouchi business district, Tokyo, after rain. This photo was taken in 1960; between the 1960s and 1980s the entire district was demolished and replaced by high-rise buildings. *(Photo by Ysbrand Rogge.)*

Tokyo Station in 1954.

One of the few surviving buildings in central Tokyo, Tokyo Station, seen here in 2007, is still one of the capital's major train stations and transportation hubs.

Pilgrims resting at a Kyoto temple in 1955.

In 1963, Mount Fuji towers above Lake Kawaguchi and the original Fuji View Hotel.

Tokyo's landmark Nihonbashi Bridge, here seen in 2005, has been obscured by the Shuto expressway since the early 1960s.

The author's Tokyo residence from 1962 to 1972 was this house designed by Antonin Raymond, an associate of Frank Lloyd Wright. Built in 1933, it was replaced by two modern houses in the late 1970s.

A company outing to Nishiura Hot
Spring, Aichi prefecture, in 1961.
It started with dinner…

...followed by a drinking party. *(Photos by Ysbrand Rogge.)*

Osaka visitors at Expo 1970 pose in front of the Tower of the Sun, designed by Taro Okamoto.

Individualism on display in Shibuya, Tokyo, in 2006…but still in a group.

In 2006, crew and cleaners await the arrival of a Shinkansen bullet train at Tokyo Station.

Old women in Nara prefecture tend fields in 1997. Although the young have moved to the cities, more traditional life is still found in Japan's rural areas.

Kimono fashions, seen here in Ginza, Tokyo, in 2006, have made a partial comeback, presenting a cosmopolitan contrast with the international luxury brands that dominate everyday urban life.

A typical public-friendly sign outside a Koban police station, photographed in 2006 in Tokyo.

A walk through Tokyo's Omotesando district in 2006 provides an example of infantile fashions.

In Tokyo's Ginza district in 2007, police confront noisy rightist vans that broadcast political messages as they pass through the streets.

Visitors flock to Tokyo's Zojoji Temple to admire the cherry blossoms in April 2008. Buddhist temples such as this are popular as recreational destinations, while continuing to serve as sites of worship and to provide funeral rites.

Japan's Tokyo Tower is wreathed in cherry blossoms in this photo taken in April 2008. Both tower and blossoms are iconic of Japan: At 1,091 feet (332.6 meters) this tower has been the world's tallest self-supporting steel structure since it was built in 1958. Cherry blossoms are Japan's unofficial national flower, and each spring people from around the country celebrate their beauty with *hanami,* or cherry blossom viewing parties.

This may well reflect the prevailing trend to search for a "new identity" and the uncertainty the growing individual felt in a predominantly group-oriented society.

Looking for Love—or Not?

In both written survey answers from and conversation with adults, romance and sex were hardly mentioned as important lifestyle factors. Surprisingly, it seemed to have no more weight with the students. I suspect some dissembling here, for there was and is ample evidence that Japanese society is as preoccupied with sex as any. Perhaps the word "romance" confused them. Courtship and emotional love were less common in Japan, where couples intent on marriage traditionally met through formal introduction. Although that custom is now largely a thing of the past, the art of courtship apparently still has some distance to go before the modern Japanese woman finds it satisfactory.

The popular press often comments on the "clumsiness" of men in going about winning the hearts of women. Some young men prefer to stay at home with their mothers rather than venture into this unaccustomed territory. Sexual energy is often channeled into solitary pursuits, some of them strange, even weird. Sexually explicit video games and manga cartoon books of a deviant nature have been thriving. Porn Web sites catering to every sexual need and fantasy are hugely popular, some offering programmable virtual "fantasy women." (As yet, there is no sign of "fantasy men," although given the way things are going, this omission is bound to be put right before long.)

A Japanese friend of mine, retired as president of a prominent media company, had this to say about the phenomenon: "The mothers pamper their sons, happy to have them at home. The fathers are useless and away most of the time. Is it any wonder that the sons become their mothers' lovers?" One must hope that he was referring to extreme cases, but there is no denying that there is frequently something unsavory about these fully grown men refusing to leave the warm nest.

And what is one to make of all those older businessmen paying for sex with sixteen- or seventeen-year-old schoolgirls dressed in a sailor's uniform and white socks? We're not talking about the perversion of a few but (although the media may have overhyped the phenomenon) a social problem serious and widespread enough to be known by a special name, *enjo-kosai*, meaning something like "assisted dating." Most of these girls, beeped up after school on their little cell phones for a dinner or karaoke date with a "helpful uncle," are apparently not bothered by guilty feelings. They are just "doing what they feel like" to earn pocket money to buy some coveted big-brand accessory. Even when the date leads to sex, as is usually the case, they claim they just do it "for fun," and some stop doing it after a while. They don't regard themselves as prostitutes, although press reports claim that many in fact end up as such.

And I haven't even mentioned the reputed sharp rise in female infidelity and divorce. Clearly sex and romance receive far more attention than my findings would suggest. Perhaps, like so much else in Japanese society, they are subjects one prefers not to discuss.

Who Wants an Intelligent Lover If You Can Have a Cute One?

A related phenomenon is the streak of "infantilism" in Japanese culture referred to by such social scientists as Sharon Kinsella and Yamane Kazuma. It was not unknown during mid-Showa but became particularly noticeable during and after the bubble. The evidence for this is indeed ubiquitous, in people's behavior, advertising, popular culture, and the service industry. Banks use childish cartoons on their ATM machines, and the police do the same in their public relations to project a citizen-friendly image. The jingles in television commercials frequently feature little-girl voices. The anime and manga industry is replete with infantile fantasies.

Young women are especially susceptible to this extended childhood. Wanting to be thought of as *kawaii* ("cute"), they often talk, gesture, and dress like little girls, while hugging soft toy animals and clutching childish handbags. Some restaurants even cater to this puerile tendency among their grown-up female clientele by offering *otona no tame no okoosama ranchi* ("children's lunch meant for adults"), a cute array of tiny, colorful savory and sweet portions, arranged on a plate and topped with a little doll or paper parasol!

In the eyes of those who consider childlike qualities as desirable (and they may well constitute the majority), a kawaii girl or young woman is not just cute but also vulnerable, innocent, sweetly selfish, adorable, pure, and inexperienced. This seems to be a good fit with the preferences of those men interested in marriage. I am told that the majority of well-educated men will still choose for a wife a kawaii girl over the more sporty, independent, capable, or intellectual types.

This prevalent male predilection for the child-woman may well have something to do with the hierarchical, confining nature of traditional Japanese employment—by no means dead even now—and the frustrations it engenders among young and mid-career employees. In exchange for security and prospects of steady advancement, the traditional employer expects submissiveness, even from its most intelligent and well-educated workers. The resulting suppressed anger and hurt self-esteem have no outlet at work, as complaints are seldom entertained and confrontations discouraged. It is not difficult to imagine that in the conjugal sphere these men unconsciously seek what they are deprived of at work: control and respect. The reassuring presence of the kawaii wife waiting at home to serve and comfort him is just what he needs to restore his battered ego. As James Michener put it in his 1950s bestseller *Sayonara,* "Japanese women make their men feel important."

Thus is desk rage sublimated and defanged. But this daily diet of grudging docility on the one hand and soothing palliation on the other is hardly conducive to character building. It takes a man of real mettle and conviction to assert himself amid all the patronizing and mollycoddling, and to understand that engagement rather than passivity is the way forward. But if he does, he might just find himself alone. For despite all the changes forced upon it by the challenges of globalization, Japanese society hasn't completely shaken off its nanny-state character. Your employer is still expected to look after your career, your wife after the comforts of home—having replaced your mother—and the state after everything else. By comparison, in the words of a Japanese woman quoted elsewhere in this book, "Europe is a land of grownups."

I want to stress that there are many exceptions to the picture just painted. The post-bubble shake-up of Japan's business and society did not fail to have an effect on work relations and personal lifestyles. At the same time, many men and women found it hard to change their habits and preferences.

What Happened to Dreams and Ambitions?

Among the personal priorities I inquired about in preparation for writing this book, cultural pursuits such as attending concerts or visiting museums found favor among some of the adults, but none of the students mentioned them. The more personal quests such as religion, spiritual disciplines, and philosophy, hardly came up either, and neither did such social concerns as helping people in need or the environment. On the other hand, no one mentioned getting rich or running for political office as a goal in life!

The impression I gained of the adults was of a comfortable people living in the present, bent on travel, and devoted to family and friends but with no great career ambitions and little passion. The younger generation seemed hardly more inspired. The absence of any kind of tangible life goal among the thirty-odd students from renowned universities I questioned is glaring. The dreams they wanted to realize were not articulated. This certainly confirms what I was told about the limitations of the educational system, notably its failure to breed independence and clarity of thought.

To the extent there was any expressed dissatisfaction with life—and there was quite a bit of that—it was to do with banal concerns such as a need for better housing and relief from boredom. Again no articulated goals, just vague, unfocused dissatisfaction with the status quo.

The Japanese Way: Acquiescence

Yet among the bland pronouncements I found once again hints of that understated, inward-looking quality and *integrity* that I have always seen as the mainstay of this culture. The Japanese as a whole never have been, and are not generally today, given to hyperbole or self-assertion. Many seem to have a well-honed aversion to taking the initiative, preferring instead to practice what might be called "intelligent acceptance" of one's circumstances: the weather, noisy children, unreasonable bosses, long commutes, obnoxious in-laws. One's station in life. Life in general.

It is tempting to equate this attitude with fatalism instead of intelligence. But there is a distinction between blind surrender to the consequences of one's birth, and the positive interpretation of a reality that, at least for the present, one cannot or does not wish to alter. The former is a submissive, defeatist state of mind, impelled perhaps by abject poverty, and it lacks hope. The latter approach to life, traditionally common in Japan, is intelligent in the sense that, while it accepts that changes to the prevailing reality should not be forced, it recognizes the possibility of a change in circumstances. This attitude is marked by a muted alertness to the immediate surroundings. For its nourishment it requires no manifestos or compelling philosophies, perhaps not even a personal dream. What it does need, besides a good education, is continuous reaffirmation of the existence of social channels and personal networks, any of which could act as conduit for change, or at least for optimal functioning.

The reader might dismiss the previous paragraph as a complicated way of describing the "open mind." But what we are talking about here is something more subtle, the kind of attitude to life coveted by those in the West who are exhausted from the excesses of an aggressive and opportunistic society, where sensitivity, introspection, and integrity seem lost commodities. What they look for is a fully informed but *calmer* and more *honest* way of dealing with the rigors of contemporary life. Some seem to find it in this alternative "Japanese" approach, which, though by no means universally followed even in Japan, nevertheless can be said to be a distinct product of Japanese culture.

The obvious downside to nonassertiveness is vulnerability to manipulation and exploitation by high-handed superiors and unscrupulous rulers. Below its facade of contentment hides a worrisome defenselessness to exterior forces, rooted in what at best is an accommodating disposition but too often can only be called indifference.

How to summarize my discussions with so many men and women of all ages at a time when Japan was still busy maneuvering its way out of the stormy strait? At the risk of simplification, I would say that, for all of the transition's severe dislocations, most of those affected were adjusting remarkably well to the changes. Emotional reactions and identity crises were unavoidable, but in the end the vast majority of the people evidently decided that the clock could not be turned back. That realization helped Japan weather the Magellan passage. But was it enough to steel it for what lay ahead?

Chapter 23

The Slow Escape from Insularity

The influx of foreign businessmen and freelancers of every kind that had been a feature of the boom years accelerated after the bubble burst, as Japan's weakened financial conditions and changing attitudes to foreign involvement in the economy opened up ever more opportunities for outsiders. This trend naturally had an effect on the way Japanese experienced the presence of foreigners in their midst.

By the Magellan decade, the days when things Western were referred to as *batakusai* (smelling of butter)—still common in mid-Showa—were long past. Europeans no longer necessarily stank, although their bathing habits and frequency of sock changes still did not always meet Japan's high standards of hygiene. (My wife remembered vividly being "nauseated" as a child by the odor emitted by the Europeans she encountered in the Yokohama Grand Hotel).

Overall though, interest in and knowledge and acceptance of Western culture in all its manifestations became truly widespread during the 1980s and 1990s, incomparably greater than our own vis-à-vis Japan's. Interracial relationships and marriages become commonplace, and international socializing in general more natural and relaxed. Rural folk were not always as accommodating as urbanites, as illustrated by anecdotal reports of Westerners occasionally (even today) being refused entry to Japanese local bathhouses because of native objections to their presence. But such stories were the exceptions.

I was curious to learn how the average Japanese viewed this gradual transformation of their society, and I decided to ask around. What I found was increased tolerance mixed with apprehension. Many adults and most students I questioned said they welcomed the increase in the number of foreign residents, as it made Japan a more cosmopolitan society. Some felt, interestingly, that without a vibrant, integrated foreign community, Japan would never break out of its insularity. But there also was noticeable uneasiness about the prospect of a multiracial Japan. Many preferred to see only foreigners from developed countries, or students who didn't stay on after graduation.

In fact, the number of foreign university students in Japan had been increasing year by year, from 45,066 in 1990 to 121,812 in 2005.[8] Almost 80 percent were from China and Korea, and another 30 percent were from elsewhere in Asia.

In spite of this trend, the *Japan Times* reported that non-Japanese Asians studying in Japan and intending to stay on after graduation faced "diminishing job prospects amid language and cultural barriers [and] a hermetic corporate culture. Society is not yet ready to accept them," said the paper. One problem, continued the article, is that foreigners cannot grasp what is meant by "tacit understanding," a manner of implied communication that is a characteristic of corporate life in Japan. This leads to friction between "what the companies require and how [foreigners] behave."[9] Even so, the evident support that I have encountered, particularly among students, for more foreign residents and a less insular Japan is heartening.

These findings, for what they are worth, confirm my personal experience that during and after the bubble, relations between Japanese and foreigners lost much of the formality and reluctance of the past. Many Japanese now seem quite comfortable in the company of non-Japanese, even when a lack of English (or Japanese, on the foreigners' part) limits communication. Education, travel, and prosperity, and the receding shadow of the lost war, obviously have done their salubrious work.

So has Japan become more or less foreign-minded than a generation ago? By the superficial yardstick of popular culture and lifestyles, I would say "more." At the same time, there appears to be, paradoxically, a low level of interest in what goes on in the rest of the world, as evidenced by a 2004 BBC/GlobeScan poll about the United States' impact on world events conducted in twenty-one countries. In that survey, the Japanese scored consistently *lowest* in the percentage of respondents expressing an opinion. Only between 25 and 50 percent of those polled expressed an opinion to a range of questions, compared to 75 to 95 percent in China, South Korea, and major Western countries.

While there may be other nations with an isolationist approach the world, their motivation tends to be different. America's latent isolationism, for example, is rooted in self-sufficiency and the presumption of invincibility. Japan's inward-looking stance may well come from quite the opposite source: an abiding sense of vulnerability and the consequent wish to avoid the limelight and stay out of trouble.

So What's the Problem?

The lack of interest in what goes on in the world may explain why—according to one of my Japanese friends, a fluent English speaker in her mid-thirties—the apparent increased ease of social mixing between educated Japanese and Westerners is less the product of natural inclination than of deliberate effort. "From early childhood, we are told that we should be assertive in our relations with Westerners," said my friend. "It's hard for us to do so because it is against our culture. But we learn. Yet even now the moment I switch to English I become a different person, a stranger to my true self."

Nevertheless, every other person I interviewed during the Magellan decade said they would consider emigrating to another country, if Japan's economic problems got worse and would affect their job or standard of living. This was a remarkable finding, particularly when seen in conjunction with the answer to another question, "Are you proud to be Japanese?" Nobody said they weren't, but again every other person said they were "neither proud nor not proud" of being Japanese. This could indicate two things. One, that being born Japanese was seen as a simple fact, not worthy of pride, which is a feeling that assumes some kind of achievement. The other interpretation, offered by some people I spoke to, is that many Japanese have an inherently negative attitude to their own country, which, if true, could issue from the long-held doubts about their real identity as Japanese discussed earlier.

The End of an Era

The Imperial Palace Plaza, Tokyo. 1 PM, January 7, 1989. The emperor died this morning at 6:33. Businesses have been invited to stay closed for two days. So far I've seen no closed shops, although the banks hang their flags half-mast. Here, in the vast but still almost empty Plaza, the public part of the Imperial Palace grounds in central Tokyo, the atmosphere is a cross between solemnity and blatant curiosity seeking. Six itinerant priests of the Myouhouji sect just passed by in single file mournfully beating their drums. But most of the people who have come to the Plaza seem more interested in clicking their cameras than in sparing a thought for their dead emperor. I entered the tent to sign the visitors' register. There was no line. I signed not as a mourner or loyal subject, but as "witness."

The historic importance of the day is undeniable, marking as it does the end of a long and controversial life that witnessed Japan's dramatic ups and downs and its reemergence as world's second-largest economy. In the name of this fragile man, a disastrous war was waged, although the extent of his personal involvement remains unclear. At least he is credited with having made the decision to end the war, thus saving countless lives. His death closes a troubled chapter. It sets his country free....

Views on Japan's Future

Throughout my interviews and casual conversations with over one hundred Japanese men and women of every age group and walk of life during the latter part of the post-bubble decade, I tried to elicit some kind of viewpoint from them about the course of their nation, with an eye to the future.

Roughly half took up the challenge, expressing a wide range of opinions, both in defense and critical of Japan. Among the more startling views was the fear that, unless Japan adjusted more swiftly to the great changes in the world, it would be defeated by Korea and China. To that end, Japan must admit more immigrants, even at the cost of a dilution of people's values and an increase in crime, because Japan cannot survive without imported labor.

My interlocutors showed little confidence in politicians and bureaucrats, calling them deceitful and corrupt. "I can't stand octogenarian politicians, celebrity politicians, and political dynasties," said one cynic. "We've got all three." Skepticism about individualism surfaced repeatedly, the upshot of most comments on the subject being that Japan should both welcome and shun individualism. One expressed it eloquently in this way: "We must learn to live with the dichotomy. The key to our future identity may lie there." There was much more, most of it betraying uncertainty about Japan's national character and anxiety about the future. But the frustration was more with the way that the country was being run than with its fundamental values. The "trivial" debates in the Diet were attacked and the Japanese tendency to follow others ridiculed, as was the politicians' inability to make decisions. But many argued that Japan must do everything in its power to preserve and propagate its strengths and virtues: tolerance, wa (harmony), sensitivity, love of peace, and its position between Asian and Western cultures. Some pointed to Japan's "successful foreign policy" in not getting involved in a single war since 1945. This was not blamed on fear or selfishness, or the anti-war constitution, but was credited to the people's genuine abhorrence of armed conflict. The world would "lose its balance" if Japan turned militaristic, "like the United States," was a view expressed more than once.

Self-criticism notwithstanding, the overriding impression I took away from my meetings and discussions with Japanese of all age groups—and most especially the young—was that of a deep attachment to their land and culture. Even those who most strongly attacked their country's weaknesses didn't waver in their loyalties.

Most were agreed on two fundamental issues: that Japan would never have a revolution and that its economy would never collapse. Given the ongoing trials of the Magellan decade, this was a remarkably optimistic view. Was it wishful thinking or an expression of confidence at the way Japan's business leaders—and even those detested politicians—had responded to the crisis so far? Did it reveal hope for progress toward a more diverse and rejuvenated society? Perhaps.

But the changes brought about by the bust were still tentative. And my interviews so far were with a cross-section of Japanese urbanites, none of whom could be considered to belong to the corporate or political elite.

Among those who did, and whom I questioned subsequently, opinions varied. Of particular interest was my long interview, in 2002, with a former high Japanese government official I had known for over thirty years. Although officially retired this well-known gentleman was still active in various multinational commissions. I solicited his views on Japan's future direction. His answer was forthright.

Foreigners Wanted!

Japan, he said, was suffering from complacency, the result of "excessive" job security in the past and of the educational system, which was devised to enhance minimum and average standards, not to turn out leaders. The seniority system provided no incentive either. Against this background moods could swing easily between excessive optimism and excessive pessimism, the latter not free from an element of masochism. He referred to "repeated mistakes in macroeconomic planning, both fiscal and monetary," and bemoaned the delays in deregulation—in distribution, construction, property development, and financial services, including banking.

In the opinion of this articulate ex-bureaucrat, the Japanese were overregulated and overprotected, and he added half seriously that what was needed was "a foreign impetus—foreign leaders—to get us out of the rut."

What kind of impetus? What leaders? True, *gai-atsu*, or foreign pressure, had sometimes helped Japan resolve intractable financial or trade issues, as in the 1970s, when President Nixon's bold overture to Mao's China and his decision to break the dollar's link to gold, put Japan on the spot and forced it to make overdue policy changes of its own. But weren't we talking about even more fundamental matters this time?

What my friend was actually referring to was hands-on involvement. Foreigners taking over. Something along the lines of what was achieved at Japan's Nissan Motors, where Carlos Ghosn—a Frenchman born in Brazil to Lebanese parents—was appointed by Nissan's controlling shareholder Renault as Nissan's CEO in 2001. Ghosn had succeeded in turning the ailing company around with a minimum of disruption, making it profitable again. Surely, he said, Japan's debt-ridden banking sector could benefit from similar treatment. What was needed was a change in the law to permit foreign majority ownership of banks and other financial services companies.

But he wouldn't stop there; he wanted Western experts as puppet masters at the government level, running things behind the scene, as "under our present system, we are unable to do a proper job." He waited for my reaction, but before it came he said quickly, with a mischievous smile: "Just joking."

Whether he was serious or not, my friend's prescription stood little chance of realization, least of all at the government level. Quite the contrary. As you will see in Part Four, the economic recovery from 2003 onward was accompanied by government efforts to redefine Japan's identity in a nationalistic context. In such a Japan, the role of foreigners could only diminish.

The Magellan decade had been rough sailing, and the vessel called Japan emerged from it with its sails tattered, its stores depleted, and its passengers shaken. But the sorely tried crew had learned a thing or two on the way. With hard work and a bit of luck, they mused, the ship could be repaired and made ready for the storms ahead.

Part Four

Overcoming Showa

What an extraordinary leap it has been from the 1950 Spartan reality of iron cauldron bathtubs wood-fired from below to the soft 2008 comforts of sissy heated toilet seats and no-touch flushes. From open drains and the pervasive odor of septic tanks to spotless streets and remote-control home climate systems. And from grimy steam engines to the super-efficiency of luxurious, accident-free bullet trains.

Europe has been left behind. Even America in some ways struggles to keep up. Japan is among the most advanced consumer societies on earth today. It is awash with gadgets and reveling in a riot of fads and fashions, with quaint new jargon to match, anchored in borrowed English, or French, or Italian, whatever fancy or the market might dictate. It's a cool, safe, high-tech urban society of 125 million consumers supplying the world with desirable products while minding its own, very Japanese business.

But notwithstanding the superficial glitter, redeemed from the boom-to-bust decades, new challenges have replaced the old ones: a declining population, the rise of China, the perceived threat from North Korea, globalization and its effect on Japan's insular tendency, the widening gap between rich and poor, impoverishment of rural areas, apathy among the young—to name some of the most pressing.

Once again, the Golden Age of Showa is back in the news. Many are nostalgic for its certainties and optimism. The political right wants to bring back Showa values, enhanced by pre-Showa notions of proud nationhood and patriotism.

But longing for an era that will never come back tends to sap the will to move forward and get on with unfinished business. And so it is with Japan. To idealize Showa's accomplishments and undoubted strengths hampers a cool appraisal of their downside: the unsuitability of some of the methods developed during Showa to the new realities of the Heisei era—which began when the current emperor, Akihito, ascended to the throne in 1989—and indeed to Japan's long-term interests.

For example, the overprotection of the people from all manner of harmful influences and, indeed, from the need to think for themselves may have fitted Showa conditions but is not appropriate in this age of far-reaching global interaction. Similarly, unquestioning loyalty to one's seniors, group, employer, and nation—a necessity at a time of reconstruction and catching up—can become an excuse for spineless docility when changed circumstances call for more critical attitudes and imaginative solutions.

I am well aware that some of these time-honored concepts are already under siege, notably in business circles, where performance counts more these days than kowtowing to the boss, and corporate policies are more likely to be shaped with a view to the global market than to ingratiating oneself with the authorities. Yet the old thinking is still stubbornly alive among the mandarins and the political establishment, as illustrated by a report in the *International Herald Tribune* of February 28, 2008. The paper reported that a Japanese government panel planned to introduce a new law that would effectively censor Internet news sites in the same way that the big newspapers are already controlled in Japan: by making Internet service providers directly answerable to the government.

Even in academia, hierarchy still often trumps intellectual credentials, as the following example illustrates. I was told about a certain Japanese lady who had earned high academic acclaim for her groundbreaking work in a European country. After returning to Japan, she looked for suitable academic employment. She attended a conference and the head of the conference, a university professor, agreed to see her. He asked her to outline her academic achievements. After she had done so, the professor's reaction was: "The first thing you must learn is humility!" (*Mazu kenson o shirinasai!*) And that to a mature scholar in her mid-forties, known for her modest and respectful demeanor.

Another indicator of what many social scientists, Japanese and foreign alike, have called the immaturity of Japanese society is the ongoing emphasis on the cute, unspoiled, and childlike in everything from advertising to television shows to what is considered desirable in the "ideal" bride. As discussed in Chapter 22, this predilection points to a lingering infantilism in Japanese culture that is out of step with the requirements of a fully mature society. What to think for example of the nominally adult television weather "girls" and young variety-show personalities who with their voices and body language imitate the behavior of little children? Or of that sweet cartoon of a flying mouse you find on the facade of many a *koban* police box, those small neighborhood police stations manned by two or three officers to assist the locals and keep an eye out for lawbreakers. Police officers as harmless, huggable creatures?

Even the central government has been enlisting the help of adorable cartoons, such as cutesy characters posing in front of tanks, to promote a "softer image" for Japan abroad. The idea is that warm feelings for Japanese anime and manga pop culture can translate into warm feelings for Japan's foreign policy. Critics both foreign and domestic contend that offering child-like icons rather than explaining the facts may work in Japan, but the outside world is not so naive.

It may well be argued—as I would if put on the spot—that none of these supposed negatives have proved a liability so far. After all, Japanese society today is functioning smoothly, is largely free from the kind of internal confrontations and security threats that plague most Western nations, and is provided with better public services than most countries in its league.

True enough. But what about the future?

What Happened to Japan's Silences? And to Patience?

November, 2005. Impatience is rife in this society—one expects to be served promptly, in shops, cafés, convenience stores, supermarkets. It's different when the waiting is for traffic lights or government officials, then the reservoir of patience seems bottomless. But otherwise there is little tolerance for any kind of delay: elevators, a line at the till, even a car stopping to unload passengers.

Shopkeepers and café personnel forestall customers' impatience by asking them instantly and often in shouting voices, the moment they enter, what they want, before they have had a chance to glance at the wares or the menu. Yet no one flinches at this treatment. Is it because shoppers don't want to be left alone for a moment? Because unasked-for attention equates with "good service" in this action-driven society?

During an upmarket guided visit to the wooded splendor of the ancient Enryakuji Temple near Kyoto, the guides constantly reminded us in loud voices (1) not to leave anything behind; (2) where we could find the toilets, although the huge signs were self-evident; (3) to stay close together, and, irony of ironies, (4) to enjoy the peace and quiet of the temple grounds at our leisure!

Cell phones are not allowed on trains and buses and other public and most private places, "because they annoy others." Yet no one complains about the constant stream of often repetitive announcements on those same buses and trains, at stations, and everywhere crowds gather.

Many Japanese tourists are understandably dismayed by the lack of helpful signs and announcements and the generally "backward state" of Europe's technology. In Japan "systems" are expected to work punctually and perfectly at all times. A Japanese friend of mine broke her nose because an automatic door "that should have opened" didn't. She had not allowed for the possibility that the door might not be fully open at the precise moment she was to pass through it. Caution was considered unnecessary because the door "should have opened."

Chapter **24**

New Challenges, Old Medicine

For a fair appraisal of Japan's long-term prospects as a peace-loving, affluent society governed by the rule of law, it may be helpful to take a brief look at the country's post–Second World War history, as it may offer a clue as to the relative strength of the country's democratic institutions—and hint at some roadblocks to a new era of prosperity.

During the early years of the Occupation democratic ideals, half-remembered from the brief, exhilarating "Taisho democracy" years of the 1920s, were pursued with astonishing zeal. For a nation until so recently immersed in myths of imperial divinity and racial superiority and subjected to the strictures of military government, the apparent ease with which the new order was embraced exceeded all expectations. But rather than Japan gratefully receiving the gift of freedom from the generous hands of the victor—a perception not uncommon in the United States—it was the parched soil of the country's deprived decades that made the speedy absorption possible.

To the consternation of the more conservative elements on General MacArthur's staff, however, Japan's fledgling democracy became dominated by left-wing ideology, leading to the popular discrediting not only of wartime leaders and rich and powerful families but also of American-style, supposedly "democratic" capitalism. Powerful labor unions sprung into being, and Communism found wide support among students, teachers, and intellectuals and infiltrated labor unionism.

The Korean War, which broke out in 1950, offered Japan its first real chance since capitulation to get its export industry going. The "special procurements" for the American (and other UN) forces fighting on the Korean peninsula provided a sorely needed shot in the arm of the economy still struggling to recover from wartime devastation.

But the vision of Japan's leaders in the early 1950s of a strong, modern economy built on technically advanced products did not agree with American expectations for Japan as a humbled, second-rate nation content to earn a decent living producing labor-intensive products for its own market and its Southeast Asian neighbors'. These leaders didn't see a future role for Japan in competition with the sweatshop labor of countries such as China and India. What they decided Japan needed was a highly educated workforce and the engineering skills capable of developing the products that would put Japan ahead in the coming race. For these plans to bear fruit, it was necessary to lay the basis for long-term peaceful labor relations and political nonactivism.

Democracy, but with a Twist

The solution was brilliant. While continuing to extol democratic ideals and institutions, the governing elite began to systematically instill concepts of social organization and morality that were in all but name based on neo-Confucian teachings. Confucius (550–479 BC), one of China's most influential historical figures, emphasized the importance of education, family loyalty, work ethic, conformity to traditional standards, honoring of ancestors, and unquestioning obedience to superiors. These ancient traditions were adapted to the post-war world, fostering group discipline and loyalty to hierarchical seniors and the larger unit—the employer, the government, the nation—to which personal needs and interests were to be subordinated. In a sense, this was a reemergence of traditional, Tokugawa-era thinking, which had largely survived the Meiji Restoration, albeit in the form of a compromise with the modernizers, who advocated refashioning the Japanese state on the German pattern. It was briefly challenged—as you have seen—by the idealism of the short-lived Taisho Democracy after the First World War, only to be resurrected with a vengeance when the militarists rose to power in the late 1920s.

Although discredited by defeat, the neo-Confucian spirit lingered. Ethical tenets such as *on* (obligation) and *giri-ninjo* (duty and humanity) were still alive in society. It was a logical step to graft the post-Occupation policy of single-minded dedication to economic recovery and expansion onto this body of remembered ethics.

The nation's best brains were recruited through the filter of demanding state examinations and placed on the slow but steady promotional ladder ultimately leading to the highest positions in the *kanryo*, the bureaucracy. The kanryo was charged with overseeing and regulating all aspects of society as well as ensuring the continuity of the nation's essential values and systems. Being career civil servants rather than political appointees, they constituted the real government. The politicians, with their usually short terms of office and preoccupation with factional struggles, fundraising, reelection campaigns, and personal vendettas, were heavily reliant on the solid rock of the kanryo establishment.

Work Now, Spend Later

Japan's ensuing rise to economic world power was thus made possible and supported by the triple pillars of an elite bureaucracy, a straightforward fast-growth policy, and a highly skilled and disciplined workforce. Disciplined—and docile: in order for the system to function optimally, it was essential that the workforce be kept politically passive. There was a paradox in this, as the workers also had to be highly educated to meet the needs of the ambitious growth goals.

The high savings rate resulting from strict personal financial discipline (another fruit of education) and "postponed" consumption helped finance the large investments needed for building the industrial and public infrastructure. (The rest was borrowed from the foreign banks.) Above all, the public's belief in the wisdom of their nation's course and their sincere commitment to it ensured its sustained success through the decades, culminating in Japan's rise to its exalted economic position.

Japan may well be the first advanced society to have inspired, during the hard-working decades of Showa, an almost universal belief in the moral imperative of group-centered behavior—and the attendant sacrifice of personal needs and preferences. That this was achieved through systematic indoctrination devoid of coercion, within a nominally democratic framework, makes it all the more remarkable. It was the kind of result utopians and dictators have vainly tried to achieve elsewhere by ruthless means. But in Japan there was no need for an autocratic regime imposing harsh standards of behavior on an unwilling population, with severe penalties for violators.

The Japanese themselves by and large identified with their government's objectives, apparently regarding it as necessary and reflecting the nation's "true spirit," rather than merely a political program of the ruling establishment.

Strange Bedfellows: Deference and Democracy

The question confronting us here is to what extent the Showa-style democratic tenets and social values described above are still a fact of Japanese sociopolitical life today and how they may be expected to impact Japanese society in the decades to come.

One way of gauging the level of popular political engagement is to take stock of the people's reaction to the bust. There is no doubt that the financial collapse left the population in shock. But the debacle was not laid at the door of its rulers. After half a century of enjoying the protection and rising living standards made possible by the prevailing system, the electorate could not or refused to see beyond its confines. People remained deferential to the executives—if not in their heart (many despised politicians and bureaucrats alike), then at least implicitly, and took no action against them.

What Japan seemed to be lacking was a democratic imperative. In the absence of strong and effective political involvement on the part of the electorate, the governing elite had always been pretty much left to run the country as they saw fit. And as their loyalties were first and foremost with their own and their party's perpetuation, changing the status quo was seldom in their interest.

In this climate only an acute "sense of crisis," preferably one occasioned by some major global event or pressure from a superior power such as the United States, could force them to act, such as President Nixon's 1971 recognition of Mao's China, an event that forced Japan to follow suit. A more recent example occurred in 2002, when in response to sustained international pressure, Japan finally decided to cancel all debts owed it by the world's poorest countries, the last of the G8 creditor countries to do so.

Evidently, the collapse of the price bubble was in a different league. It did not become the trigger to fundamental change. Being an internal event, it was treated with local medicine. It inevitably resulted in some needed adjustments in the methodology of government and big business, but the structure of society was left untouched. The bureaucracy retained its power and could continue to count on cushy post-retirement jobs. The national debt, already the highest in the world as a percentage of GDP, kept on rising; as of June 30, 2007, it stood at 836 trillion yen, roughly $7.5 trillion, or 150 percent of GDP.

Yet Japan's reliance on traditional values and the belief in its ability to overcome every setback appears to have survived the turmoil. For now at least, the critics who said Japan was finished were left to look ridiculous, even as, paradoxically, the notion of an essential "Japaneseness" sustaining it, is under siege, as discussed in Chapter 21.

As you will see in the remaining chapters, it is doubtful if Japan can afford to go on resisting change in the years to come.

Chapter **25**

The State of the Nation

J apan's Liberal Democratic Party (LDP)—the party of big business, vested interests, and the military alliance with the United States—has been in power almost uninterruptedly since the early 1950s. How does the current generation of this ingrown conservative leadership view the situation in Japan in the first decade of the twenty-first century? Let me make a guess, based on statements and warnings by assorted authoritative political and media sources over the past several years:

> Society is becoming unruly and diverse, young people reject their elders' values, school children are rebellious, and morality and manners are crumbling. Bullying and absenteeism in schools is rife. National pride is at low ebb, the birthrate has dropped precipitously, and interest in marriage is waning. Millions of young people prefer casual work to steady employment. Profligate consumerism has replaced time-honored, aesthetic frugality. Blind adoration of everything Western has eroded respect for Japan's own rich cultural heritage. The nation's spiritual basis is in grave danger. China and South Korea keep nagging Japan about its wartime actions, while fast grabbing its overseas markets. North Korea has refused to account for kidnapped Japanese citizens and aims rockets at Japan. China's hostility and its emergence as a superpower spell serious potential security risks. The Japanese public shows little concern about these multiple threats to Japan's future. Complacency abounds.

Whether this is a fair summary of how Japan's leaders see the present state of their nation I have no way of knowing. But all of these issues get a regular airing, mostly in conservative circles, as problems to be "solved." And the solution most frequently suggested—and meanwhile partly being written into law—is that neglected or discarded principles should be brought back, love of country instilled in the classroom, and Japan's unique traditions safeguarded. The virtues of the Showa era are being extolled in the national holiday Showa Day.

In a policy speech shortly after his election as prime minister in September 2006, Shinzo Abe promised to bring back Japan's confidence and pride. Using the slogan "toward a beautiful Japan," he announced that family values and traditional virtues were to be revived, and education reformed to serve these goals. Reactions to his patriotic program ranged from approbation to indulgent smiles to scathing dismissal. Opposition parties in the Diet criticized the speech for its "nationalistic and authoritarian" undertone.

Lending credence to this criticism, within a month of his "beautiful country" speech, there were persistent media reports of bureaucratic manipulation and intimidation at Abe's press briefings. The prime minister himself returned his salary for three months to show his responsibility for organizing a series of "town meetings" on educational reform and other government policies, which were billed as opportunities for the public to raise issues but, it turned out, were dominated by people paid to ask predetermined questions.[1]

Abe stumbled within a year, less on account of his naive slogan and patriotic program than because of scandals and serious failings of his brief administration. Several members of his cabinet resigned to show they were taking responsibility, and one committed suicide. The loss of the ruling party's control of the House of Councilors (the upper house) in the general election of July 2007 sealed Abe's fate.

Does this mean that his vision of a proud Japan observing traditional values was merely a political gimmick that will soon fade into oblivion, together with the man that launched it?

"Bring Back Bushido!"

Apparently not. Some, especially older, Japanese support moves to roll back the rising tide of social diversity. And that is what worries those who want to see a more open, internationalist Japan. The unease was increased by one of Mr. Abe's major initiatives: the revision of the Fundamental Law on Education, which involves among other things the compulsory teaching of patriotism in the classroom. The concern in liberal circles that in a group-oriented society with little tolerance for individuality this could easily be exploited by nationalists aiming to revive pre-war "traditional" values, proved not strong enough to prevent passage of the bill. One elder statesman, former Prime Minister Yasuhiro Nakasone (1982–1987), suggested that "the administration should strive for a society that restores the spirit of *bushido* [the fundamental code of samurai behavior], which involves self-sacrificing dedication to the public interest."[2] This is an unusual way to describe bushido. In his 1905 bestselling book *Bushido: The Soul of Japan*, Inazo Nitobe described bushido as "the code of moral principles which the samurai were required or instructed to observe.... More frequently it is a code unuttered and unwritten.... It was an organic growth of decades and centuries of military career." Bushido was, in some respects, analogous to the medieval European concept of chivalry, in which loyalty to one's lord stood uppermost. Bushido included the willingness to take one's own life, typically by disembowelment, to atone for a loss of honor or to avoid capture. The last time it was used in a national context was during the Second World War when Japan's military invoked the bushido spirit to encourage soldiers to commit suicide rather than surrender. The young kamikaze pilots who volunteered for one-way suicide missions were similarly inspired by bushido.

Granted, this was only one aspect of the rather elusive tenets of bushido. Perhaps Mr. Nakasone meant to broaden its meaning to include selfless public service in a democratic society, and the moral superiority of honor and total dedication over materialism. Yet, the word itself evokes disturbing associations.

Loyalty First

A Dog of Flanders is a sentimental novel written in the early 1870s by Ouida, the pen name of British author Louise De La Reme. It tells the story of the Flemish boy Nello, an orphan brought up by his grandfather, and his faithful dog Patrasche. Nello is illiterate but is talented in drawing and dreams of becoming a painter, but he fails to win a prize when he enters his work in a junior art contest. When his grandfather dies Nello is falsely accused of causing a fire. Having no place to go he escapes, with Patrasche, his goal Antwerp cathedral and its Rubens masterpiece, *The Elevation of the Cross*, which he had always wanted to see. Battling snow storms they finally make it to the cathedral on Christmas Eve. Overwhelmed by cold, Nello and his dog freeze to death while gazing at Rubens' great painting.

The book is much loved in Japan, but less so in Europe and the United States, where Nello is seen as lacking a fighting spirit—a loser passively accepting his fate. Even so, in America it has been made into a movie no less than five times, but each time revised to have a happy ending.

On 27 December 2007, the *Daily Yomiuri,* a leading Japanese newspaper, reported that a Belgian film maker, Didier Volkaert, intrigued by the different Japanese perception of the book's conclusion, had made a documentary on the Japanese fascination with the book's tragic theme. He was bemused by the streams of Japanese tourists that regularly flock to the cathedral to tearfully gaze at the Rubens painting. He concluded that what drew the Japanese to the novel was their identification with the "nobility of failure" in quest of a higher goal. They recognized the value of loyalty as a supreme good in itself.

The political far right clearly has sensed an opportunity to reclaim some of the ground it lost since the end of the war. Its agenda calls for a return to the simpler truths and symbols of pre-war Showa: the flag, the national anthem, discipline, and patriotism. It demands a more assertive and powerful Japan, uncontaminated by "foreign" ideas or bullying neighbors. Its rhetoric is often strident, its actions and utterances apparently oblivious to concerned voices from within and outrage from abroad, if not actually courting it.

That the new patriotism has gained support is evident from the popularity enjoyed by Tokyo governor Shintaro Ishihara, a maverick known for his aggressive nationalism and outrageous, often anti-Chinese outbursts. Under his administration, Tokyo schools have been ordered to require students and teachers to salute the flag and sing the national anthem (both still controversial symbols in the eyes of the political left which associates them with Japan's aggressive wartime policies) at school ceremonies, and to "punish" those who disobey. His provocative statements and actions—some of which he claims not to really *mean*—are hailed by many as a breath of fresh air, challenging as they do the stultifying dullness and horse trading of traditional party politics and the low-posture, head-in-the-sand foreign policies of the Showa era. They clearly appeal to those who want to see a prouder, less apologetic Japan. Some of my Japanese friends, long-time readers of the comparatively liberal *Asahi Shimbun* daily, have canceled their subscription because they now find it "too left-wing." They have clearly come under the spell of the patriotic governor.

But even right-wing politicians like Abe and Ishihara stay well clear of the noisy shenanigans and intimidating swagger of the ultra-nationalists, Japan's answer to the neo-Nazis, a tiny but vocal element advocating the return of direct rule by the emperor as sacred and unimpeachable sovereign-priest of the nation. Their tactics (which are known to include personal threats and suspected support for assassinations) are enough to scare some journalists and other media and public figures away from, for example, examining Japan's alleged wartime atrocities or depicting the imperial family in a human light.

But even without the "help" of the ultra-rightists, the neo-conservatives' rhetoric and actions have proved to be highly controversial abroad and have soured relations with China and South Korea. Far from raising Japan's stature—the avowed aim of recent governments—they tend to feed lingering resentment over Japan's past behavior and foreign suspicion of Japan's true nature and motives. This distrust is understood by many of the well-educated urban young and not-so-young in Japan, but their calls for full recognition and genuine contrition over Japan's wartime actions, "like Germany," are feeble and have little political impact.

Instead, the vast majority of the people clearly do not wish to raise the ghosts of an unhappy past. This factor and the widespread lack of political commitment, combined with an ingrained tendency to leave problems for "those in charge" to solve, make popular action over this or, indeed, any other serious issue highly unlikely.

The Appeal of the Men of Action

While the chances of a revolution in Japan are next to zero, the fears of those who are worried about a return of an assertive nationalism are by no means groundless. A bright young academic and aspiring LDP politician recently put it to me this way: "We Japanese are inclined to follow leaders who represent extremes." A professor at a leading Japanese university added that "we tend to admire men of action, who dare to talk tough and are seen to be acting boldly." Men willing to take the bull by the horns, he meant. Any bull. It matters less what they stand for than that they *do* something.

Abe's predecessor, Junichiro Koizumi, was such a man. It was not so much his policies as his bold statements ("I will destroy the Liberal Democratic Party"), daring actions (he expelled a large number of parliament members from his own party for daring to vote against his proposals), and distinctive hairstyle that earned him great popularity during his term of office (2001–2006). The privatization of Japan Post, the mammoth postal savings and insurance system, the chief item on his agenda stubbornly pursued under strong US "encouragement," was accomplished without significant protest from the electorate, even though its economic and social necessity was debatable. Japan Post was said to be the largest holder of personal savings in the world. With over 224 trillion yen ($2.1 trillion) of household assets in its savings accounts and 126 trillion yen ($1.2 trillion) in its life insurance services, its holdings accounted for 25 percent of household assets in Japan. Japan Post also held about 140 trillion yen (one-fifth) of the Japanese national debt in the form of government bonds. American interest in the system's privatization was obviously driven by the expected investment opportunities for US business.

Shintaro Ishihara is another man of action: he retains his large following mainly on account of his controversial, headline-grabbing posturing and statements and despite the actual *unpopularity* of some of his policies.

Rather than critically examining a party's policies, Japanese voters these days really do seem more interested in theatricals and confrontational rhetoric. And the promise of "action."

As of this writing, the political waters have calmed somewhat. The hapless Mr. Abe's successor, Yasuo Fukuda, again drawn from the ruling Liberal Democratic Party, though dour and uninspiring, has at least taken care not to offend either his domestic left-wing opposition or the leaders of South Korea and China. But contrary to Koizumi, he is a creature of the old guard, the clique of LDP stalwarts with their vested interests and lack of vision. The jury is out on whether Fukuda, or indeed *his* successors, will actually be able to set Japan on a new course.

Chapter 26

What Has Changed

When critics maintain that Japan hasn't changed and will never change, they are usually referring to the mentality of its governing classes or the essential character of the people. We may agree or disagree with such assertions, depending on our point of view.

If we confined ourselves to the more tangible and measurable, the evidence of major changes over the past decade or so is persuasive. They have occurred first and foremost in the management of the nation's economy: corporate restructuring, financial reform, opening of markets to foreign competition, extensive outsourcing, and impressive technological advances. The results of these transformations have been showing up in a stronger performance of the usual economic indicators—and a more optimistic mood among big business and the public.

The reforms have also had a severe impact on social conditions. With less job security, a shrinking middle class and a widening income gap, Japan's profile has grown closer to that of the advanced economies of the West. In addition, the declining birthrate and ever-increasing lure of Tokyo and other large urban centers has caused serious depopulation and impoverishment of many rural areas.

The Ubiquitous Foreigner

One of the consequences of the liberalization of foreign investment and imports since the 1980s has been a sharp increase in the number of foreign expatriates and long-term residents.

The Japanese have become quite accustomed to their presence. The days when Westerners were stared at are now only dimly remembered. As of 2005, the actual number of Europeans, North Americans, Australians, and New Zealanders living in Japan (mostly on three-year residence permits) was still only about 139,000, or 0.11 percent of the total population of 127 million. However, they have become at least as well accepted as, say, Japanese living in London or New York or Amsterdam, and increasingly well integrated. (Incidentally, the number of Japanese living abroad in 2005 was 1,012,000, of which 640,000 live in Western countries, more than 4.5 times the number of Westerners in Japan.)

Marriages of Japanese to foreigners have increased sharply in recent years. In 2000, they already reached 4.5 percent of all new marriages nationwide and as high as 10 percent in Tokyo. Most of these involve Asian wives for Japanese husbands, and Korean and Western husbands for Japanese brides.

The popularity of Western men among young Japanese women is graphically illustrated by a recent prominent mobile phone advertising campaign by KDDI, a quintessential Japanese corporation, showing a young woman making a phone call to a Spanish-looking young man. Such images were unthinkable during Showa. Some marriage brokers are doing a brisk trade finding suitable Western husbands for affluent Japanese (career) women able to shell out a nonrefundable search fee of up to one million yen (around $10,000.)

Why Western men? A clue was provided by a popular Japanese TV program at the end of 2005 entitled *Men Who Can't Get Married.* It listed some of the complaints young Japanese women harbor about Japanese men, such as: they have nothing to say, lack guts, can't make up their mind, are not assertive, have too many demands, neglect their appearance, want their wife to stop working.[3] An old chestnut that is said to still hold true of certain, mostly older, Japanese married men is that their after-work conversation with the wife is limited to three words, uttered as grumpy commands: *Furo! Meshi! Neru!* (Bath! Dinner! Bedtime!). With this kind of reputation, whether deserved or not, and the no doubt idealized image many Japanese women seem to have of Western men, it is no wonder that many Japanese men can't find a wife. In some companies almost every employee is single. The housing sector has responded to this new market by building numerous high-rise blocks of single-person apartments.

The many Western, Asian, and other foreign residents now working in Japan also are having an impact on the business scene. Their practical, flexible ways of approaching problems sometimes give them an edge over their more formal, cumbersome local competition. A case in point is the following. In November, 2006, I called Sony's customer service in Tokyo to request a replacement for the defective keyboard on my Sony laptop, which I had bought in London. They first asked a number of questions, including my full personal details, down to e-mail and home address, and then told me they could not provide parts for products bought outside Japan. After some searching, I found a small American-run IT service company in Tokyo. I rang them up and told them what I needed, emphasizing that the product was bought in the United Kingdom. "No problem," was the answer. They gave me a price, I accepted it, and lastly they asked my name and phone number.

Because of their still relatively small numbers and their predominantly expatriate status, Westerners are not perceived as a threat to Japan's security or cultural identity. For the same reason, and despite its trappings of a great metropolis, Tokyo cannot (yet) be called a truly *cosmopolitan* city: apart from a handful of Tokyo neighborhoods favored by foreign residents, the street scene in Tokyo and, even more so, other major cities continues to be quintessentially Japanese.

The New Japanese Woman

In this area, there has been conspicuous progress from the early Showa days of placid housewives serving their husbands' every need. Not only do women demand a more equal role, but if they are dissatisfied with their marriage, they are much more likely to get a divorce than in the past. An estimated one in four Japanese marriages now breaks up. A new law that became effective April 1, 2007, considerably eases the older woman's path to divorce: it requires half of the husband's pension to be paid to her after their marriage is dissolved. There has been a sharp increase in "retirement divorces" since the law came into effect, 90 percent of them at the wife's request. The reason stated most often is that they can't get used to having the retired husband at home full-time!

There has also been, among young, unmarried women, a shift in perception of what their role in marriage should be. In post-bubble Japan, the traditional cliché of the *otonashii* (quiet, obedient), *kawaii* (sweet, cute) wife has been steadily losing ground to the wife as equal partner—modern, well educated, often with a career of her own. This new woman was strikingly illustrated on a recent poster of a leading Tokyo department store advertising its "wedding packages." It showed an independent bride, looking over the groom's shoulder, away from him, into a world of her own.

The problem, as explored in the earlier discussion of infantilism in Japan's culture, is that most Japanese men don't value such independence, with the result that more and more young people end up staying single.

Perhaps it is partly due to this stubborn male resistance to female emancipation that gender equality in employment so far has been an elusive goal. Although women have been making inroads throughout society, their career seldom lifts them above the middle ranks.

One indication that Japan still has a long way to go in this area—despite the progress achieved—is its ranking in the Gender Empowerment Measure (GEM) of the United Nations Development Program, which tracks women's participation in politics and business. In 2007, Japan was ranked 54th out of 93 countries, compared with Australia's 8th, Canada's 10th, Britain's 14th, and the United States' 15th. Among Asian countries, Japan ranks well below Singapore (16th), while China and South Korea both trailed Japan at 57th and 64th, respectively.

Clearly, Japanese women have yet to break the glass ceiling. Only 9.4 percent of parliamentary seats in Japan are occupied by women, putting the nation in 131st place out of 189 countries surveyed. In business and academia the situation is even worse, with—for example—only 3.7 percent of department chief positions in private sector companies and 2.5 percent of professorial posts in science and technology being occupied by women. A (male) perception that a career in science or business is somehow not "attractive" for a woman may have something to do with the low female representation in these fields.[4] Another yardstick of lagging gender equality in Japan is the persistent wage gap. According to the International Labor Organization (ILO), employed women in Japan earned on average one-third less than men.[5] (The gap has been widening: from 31.2 percent in 2004 to 32.9 percent in 2006.)

The main areas where women have become successful and fully accepted at all levels tend to be the independent and professional occupations such as retail, design, fashion, broadcasting, journalism, sales, teaching, medicine, and entertainment. When no established, male-dominated hierarchy is involved, women are quick to make their mark, often proving to be more assertive—and effective—than their male colleagues.

Notably among young independent women, inconsiderate manners are no longer rare, scaring off not only those men who still prefer the traditional feminine virtues in their prospective brides, but the more conservative public in general. On the street these types stride arrogantly ahead, heedless of other pedestrians. In the workplace they often bully younger male colleagues. It is as if, in their handed-down mode of black-or-white thinking, these women have thrown a switch—from pliant sweetie to assertive bitch, as if there were nothing in between.

Whether in reaction or by coincidence, the trend with many young men is in the opposite direction. Softness and gentleness are in vogue there. "The new Japanese woman," according to a recent newspaper article, "is robust, bursting with energy.... In stark contrast, it's the men who want to be slender, vulnerable, and protected.... The term 'kawaii' used to be something that described women.... Now...more young men aspire to be cute."[6] (That this trend may not be confined to Japan is suggested by certain recent ads of the European fashion industry depicting weak, submissive men alongside strong women.)

Whether such role reversal is symptomatic of an emerging aggressive feminism in Japan, or more likely, a rejection of Showa-vintage constraining conformity, it does represent a break with the carefully nurtured social mores of the past, which were traditionally instilled at home and constantly reinforced at school and work.

Fortunately, instances of inconsiderate behavior are still the exception. By and large, Japanese society continues to be characterized by a high degree of civility.

The Salaryman: Not Extinct, but Reprogrammed

As discussed in Chapter 18, one Showa institution that has undergone drastic change is that of the salaryman, not on account of female competition but due to the changed economic environment. Since the bursting of the economic bubble in the late 1980s, there has been extensive restructuring of corporate Japan, often involving dismissals of loyal, older employees.

Economic necessity has brought about rigorous revisions in employment practices. The career escalator is not nearly as reliable as it once was, and merit-based promotions and pay have become fairly widespread. Foreign interests have taken over or invested heavily in many a Japanese household-name company, and the promises and threats of globalization have become everyone's concern.

Meanwhile, necessary belt tightening even among Japan's top corporations and banks has drastically cut into the funds available for entertainment. Upmarket restaurants and nightclubs have suffered a sharp drop in business. And those annual or even twice-yearly company outings to the spas, for so long a staple of the salaryman's life, are another casualty of the leaner times.

Yet the salaryman as a social species seems to have survived reasonably intact, judging from the unchanged long working hours of my company-employee friends and the morning scene at any major railway station. Rush-hour crowds are heavy in any large city, but in Japan they seem particularly monolithic. Japanese men—and increasingly women, too—on their way to work *charge* rather than walk.

In the evening the pattern tends to be different, more relaxed, as many of these same men and women are not really going home. They are on their way, in groups, to some watering hole or other to drink and eat together to welcome back or see off a colleague, or simply reaffirm their loyalties, Showa-style. And if they are not joining a drinking session, they are most likely still in the office, until eight or nine or ten PM, for that Showa habit has been hard to kick as well.

For now, organized Japanese society is still largely held together by the group ethos that for so long has been the source of Japan's success. But it is clearly under siege from an emerging, more demanding leadership culture, with increasing emphasis on individual ability, especially at the management and specialist level.

What has also changed is the unquestioned acceptance of a salaryman's career as the norm for aspiring young men—and their even more ambitious parents. Dropping out, striking out on your own, going abroad, taking a gap year or two—during Showa those were unthinkable options, firmly condemned by parents and the social environment. That is no longer the case.

Since the end of Showa, parents' influence over the career choices of their offspring has declined markedly. Today's young men and women increasingly take their future into their own hands, often refusing marriage and steady employment even as they "temporarily" rely for sustenance on indulgent parents.

Melding Tradition with World Culture

The new century with its ever-more Western-style living is witnessing a vigorous revival of many traditional Japanese arts, crafts, and fashions—sometimes in modified form to appeal to contemporary tastes. The number of haiku practitioners runs into the millions, and many children choose calligraphy from the optional art courses of their school curriculum. Kimono stores are thriving once again with new designs after decades of decline. Kabuki, Noh, and *bunraku* (puppet theater) performances are solidly sold out.

Sake brewers and the producers of *shochu*—a strong, formerly "working class" distillate that has become fashionable—are manfully and often successfully confronting the onslaught of wine onto the nation's dining tables by trumpeting their products' ancient lineage or exquisite flavors, and broadening their product line to complement different kinds of food. And television costume dramas and samurai series, never out of favor to begin with, are as popular as ever.

What we are witnessing is not, however, a return to Japanese traditions at the expense of Western-style arts, crafts, and fashions, but a broadening of the cultural palette to accommodate all colors and shades, old and new, whatever their origin. Every conceivable style of music and dance is available live in Tokyo and other major cities. Every kind of high and low cuisine can be found in the list of restaurants. The superbrand stores are among the world's most lavish, even as some of the women gazing into their windows may be got up in punk—or kimono. Japanese art and design are at the cutting edge of creativity, combining traditional themes with totally new concepts. Japan is a major force in almost every field, from architecture and contemporary dance to fashion design and the burgeoning cartoon world of manga and anime. In Japan, the popularity of cartoon books, magazines, and videos has eclipsed that of conventional books.

In short, Japan today is a major center of high and popular culture spanning East and West. Precisely because of its receptivity to multiple influences its creative range may well be wider than anywhere else in the world.

Japan is the world's largest market for luxury goods, accounting for a whopping 40 percent of global sales. When I asked the president of Louis Vuitton's highly successful Japan operation how he explained this frenzy for big brands, he looked at me quizzically. "What do you mean?" he countered. "Every woman wants quality. It is a natural thing."

Every woman indeed. The Japanese market for prestige fashions crosses conventional class boundaries. Women from all backgrounds and age groups, urban or rural, aspire to owning at least one or two superbrand items, say a Prada product or a Kelly bag from Hermès. But rather than a careful search for quality, more often it is their way of expressing their individuality and "personal" taste, even if that taste conforms to the current trend and is shared by countless others.

When strolling through the Ginza district one cannot escape the impression that shibui, the defining austere mid-Showa aesthetic, has had its day. It has gone the way of frugality and modesty and quiet good manners. Clearly, world fashions rule the roost. Perhaps in time, when the initial, pent-up craving has been satisfied, tastes will evolve to reflect acquired self-confidence and experience and personal creativity, rather than obeisance to the tyranny of the monster brands.

Anti-Establishment Trends and the Newly Self-Employed

The most significant development of the post-Showa era may well be the emergence of a huge number of people not in regular employment. As discussed in Chapter 14, this pool, possibly millions in size, includes a new breed of entrepreneurs as well as intellectuals, artists, designers, and other self-employed men and women who have turned their backs on traditional employment to strike out on their own.

With their very independence these various kinds of free spirits largely flout such Showa concepts as group identity, absolute loyalty to an employer, and risk avoidance. They don't follow suit—they chart their own course. Some of their initiatives, particularly in the business sphere, have infuriated the establishment, and not all are successful or wise. But they were and are the sorely needed spice in what during Showa had become a rather complacent, bland social stew.

This unconventional behavior is not necessarily a conscious protest against the confining ways of the past and the reactionary trends of the present. It is not a dissident political movement. Yet the very existence of such a growing nonconformist element is evidence of an increasingly diverse society. Even the millions of freelance manual workers and social dropouts, passive though their attitude often seems to be, reinforce the sense of growing social heterogeneity, while sorely testing time-honored institutions and work practices.

Another, perhaps related, phenomenon is the emergence of large numbers of volunteers to help in all kinds of social and emergency situations. The nascent movement got a big boost by the Great Hanshin Earthquake of January 1995, when over 6,000 people died in Kobe and its suburbs and 220,000 were left homeless. In the absence of timely government help, nongovernmental organizations, private companies, yakuza gangsters, and above all, individuals from all over Japan flocked to the stricken area. In the three months following the disaster, an estimated 1.2 million volunteers organized and helped in the relief efforts. Since then, countless volunteer organizations have sprung up, many providing assistance in poor countries.

That humanitarian aid sometimes runs up against ingrained prejudice against people down on their luck is illustrated by an article in the 2005/2006 activity report of Médecins Sans Frontières (MSF; Doctors without Borders). In Japan, MSF wants to offer medical care to the thousands of homeless persons who are effectively excluded from the country's universal healthcare system. "MSF has made several attempts," the report states, "to establish a fixed healthcare center in the area [near Osaka], but discrimination against this population is fierce and widespread and has prevented the establishment of a fixed clinic. MSF has met with continual opposition from some of the local communities and authorities."

Nevertheless, countless volunteer initiatives are making their mark on Japanese society.

After the Earthquake

Kobe, November 1995. Arrived last night at the newly opened Kansai Airport from Sydney in a gale and driving rain. By hydrofoil in 33 minutes at 47 miles (75 kilometers) per hour to Kobe port, thence by taxi to Kobe Bay Sheraton Hotel, on Rokko Island. The hotel is undamaged, but the effect of the great earthquake that hit the Kobe region in January is evident even here on this reclaimed land: cracks and level differences of up to a yard (meter), and sagging pavement. The government was slow to react to the disaster. Most of the relief work was done by volunteers from all over Japan.

From my window I look down on a sea of neat barracks in orderly rows, packed tightly together over a large area. The taxi driver told me these are temporary quarters for survivors of the quake who lost their homes and are waiting for government decisions on rezoning, including widening of roads, before they can rebuild. This may take years. You'd not guess people are living there but for the lit windows. It's utterly tidy and uncluttered. The driver told me much of Ashiya/Kawanishicho where I lived in 1956 and 1957 is destroyed, including his own house. Dozens were killed in this section alone.

Today fine but windy and quite cold. Walked through Sannomiya, Ikuta, and Motomachi. The Moche building on Kyomachi (where I once worked) is gone, so is the Kobe Oriental Hotel, where we held our wedding reception back in 1959. All collapsed or damaged beyond repair.

Went to Ashiya and walked around Kawanishicho. Of my old house only the wall with its massive gate is still standing. A friend's concrete house, in Kobe's Nagatacho, survived the quake, but he pointed to a few neighboring houses that did not. "Some people got killed there under the collapsed roofs."

Equally, there is ample evidence of the growing power of consumer organizations and local action committees that guard the interests of citizens in matters of health, safety, and the living environment.

The penetration in the past decade or so by large and small foreign businesses, as well as by foreign architects, designers, and other professionals, has further enlivened the urban scene. The growing popularity of international schools among Japanese parents dissatisfied with the declining standards of Japanese education discussed in Chapter 32, is another telling sign of social change.

No Nuances Please—We Are Japanese!

One change in Japanese society that is at least as surprising as the massive shift to conspicuous consumption seen between the early years of Showa and the excesses of the 1980s—and today—is the embrace of concepts like "if you're not a winner you're a loser" and "if you're not for me, you're against me."

I always thought that this mentality was more at home in America than in Japan. Given the notoriously *aimai* ("vague") Japanese response to situations requiring decisions or taking sides, this newly evident black/white, either/or approach to life seems oddly out of place. Nonetheless, the media has widely adopted it as if it were a fundamental tenet of life, making us believe it is the new reality, and we had better get used to it.

I have had my own brushes with the new requirement of decisiveness and taking sides, as when I am asked whether I am for or against Japan. A well-known business magazine interviewed me at length, while a photographer took

120 portrait shots of me, and then decided not to publish the interview. They had "mistakenly" thought I was unreservedly pro-Japanese. When it turned out I was neither "for" nor "against" Japan, the editor lost interest.

This baffled me, convinced as I was that the magazine's readers would be interested in a nuanced exposé. But I was wrong. From my experience in the 1960s and 1970s, I had retained the belief that more than Westerners, Japanese had a deep awareness of life's many shades of grey, which called for contemplation and analysis before making a commitment. Now I must modify that belief. The likely reason for the much-observed reluctance of many Japanese to express or appreciate balanced opinions is that nuances do not sit well with the group mentality. After all, group thinking depends on broadly agreed or handed-down positions. It does not allow for subtlety or individual interpretation. It essentially leaves you only one choice: toe the line, or be ostracized.

It could therefore be argued that the very nature of the traditional Japanese group culture—which continued flourishing during Showa—must be held responsible for some of the changes in behavior one sees today.

Its erosion since the end of Showa without a clear, well-taught alternative taking its place has thrown many young Japanese women and men off-balance, leading at times to extremes in their search for a new identity.

Already the cumulative effect of these new forces is making itself felt. It is becoming harder by the day to justify that favorite pastime of the classic Japan-watcher: passing judgment on "the Japanese." Sweeping generalizations are no longer tenable, if they ever were. That alone is a sure sign of the diversity that has crept willy-nilly into Japanese society. So is the genie out of the bottle?

Well, not quite.

Chapter 27

What Hasn't Changed

A Japanese academic friend of mine concluded in 2007 that "nothing has changed" when no one in his department congratulated him when he was awarded a high academic honor. No one, that is, except a European member of the team. The home-grown scholars stayed sternly silent. My friend, who received his doctorate in Britain and published several books and papers abroad, had become used to the spontaneity typical of collegial relations in the West. He sensed that his cross-cultural background and activities had stirred up resentment on his home turf.

Not that anyone ever said as much. The system is too subtle for that. Both hierarchical and peer relations are still governed by a dense, unwritten code that one acquires largely through osmosis, by growing up in its embrace. In this network of minute rules of behavior and patterns of thinking, individuals are like the pixels in a digital image: separate but interdependent. The pixels don't touch, but they are constantly aware of each other's presence and are incessantly reminded to keep their place in the total scheme of things, to preserve its integrity and ensure its continuity. Asian students attending Japanese universities are still discouraged from staying on after graduation to find work in Japan, "because they will not be able to fit in."

In such a system, change comes slowly. Here are two reminders (out of many I could cite) of stubbornly surviving customs and attitudes that seem no longer appropriate:

- The government's avowed intention to stamp out the corruption-inducing practice of *amakudari*—retiring bureaucrats landing private-sector jobs in industries they once oversaw—has been meeting deep-rooted resistance. The agency it set up in 2000 to help public servants find "unsuspicious" post-retirement jobs, has so far been successful only *once*.[7]

- In response to an April 2005 train accident caused by a hurried driver, West Japan Railway Company announced in May 2005 that it would replace punitive measures against train drivers running late with "educational programs." However, in February 2007 the company's vice president *defended* punitive programs as necessary "to protect the public."[8]

A Future Candidate for Amakudari

Aomori prefecture, 1968. At Hirosaki Station, I witnessed a stark example of the crooked ties between politicians and business. A local politician elected to the national Diet was seen off by a horde of well-wishers pressing gifts of cash on him, while beseeching him to take care of their interests in the capital. By the time he boarded his train all the man's pockets were literally bulging with wads of banknotes, some of the money spilling out onto the platform and left lying there as mute witnesses to a corrupt system.

Many Japanese object to the mindless clinging to outdated ways just because they are the traditional "Japanese" way. Some highly educated Japanese have expressed to me their dismay over their countrymen's ingrained habit of disparaging themselves, not in the British, half-humorous, self-deprecating manner but by making a show of their own worthlessness. "We never stop apologizing, bowing our heads, repeating that we are useless, that we can't do better," a columnist wrote recently. "It's time we stand up and behave like mature people."

It seems what Japanese society still lacks is informed confidence and robustness, indispensable ingredients in a successful participatory democracy.

The Undying Western Role Model

Despite the post-bubble changes in Japanese life, there is ample evidence of the continuing popular appeal of "things Western." An appeal that is often tinged with, and complicated by, self-consciousness.

Take advertising. Ads for everything from fashions and food to cars and exercise equipment and apartments use leggy foreign models, preferably blondes, and Western couples almost as often as Japanese, even though those ads are aimed squarely at the *Japanese* consumer. Hair colorings are in wide use. On a recent Sunday walk along Tokyo's busy Ginza shopping avenue (when it becomes a pedestrian mall), I was struck by the golden-brown glow overlaying the large, mostly female street crowd in the slanting late-afternoon sun. It was caused by the assembled heads, which were virtually all dyed in shades of brown. Thirty years ago it would have been a sea of black. The comment of one Japanese lady on my observation was illustrative of the power of advertising and fashion: "Just leaving my hair black makes me feel untidy—almost...*impolite.*"

When my wife and I returned to live in Japan after a thirty-year absence and were looking around for accommodation, we were attracted to a new high-rise complex featuring glamorous foreign faces and cosmopolitan living on its billboards and in its lavish brochures. We were given a detailed briefing and a long tour, but it turned out that their target market was Japanese, and the housing loans they promoted were not available to foreigners.

In personal situations, Westerners are often placed on a pedestal for reasons that are not always clear. During a recent three-day group excursion to Kyoto to attend a rare Noh theater performance at the Shimogamo Shrine and other cultural delights, I was asked by the group's leader to propose the toast at the closing banquet. Seeing that I was the only non-Japanese in a crowd of 150, I hesitated. But there was no escape. My Western looks evidently earned me this special honor. It was a quite unnecessary gesture, and judging by the expression on their faces, some of the impressive gentlemen in our group evidently thought so, too.

A particular irony of the position of Westerners in Japan is that they are often accorded privileged treatment as honored guests even if they voice serious criticism about their host country—if not more so. As one Japanese editor commented to me, "we love it when foreign writers dish the dirt on us."

That Western society is still looked up to as a model to be emulated is sometimes revealed by small incidents. A year ago, on a train ride from Amsterdam to Antwerp, I met a Japanese lady who was worried that she was on the wrong train. As we silently pulled into Antwerp station, I remarked on the lack of announcements by the train's conductor compared to Japan's constant, detailed on-board information on screens and through speakers. "*Demo, korewa otona no kuni desukara.*" ("But after all, this is a country of grown-ups.") was her comment, implying that the Japanese are mollycoddled.

Democracy: An Automatic Washing Machine?

Sometimes I think that, in Japan, democracy is seen as a kind of self-programming entity, an automatic political washing machine that does the job for you once you push the button. The notion that democracy is a vulnerable system that needs active care and maintenance, which means constant scrutiny of its elected and appointed representatives, is not widely understood.

The problem is that, as we have seen, Japan's democracy had a rather brief history. It did not arrive as the end result of a long process, but in fits and starts, beginning with the promising but short-lived Taisho democracy of the 1920s, and then, after a decade and a half of autocratic military rule, once more, rather abruptly, on the heels of defeat in war.

Japan's political scene has come a long way since then. Parliamentary government is firmly established, with open campaigning by all parties and voter turnout typically between 60 and 65 percent. Even so, the full force of a vibrant Japanese democracy is yet to emerge. The main opposition parties have so far failed to impress the electorate because they lack a clear message. They do frequently talk about the need for change but seldom offer sensible alternatives and persuasive arguments. They tend to rely more on boycotting voting procedures than proper debate. Meanwhile, politicians—of all parties—spend much time on internal power struggles and adjustment of views. During the run-up to elections, they do little more than groveling before the voters with appeals for support and "trust." They don't seek to convince with arguments—they mostly try to make voters "feel good" about them.

The voters' predictable reaction to the uninspiring spectacle of a business-as-usual political culture is to vote for the status quo. The instinct not to rock the boat and to leave everything to "those-in-charge" is deeply rooted, as is, perhaps, the longing for a return to the safety and snugness of a known past. Playing upon nostalgia, fear of uncharted waters, and the national habit of self-debasement, the sclerotic political establishment aims to exorcise the specter of an emerging diverse society.

And turn Japan into a beautiful fossil on the world's body dynamic.

The Hazards of Navel-Gazing

If you have followed me this far, you will agree that Japan's proven strengths are not in question, even in today's challenging environment. The nation has displayed remarkable resilience after the collapse of the bubble economy, and the business sector in particular has introduced some long-overdue changes in corporate management. That said, I believe that Japanese society as a whole suffers from an historic and ongoing conflict between the fervent wish to be "more like the West" and a deep-seated tendency to isolate itself. This is a cultural conundrum, the product of long and systematic conditioning whose aim was to instill a sense of national exclusivity, while at the same time urging a close study of everything Western. The result could be called Japan's existential dilemma: both shunning and welcoming Westernization. It engendered a sense of "uniqueness" among nations, of a fated and almost splendid loneliness, which functions both as a protective shield against rampant adulteration and as a justification for self-absorption.

This preoccupation with itself may have hampered Japan's smooth integration into a broad Asian political or economic structure and proved to be an ongoing obstacle to effective global diplomacy. If given free rein in the future, it may even undermine the search for solutions for some of the country's more serious social, demographic and economic challenges, most of which would benefit from more open-minded thinking.

In the following chapters, I hope to alert the reader to certain aspects of Japanese society and culture, which, if left untended, may mar the country's future. I offer these observations as my personal view, but it is a view that is shared by many other observers, Japanese and foreign alike.

Chapter **28**

On Forming Ideas and Opinions

An article in the *Daily Yomiuri* of February 26, 2005, on the study of English reported on a group of Japanese high school students selected for home stays in the United States. The host families were pleased with their behavior but baffled by the students' apparent inability to formulate thoughts. "It's not their English," was their comment. "They clearly answered yes or no [to questions but] they showed no signs of keeping conversations going further." The Japanese teacher accompanying them said: "They behave in the same way even in Japan," adding that today's students are virtually incapable of carrying on a meaningful conversation even in their own language.

This seems a harsh verdict, but it is by no means an isolated case. Even mature Japanese with a good command of English often feel awkward in the presence of talkative, opinionated foreigners, unfamiliar as they are with abstract thinking and the give and take of a spirited dialogue. In Japan having "opinions" is not encouraged.

A group of undergraduates gathered around me on the lawn of Kwansei Gakuin, a private university near Osaka, told me that they were not used to expressing personal opinions "in the presence of people we don't know." Most had attended debate classes, but they didn't like being forced to speak up. "When my assigned position is attacked during debate," one student complained, "I'm made to feel that I am *personally* wrong, and everybody turns against me." The others nodded in agreement, adding that in high school they never "discussed" anything. They just memorized what was in the textbooks. And a Japanese professor who spent several years in the United Kingdom recently put it this way: "In Japan, even in academic circles, to question is to quibble."

Another professor, a proponent of educational reform, emphasized that there is no need for every university graduate to become an eloquent, effective communicator with ideas of his own, but that there has to be a critical mass commensurate with Japan's stature in the world if Japan is to pull its weight on the global stage. Sadly, he added, apart from business, far too few Japanese these days seem to possess the requisite skills.

Anyone who has ever given a lecture before a typical Japanese audience knows that the discussion period at the end will typically be brief. Such questions as there are tend to be factual. The audience, content with listening, is not used to evaluating the information and ideas received and comparing them with their own position on the subject. Like the Osaka students, they never learned to engage in debate.

Even at funerals, everyone seems lost for words. Ceremonies, usually conducted around a routine Buddhist ritual, are formal, restrained, and impersonal. Condolences are formulaic and accompanied by an envelope containing condolence money.

The Choreography of Death

Tokyo, March 10, 2005. The funeral of our relative Miss S., who died aged sixty-three, was exemplary in its scripted perfection and solemnity of the prescribed rituals. The forty relatives and close friends were seated in facing twin rows of ten, leaving an aisle. The coffin was all but invisible in a sloping wall of white and pink lilies and lilac sweet pea. The names of those who had sent flowers were calligraphed on two prominent stands flanking the altar.

An imposing Buddhist monk in rich brocade intoned, for over half an hour, regulation sutras that were incomprehensible to all present, while we offered incense from a small trolley that twice circulated between the rows.

When the priest left those waiting outside the room—not being part of the inner circle—were invited to step up to offer incense from a distance. The black-dressed mourners, mostly women, advanced two at a time, bowing to the relatives and friends and dropping the prescribed two pinches of granulated incense into the censer, before bowing again and retreating, not to be seen again. They had not been invited to the ceremony and the repast that was to follow.

An uncle rose and uttered a few formal phrases to thank all for coming. There were no eulogies or impromptu words of remembrance. The silk-lined coffin was now lowered from the altar and we crowded around it to catch a final glimpse of the deceased. The staff handed out small bouquets made from the wealth of flowers, for us to place in the open coffin. It was a touching little ritual accompanied by much suppressed wailing among the women. But the men showed no emotion.

Six men, I included, carried the coffin to the next-door crematorium, where the furnace was waiting—one in a row of six all going full blast, for this is a busy month for dying. The coffin was rolled into the gaping mouth of the stylishly designed oven. An attendant pushed a button. We were sent to a private room for refreshments.

An hour later the oven door was opened in our presence, and the still-warm remains pulled out, placed on a tray, and then, with our help, transferred to a large urn with oversized chopsticks. An attendant explained the identity of the various bone fragments as he arranged them into the urn, which was then sealed and handed to the chief mourner.

It was all done in the best of taste, orchestrated by respectful employees, who made sure that the time frame was strictly adhered to, with no room for deviation.

The only opportunity to reminisce came after the ceremony, during lunch served in a private room. But no speeches here either, just small talk, mostly about anything but the deceased.

Breaking the Mold

The quest for personal distinctiveness seen among many young Japanese has created a need for a new framework of basic values to replace those dictated by conventional norms. The problem is that, as we have seen, the concept of "individualism," essentially a Western notion, is widely distrusted and often equated with selfishness. This skepticism can affect these youngsters' self-confidence and leave them emotionally adrift between what they reject (traditional notions of obedience and hierarchy and seemly behavior) and the elusive search for new bedrock to justify their preferred lifestyle. For some, this search may cause distress and self-doubt. For others, the need remains unconscious and is subsumed in a flight to fashion, entertainment, or dissipation.

The prevailing uncertainty—and conflicting political views—on how to prepare young minds for the changing world they are entering has hampered necessary educational reform. What is needed is the belief, both at the policy level and in the classroom, that imagination and initiative, informed by careful evaluation of the factors involved and balanced with a sense of social responsibility, is to be welcomed and encouraged, as it can be both personally fulfilling *and* beneficial to society as a whole.

But many young people have not waited for the educational system to catch up. They have discovered on their own that follow the leader is a dull game. They seek the challenges of personal initiative, and the rewards they can bring. Some discover that the imagination is a wondrous human attribute: it may not get you anywhere, but without it you may just miss the chance that it *might*.

Along with this comes, occasionally, a new willingness to take a stand against perceived social wrongs or unethical dealings. Take the case of a woman in her late thirties known to me who became concerned about certain business practices of the small company she worked for. In her opinion these practices—which had already triggered legal actions against the company—were harmful to the company and to the market it was serving. She made her views clear and, as she was in charge of the firm's public relations, prepared statements for the company's Web site, placing the alleged practices in perspective, and reassuring their client base. But her boss vetoed her initiative and told her to keep her nose out of the firm's policies. She then resigned, as she could no longer serve an employer whose ethics conflicted with her own. Her parents found her behavior "selfish": she should have been more patient and obedient.

The interesting aspect of this case, which occurred in 2007, is that this woman is by no means the strident or opinionated type. She is an average mid-career office worker of modest disposition, with only two years of college. For such a person to follow principle rather than expediency—at some economic risk to herself—represents a new and, to my mind, encouraging trend among the under-forty generation.

What Japanese society now faces is not a simple choice between collectivism and individualism, but between sticking to the static group-centered ways of the past and the dynamism of thoughtful minds set free to define their own role in a diverse society. There may be many opportunities for both approaches to dovetail. But trying to run Heisei with a Showa mindset is like retrofitting a Boeing 780 with propeller engines. It won't fly.

Chapter 29

Hidden Agonies

In Japan's traditional social structure—characterized by such factors as suppression of individual needs, emphasis on "face" (i.e., avoiding at all costs behavior perceived as shameful or embarrassing) and, for school-going children, relentless memorizing of facts in an educational system that favors rote learning over development of character—the incidence of personal stress especially among men has always been high. Socially acceptable channels of relief such as drinking parties and golf outings help balance to some extent the culture of enforced conformity, but for some these outlets are inappropriate or inadequate to soothe their troubled souls. For others, ill health or post-bubble woes, such as loss of employment, have caused a sense of hopelessness in their lives that they are unable to deal with.

Japan's consistently high rate of suicide (over 30,000 annually since 1998, the highest among economically advanced nations) no doubt is in part related to the stresses inherent in its social structure. Resorting to suicide is facilitated by the much lower stigma it carries in Japan compared to, say, the Judeo-Christian world, where it is or was considered a sin. In fact, suicide can be said to have a long and honorable tradition in Japan, especially when carried out ritually in the noble service of a lord, to atone for a grievous mistake, or in the face of a hopeless situation.

During the pre-1868 feudal period, high officials and regional lords condemned to death for insubordination or "failure of loyalty" were permitted to carry out the sentence by their own hand, at a solemn, splendid ceremony. To this day, samurai films, kabuki plays, and historical manga comics seldom neglect to slip in a *seppuku* ritual (better known outside Japan as hara-kiri) in their romanticized interpretations of history, to satisfy the apparently never-waning public appetite for examples of glorious self-annihilation.

Therein also lies the essential difference from Western graphic and cinematic depictions of the destruction of an enemy or a rival: the Japanese used to leave the deed to the condemned; we in the West almost never did. (Socrates taking his poison was an exception.) Even our tragic kings and queens were handed over to their executioners. In Japan, to humiliate an honorable adversary or a once loyal aide when he is down is not ethical, even if he is to die. Good manners must prevail to the bitter end. During the Second World War, suicide was the recommended action in the face of imminent capture—for soldiers and in principle even for civilians.

Suicide also has a respectable place in literature. In *Runaway Horses*, the second of his four-part cycle of novels under the collective title *The Sea of Fertility*, Japanese novelist Yukio Mishima describes the recruitment, in 1932, of a band of young, clear-eyed men for a noble cause that they knew was hopeless and that would end in their certain death, by suicide if not in battle, as a sacrifice to their emperor. This novel was published in 1969. Hours after delivering the manuscript of the last volume of this series to his publishers the following year, Mishima committed suicide by disemboweling himself in public, in a protest against the lost emperor-centered "purity" of his nation. The action was as melodramatic as it was fruitless, but it was not without its admirers among those Japanese—by no means only the "pre-war" generation—yearning for the certainties of the past.

That the dark appeal of self-destruction has not waned is illustrated by the following incident. On October 11, 2004, four young men and three young women were found dead in a deserted van outside Tokyo, the victims of a suicide pact arranged over the Internet. It was the largest group suicide on record in over a hundred years of record keeping. The suicide notes left by the seven young people contained few clues about their motives, other than that they saw no purpose in living, or had lost hope in finding what they wanted.

In the decade prior to 1998, the annual number of suicides hovered between 15,000 and 25,000, a rate comparable to that of most western European nations. Suicides began to increase sharply in 1998 when, in the wake of economic woes, they jumped to over 32,000. They have exceeded 30,000 a year ever since. In 2006, suicides totaled 32,155, a slight decrease from the previous year. Especially tragic are the youth suicides. In 2007, as many as 623 Japanese children nineteen and under took their own lives, 2.5 percent more than in the previous year.[9]

Suicide Web pages appear to be an increasing means of communication between (young) people wishing to end their lives but not wanting to be alone when doing it. Demands to block such pages have met resistance from human rights and free speech advocates.

The reasons for committing suicide naturally vary widely. Economic hardship and serious illness have always been leading causes, with the elderly most likely to end their lives for these reasons. However piteous they may be in human terms, such suicides are relatively straightforward. More complex are those that result from shame or social alienation.

Shame suicides are sometimes resorted to by individuals who have caused serious harm to their family, their employer, or the general public, deliberately or inadvertently, or have failed to perform their duty, with disastrous consequences. But even losing one's job can be sufficient cause to end it all, as in the case of those mainly older men who during the 1990s found it impossible to face their family and friends after being made redundant in the aftermath of the bursting of the bubble. Such suicides in particular raise serious questions about the nature of a society that places such extreme emphasis on (two-way) loyalty and group identity, making some of its members feel worthless as individuals. Their misery is often compounded by the treatment they received before finally losing their cherished jobs: relegation to inferior positions, transfers to undesirable outposts, removal from important committees, and the like.

Social alienation, discussed elsewhere, also appears to be an increasing cause of suicide among the young, and a particularly wretched one at that. The ruling elite apparently failed to anticipate the need for new directions as the period of high growth came to a close. For a while there was a lot of political talk about Japan having to become "a normal country," but if that meant a country like France or the United Kingdom or America, with their traditions of open debate and real-life personal choices, you would not know it from the way children continued to be reared and students educated. The 2006 UNICEF survey on subjective well-being among children aged eleven to fifteen cited in this book's Preface provides some clues to the root causes of unhappiness among children, and the sharp increase in youth suicides in recent years.

Emphasis on "traditional" values and outdated notions of Japan's "uniqueness" have long outlived their justification. There has been precious little recognition of the true nature of the ferment in so many lives. The sullen silence or anguished cries of the disaffected go largely unnoticed.

Whatever the individual cause, the high incidence of suicide for other than financial or health reasons continues to be a worrying aspect of Japanese society today. It seems to indicate an inability among those taking their own lives—and the unknown numbers contemplating it—to accept or identify with certain crucial aspects of today's Japan.

Some may miss the grand, national purposes and clear rules their elders were provided by the government, without finding anything worthwhile to take their place. Others may suffer an irreparable disconnect between their sensitive, searching selves and the blatantly commercialized, extroverted, shallow world surrounding them. And for most, their inability to make themselves heard in a society still reluctant to listen to the distinctive voice of the individual may often be the last straw.

Chapter **30**

The Patriotism Trap

Post-Showa economic uncertainties have caused a decline in job security, family values, and centrally formulated economic goals. This new environment has placed a premium on individual strength and resourcefulness, a challenge for which many proved unprepared. This must have contributed greatly to the social alienation of many young people and shaken their national pride.

But rather than working to ease the transition into this new environment, there are those among the people in positions of power in Japan who seek the solution in a "return to traditional values." Fearing the loss of docility among the "workers," and emboldened by their perception of the apathy and lack of direction among the young they engage in patriotic rhetoric.

New laws proposed and, in part, enacted in recent years underline this right-wing determination to reestablish patriotism in the national consciousness. The revision of the Fundamental Law on Education, which passed both houses of the Diet toward the end of 2006, calls for the compulsory classroom teaching, as a subject, of "love of one's country"—a euphemism that replaced "patriotism" as a notional concession to the opposition. Various commentators caution us that despite the milder language, the intent of the revised law remains unchanged.

Another seminal change is that, in the revised Fundamental Law, education shall no longer be "carried out with direct responsibility to the whole people." Instead, it shall be "carried out in accordance with this law and other laws." This apparently innocuous change is seen as effectively shifting control over the direction of education from local school boards to the central government.

The changes met with huge resistance from the political opposition, which refused to participate in the parliamentary vote. Japan's legal profession has also expressed misgivings about the new law.[10]

How the revised law will be implemented remains to be seen, but the government's agenda seems clear enough, especially when viewed in the context of other developments over the past few years. To recap:

- The ongoing controversy over the rewriting of history textbooks to place Japan's wartime record in China and other Asian countries in a more favorable light

- Recurring attempts by LDP politicians to rescind the 1993 government apology over the wartime treatment of Korean "comfort women" as they were "nothing more than prostitutes." (The phrase "comfort women" is a euphemism for the thousands of Korean and other Asian women, as well as a large number of Dutch women in Indonesia, who were forced into prostitution by or with the connivance of the Japanese military before and during World War II, to serve Japanese troops.)

- Former Prime Minister Koizumi's annual visits to the Yasukuni Shrine, which glorifies Japan's wartime actions

- The compulsory greeting of the flag and singing of the national anthem at school ceremonies in Tokyo and elsewhere—on pain of punishment for teachers and pupils that refuse to obey

- Late in 2007, another government attempt at censorship, this time by ordering publishers to strike from history textbooks all references to the 1945 incident in Okinawa, where an estimated seven hundred civilians were coerced by the military to kill themselves, rather than surrender to the invading Americans. (This government attempt met with mass protects in Okinawa prefecture, forcing the authorities into an unprecedented retreat.)[11]

As one pundit phrased it, Japan's leaders are preparing the country for the future by returning to the past. What he meant was that with actions such as those just listed, supposedly intended to better equip the nation to face the challenges ahead, Japan's leaders are in fact reintroducing the kind of narrow nationalist thinking that was typical of Japan's pre-1945 leadership.

In the minds of independent Japanese commentators, it is deeply regrettable that Japan's leaders are trying to fix the social problems caused by the loss of Showa-era certainties from the top down, by requiring more conformity and insulating children against the harsher truths about history and human nature, instead of taking measures aimed at strengthening self-reliance and individuality and thereby creating a more robust citizenry. After all, those commentators argue, the prevailing apathy is not about life and its potential but about stale and corrupt politics and the outdated, uninspiring notions of a bygone era.

Patriotism—A Malleable Term

We may well ask why the very term "patriotism" has stirred up such vehement resistance in Japan. Is there actually anything wrong with being a patriot?

In *The Patriot*, Samuel Johnson (1709–1784) (British author and compiler of the first comprehensive dictionary of the English language) wrote: "A patriot is he whose public conduct is regulated by one single motive, the love of his country; who...refers every thing to the common interest." Nothing very controversial about that.

But Dr. Johnson is also credited by his biographer, James Boswell, with the famous remark that "patriotism is the last refuge of a scoundrel." Boswell hastens to assure us that Johnson was not indicting patriotism in general, only *false* patriotism. What is false patriotism?

In a highly advanced society like Japan there should be no need to "teach" love of one's country in the classroom, just as the school is not the place where children should learn to love their parents. *Healthy patriotism* should grow naturally from the bond one feels with one's place of birth enhanced by an intelligent understanding of one's nation's history—warts and all—and a clear sense of personal identity fostered through upbringing, education, and experience.

Conversely, an educational system that overemphasizes the value of group identity, obedience, and collective effort and disparages the value of the individual creates a need for centrally formulated values and national goals. During Showa these values and goals were relatively innocuous being primarily expressed in economic terms, but in the post-Showa era of globalization this has become inappropriate and has been largely abandoned. Instead, the teaching of patriotism is now justified as a way to strengthen discipline and national pride and as a necessary medicine to fight the prevailing apathy. This I would call unhealthy or false patriotism.

For such a road, once chosen, can easily lead to a nationalist agenda, with its slogans and flag waving, its sanitized version of national history, and its demand to "revere the sovereign." Control of the media is the logical next step. If hijacked by ultra-right forces, politics could swiftly descend into a new authoritarianism in which democratic rights and values are increasingly trampled upon—always under the cloak of patriotism.

I well remember a classmate of mine in German-occupied Holland when I was eleven or twelve years old. The son of a Nazi collaborator, he often wore the uniform of the Jeugdstorm, the Dutch version of the Hitler-Jugend, the Nazi youth brigade. Asked why, he answered proudly "because we are patriots." Obviously, this boy employed the word innocently, having been taught that it was noble to be a patriot. But I remember my revulsion at his use of the word. It drove home to me the hard truth that the term could be—and was in fact being—abused by the government to justify their despicable wartime policies. It made me forever suspicious of government appeals to "patriotism"—anywhere.

Even in peacetime, the word patriotism often carries negative connotations. It evokes images of grand military spectacles and rousing rhetoric.

That Japan's ultra-rightists have been trying to influence Japanese politics by almost any means is beyond question. Their sinister black propaganda vans have been polluting the Tokyo air with high-decibel slogans and songs for years, and there are frequent reports of intimidation of anyone daring to say anything critical of the imperial family or Japan's wartime behavior.

Instances of rightist coercion abound. A senior LDP politician's home and office was set on fire in August 2006 by an ultra-rightist as punishment for the politician's criticism of Prime Minster Koizumi's repeated visits to the Yasukuni Shrine.[12]

In the same month, the Japan Institute of International Affairs, a think tank funded in part by the Ministry of Foreign Affairs and headed by a highly respected former ambassador to the UN, decided to pull an article criticizing then Prime Minister Koizumi's "attempts to revive the cult of Yasukuni" from its Web site, after severe condemnation of the article by a leading right-wing columnist and supporter of the movement to deny Japan's war crimes.[13]

Is there a real chance of Japan's government being taken over by such extremist forces? I doubt it. The ultra-rightists are a relatively small band of fanatics not taken seriously by the vast majority of the population. But there is a well-founded fear that with their strong-arm tactics of intimidation they may succeed in silencing any mass-media voices critical of their nationalist agenda, without effective protest from a passive electorate. This development would not bode well for open debate in Japan.

Emperor—Or President?

Perhaps this is a good place to consider briefly the position of Japan's monarchy. For any discussion about Japanese patriotism or, indeed, any study of how the Japanese see themselves as a nation, sooner or later arrives at the gates of the Imperial Palace in Tokyo.

Many, if not most, Japanese have always seen the imperial institution as an integral element of the Japanese identity—whatever uncertainties they may otherwise harbor about that elusive concept. But another segment of the population, chiefly those calling themselves left-wing or progressive, is less supportive of the monarchy. Some of them have expressed to me, in private conversations, the need for a change in the "emperor system," even its abolition, to free the country from an "intolerable constraint" on its quest to become a truly advanced, modern power. To place these rumblings in perspective, let us consider briefly the Japanese monarchy's history.

The lineage of the imperial family can be traced back almost two thousand years, if one is prepared to equate adoptions with natural births and accept children fathered with concubines as legitimate offspring, both ancient practices in Japan. During the decades leading up to World War II, the emperor was worshipped as a divinity, a claim he publicly disavowed after Japan's surrender. Over the centuries, the imperial house has survived rebellions, civil war, usurpation of power by shoguns, and the threat of abolition by a victorious America. Under the new, democratic constitution of 1947 the emperor became "symbol of the nation."

Compared to the more approachable monarchies of northwestern Europe, with their bicycling and divorcing royals, the Japanese imperial family, despite its de-deification, still lives a closely guarded, distant, and very formal life. The public appearances of the emperor and empress are even more strictly choreographed than those of the British queen and her consort, and largely confined to official functions.

The failure of Crown Prince Naruhito and Princess Masako to produce an heir to the throne in a "timely manner" had the nation exercised for years. The absence of a male heir would mean the end of the monarchy since under the postwar constitution illegitimate or adopted children could no longer succeed. The anxiety ended, more than eight years after the couple's marriage, with the birth of a baby girl in December 2001. Yet this joyful event presented the nation with a dilemma: wait for a further birth, of a male heir, from the then thirty-seven-year-old crown princess or amend the constitution to permit a woman to occupy the Chrysanthemum Throne. (The birth, in September 2006, of a baby boy to Princess Kiko, wife of the emperor's second son, resolved the issue of succession for the time being.)

But the media handled even this story, with its potential for intimate probing and unseemly rumor that would have a UK-style tabloid press salivating at the royal couple's bedroom door, with considerable deference and restraint. Kiss-and-tell stories by former employees of the imperial household are equally absent; loyalty and discretion evidently reign as supreme virtues.

I couldn't help wondering how deep popular respect and support for the emperor and the institution he represents ran in present-day Japan, and decided to ask around.

Roughly two-thirds of the people I talked to believed Japan's emperor system makes sense for the twenty-first century. The rest said it didn't, with students more heavily against it than the adults. This suggests a divided nation, albeit with the monarchists decidedly in the majority.

The emperor's role in preserving ancient traditions and in setting moral standards for the nation was among the reasons given for retaining the monarchy. Some, mostly older Japanese said that Japan's soul has its true home in the imperial family, or words to that effect. Most showed no objection to a change in the constitution to permit female succession (though such a change is strongly resisted by the conservative establishment).

Those against the monarchy called the imperial family an abstract entity, wrapped in ritual, and a waste of taxes. Some went as far as suggesting that its continued existence increases the potential for war and invasion.

Two academics I questioned on the subject betrayed republican sentiments. They both blamed Japan's resistance to fundamental change on its failure to end the monarchy. The older professor observed that unlike all major European nations, the Japanese had never committed regicide. The younger man was even more outspoken: "The emperor should have been judged in the court and punished as a war criminal," he said. "That would have enabled us to start with a clean slate." These were obviously minority views held by radical intellectuals.

Nobody I talked to referred to the connection of the imperial house to the Shinto religion, perhaps because of lingering embarrassment over the now discredited myth of the emperor's descent from Amaterasu, the sun goddess. But the elaborate court ritual is heavily steeped in Shinto tradition and mythology, and Japan's political right, which favors a return of the imperial house to something close to its erstwhile glory, worships ostentatiously at Shinto shrines.

The person and movements of the emperor and his immediate family may only be referred to by employing special terms, not applicable to ordinary mortals, and largely unknown to the general public. After the death of the Showa emperor, the *Kunaicho* (Imperial Household Agency) released a long list of words and phrases to the press to be used in articles and television programs about the deceased emperor and the funeral ceremonies. This was more like a decree than a helpful suggestion, and it went far beyond the kind of protocol that surrounds royal funerals elsewhere. It is an instance of the Kunaicho's ongoing efforts to uphold the near-divinity of the imperial presence by shielding it from even the slightest contamination by the common people, both in word and in deed. The emperor, to this day, remains a distant and formal figure, not as remote and shadowy perhaps as his father, Emperor Hirohito, was in his day, for there has been *some* modernization in the imperial way of life, but not the warm, concerned sovereign that his subjects might want to see, either. The emperor, after all, has no official place in Japan's constitutional democracy. He is not the head of state, but "symbol of the nation."

This atmosphere of awe, systematically maintained by the emperor's keepers and connived at by the conservative establishment, has the dual effect of preserving the sovereign's essential separateness and reinforcing the people's belief in their nation's uniqueness, through its inalienable bond with the imperial myth. It is a powerful mixture, and one that is already being subtly used by the political right to further their agenda for more patriotism and a return to neglected values.

For now, these efforts are still relatively mild in scale and intensity, and chances are that they will remain so given the clear intention of the opposition to block any further drift to the right.

Chapter **31**

A Free (or Shackled?) Press

The *Principles of Democracy* publication of the US Department of State has the following preamble:

> In a democracy the press should operate free from governmental control. Democratic governments do not have ministries of information to regulate content of newspapers or the activities of journalists; requirements that journalists be vetted by the state; or force journalists to join government-controlled unions.

How does the Japanese mainstream media stack up against this statement, which can be said to reflect acceptable standards of press freedom in democratic countries anywhere?

Article 21 of the Japanese constitution guarantees "freedom of assembly and association as well as speech, press, and all other forms of expression," adding that "no censorship shall be maintained." In practice, a degree of uniformity—if not formal censorship—in reporting is achieved in Japan through the century-old system of *kisha* clubs, the exclusive reporters' clubs attached to major government, political, business, and consumer organizations for members to gain access to news and information disseminated by them. Membership is confined to a mere seventeen media outlets: the major newspapers, TV channels, and two news agencies, all Japanese. The clubs are closed to (Japanese) freelance reporters and magazine and trade publication journalists. Until recently, foreign correspondents were also barred from the kisha clubs. Persistent efforts by foreign reporters to break down the barriers resulted, in 2004, in membership in the Prime Minister's Press Club and some other clubs being opened to non-Japanese correspondents, although the process to gain admission is fairly onerous.

Reporters are free to add independent research to what they receive in the daily briefings, but more often than not, they simply report, uncritically and without analysis, what they are told. The result is what veteran American correspondent Sam Jameson in a recent article calls "shoddy journalism—as seen in the lists of [pro forma] questions that reporters at the Prime Minister's Press Club submit before a televised news conference." He continues: "Individual reporters don't seem able to ask spontaneous follow-up questions, and news conferences often end with obvious, even urgent, questions not being asked."

The system has stifled critical, investigative reporting and produced instead a precooked menu of bland copy, communicating an "atmosphere" rather than incisive analysis or well-researched opinion. The club system does have a curious side effect: it fosters political bonds between some reporters and the politicians they are assigned to cover. At times, this has resulted in groups of reporters ganging up against a particular politician and forcing him to resign. In Jameson's opinion, "Japan's media companies have not achieved their full potential. They have honed skills in fixing blame, toppling prime ministers, and setting an outer boundary for permissible government action. But they haven't developed the willpower to expose, uproot, and correct social ills, corruption, and inefficiency."[14]

Such a culture clearly is a breeding ground for political scandal. Bribery, incompetence, nepotism, fraud—these have long been normal features of Japanese politics, facilitated by the governing Liberal Democratic Party's almost uninterrupted control of the Diet's lower house for more than half a century. Having little fear, until recently, of being voted out of office, the ruling politicians usually managed to exorcise scandals rather than confronting them. Inconvenient truths are glossed over, hard evidence answered with a deep apology, if necessary accompanied by the sacrifice of some hapless minister or other. That done, the media lose interest, the public shrugs the matter off, and life goes on as if nothing had happened.

The opposition in the Diet is chronically weak and devoid of ideas, allowing the ruling party (or coalition) to patronize the electorate and keep them in a permanent state of acquiescence. And the people, steeped as they are in a culture of deference and docility, usually oblige. Many feel disgusted with politics, and some may growl and grumble, but even they will follow suit.

This then may be Japan's Achilles heel: just as in the Showa era, the electorate is passive and can be manipulated. The media are largely inadequate to their vital role as independent watchdogs and critics. Unscrupulous or extreme leaders could once again succeed in taking the country where it does not want to go. Japan's democracy may not be robust enough to withstand such an eventuality, nor the media tough enough to sound the alarm.

The Waribashi Syndrome

The Japanese use of unpainted wooden chopsticks goes back to the beginning of Japan's recorded history. Because natural wood is porous, these chopsticks are hard to clean. As the idea of eating with chopsticks previously used by others is repellent to most Japanese,[15] they expect to be given new wooden chopsticks whenever they eat away from home. The best proof that they have never been used is to present them as *waribashi*, "half-split chopsticks," manufactured in one piece, with a groove down the middle. Introduced in the nineteenth century, they have become the standard in restaurant eating implements in Japan, with some twenty-five billion sold each year.

Wooden chopsticks, especially the waribashi kind, can be said to be emblematic of Japan's deepest psychological identity, which from ancient times has been bound up with concepts of newness, purity, and natural, undecorated surfaces. The Shinto religion, traditional housing construction, art, and design all place a high value on fine, new, unpainted timber.

There is some controversy about the environmental waste implicit in discarding chopsticks after a single use, not only in Japan but also in China, which only adopted the waribashi in the 1980s. But unless the government decrees otherwise, or a massive green movement interferes, the Japanese will cling to their waribashi as tightly as the waribashi cling to each other.

It is this tightness, this cleaving to known ways and structures, that made me hit upon the waribashi as a suitable metaphor for certain distinguishing Japanese characteristics. In addition to representing an ethical and aesthetic dimension, the waribashi could also be seen to refer to values and qualities such as interdependence, risk avoidance, and obsession with cleanliness.

By implication, the waribashi—once split—represent a definitive, irreversible deed. Thus the act of splitting must not be undertaken unless there is a clear and compelling purpose in doing so. Fundamental change in Japanese society is unlikely to happen until inspired new leaders make a convincing case for breaking with the safe and known past. For splitting the waribashi.

Chapter 32

Education for the Future

As elsewhere, political and educational authorities in Japan fret intermittently over how to best educate the young, frequently clashing among each other over goals and means.

Over the past half-century, compulsory education (up to age fifteen) and the three-year high school following it, has been largely about rote learning and instilling social manners and community responsibilities. The polished civil behavior and high standard of literacy and general knowledge of the population at large for which Japan is known are no doubt due in large part to the quality of that system.

Recent years have seen a worsening of school discipline, as evidenced by rising absenteeism, bullying, and crimes committed by children. In addition, various surveys point to a decline in academic performance relative to other countries. For example, the 2006 Program for International Student Assessment (PISA) of the Organization for Economic Cooperation and Development (OECD), showed a rather steep fall in Japan's ranking in reading and scientific and mathematical literacy among fifteen-year-old high school students.

These and other warning signals finally prompted the Ministry of Education, Culture, Sports, Science, and Technology (MEXT) to start a process of reform, which it claims will emphasize matters such as "coexistence in a diverse society," "cultivating a passion for learning," and encouraging students to "think for themselves and communicate ideas effectively."

What are the actual changes introduced so far? To improve scholastic performance, class hours devoted to English and math are increased by 20 to 30 percent. Overall class hours are also expanded, but "integrated study" classes aimed at nurturing students' thinking power and creativity by opening their minds to the interrelationship between various subjects, are being reduced. This seems strange, considering that the PISA tests—which MEXT takes very seriously—do not primarily measure basic skills such as reading, writing, and arithmetic but rather students' ability to investigate and resolve questions on these subjects using their own acquired knowledge.[16]

Overall, there is little indication that the reforms constitute a fundamental change in educational philosophy. It seems MEXT and the government as a whole fail to grasp Japan's real educational needs in a fast-changing world. Commentators claim that the authorities know very well what they are doing: the changes are mere window dressing, as the government has no intention of abandoning the principle of wa and group-based thinking or promoting liberal ideas about such subjects as political consciousness and pluralism.

As for the decline in discipline, the government's response has been, as we have seen, the introduction of mandatory classes in patriotism and a renewed emphasis on obedience. How obedience is actually taught was made clear by a scene I watched last year. A group of elementary school boys were waiting for the start of a guided tour of the Shiba Water Supply Station in Tokyo. The teacher used the time to drill his charges in the art of *saikeirei*, deep, 90 degree bowing and shouting *Ohayou-gozaimasu!* (Good morning!). He pushed their heads down when they didn't bow deeply enough.

This brief overview is not an attempt to analyze the deeper causes of the problems in Japanese education, nor the best way to treat them. There are complex and sensitive issues at stake here, which should properly be assessed by experts. Suffice it to say that the dizzying events of Japan's bubble-and-bust economy and the social changes that came in its wake have not left the young untouched. Neither have the cell phones, video games, portable computers, and other new technologies that have complicated the lives of young Japanese, as they have the lives of children elsewhere in the developed world.

What seems clear however is that, whatever the problems in the existing educational model, their resolution must reasonably include a much larger place for enabling children to develop their unique potential and divergent thinking ability, and equip them to assume responsibility for their own futures.

If such a philosophy seems a sound basis for middle and high school education, it must be equally true, if not more so, for the institutions of higher learning. Roughly half of all Japanese high school graduates go on to university. There, in the classic higher education model, the students' critical and analytical faculties are further developed, and they are prepared for independent life in a complex society.

But this is not the way a Japanese university education is generally experienced. As in Showa, the primary purpose of a four-year university education today is to qualify the student for employment in industry, finance, or government. Since graduation is practically a given, there is no great pressure to achieve academic excellence or master analytical skills except for individuals aiming to pursue an academic career. No wonder the impression persists that university is meant more for forming friendships, engaging in sport, and generally having a well-deserved break between the rigors of the university entrance exams and the future of corporate servitude, than for growing into an intellectually and emotionally mature adult.

And What Is Your Real Age?

In fact, the Japanese school system, from middle school upward, seems to swaddle children in a kind of prolonged childhood. The Tokyo law professor I quoted in Chapter 19 voiced a rather extreme view on the matter. "The mental age of male students aged eighteen these days is about 60 percent of what it was in the 1960s, twelve instead of eighteen, and *going down*," he said. "Girls: maybe 70 percent, which makes them a mental fourteen when they enter university." And what about graduate students? "Their mental age is that of an undergraduate."

The professor's harsh assessment may be a blatant exaggeration, intended to provoke. Yet no thoughtful visitor can escape the impression that Japanese teenagers—and even those in their twenties—are often more childlike (or youthful) and modest, not to say naive, in their behavior than their peers in the West. There is a disarming vulnerability about their unworldly, trusting demeanor that is both attractive and strange, and a little worrisome. It leaves you wondering how pampered kids like these are going to cope in the real world. No wonder young Japanese tourists (and the not-so-young, too) are sometimes targeted by thieves and conmen in foreign cities, and innocent or careless young women sometimes fall victim to viciousness.

When I asked the professor what in his view was the cause of this slide in intellectual levels his answer was swift: the current educational system, which emphasizes factual, rote learning, passing multiple-choice exams, and following the example of others. It was of course a well-known view, but I was surprised to hear it from his mouth. Hadn't he told me that state examinations sift the wheat from the chaff, with those who pass forming the elite and making their own decisions?

True, but he had been talking about where the current system leaves the *general* student. The best brains always manage to get to the top, whatever the system, he insisted. The average graduate on the other hand, such as the ones that made up the rank and file of the economy during the high-growth 1960s and 1970s, could be produced more efficiently by assembly-line cramming. In the wake of the anti-government student demonstrations of the sixties, he said, a formally educated but docile workforce was clearly considered preferable to an intellectually astute one.

The Importance of English

Another controversial and, in the eyes of many commentators, deeply flawed aspect of Japan's educational system is its approach to the English language. Many Japanese probably consider a reasonable knowledge of English important if not essential for their career, and most would agree that it is a great aid to the personal enjoyment of life. (Of the roughly seventy adults and thirty students I interviewed in 2002 and 2003, half the adults and all of the students said English was either somewhat or very important to their life, even if they did not need it in their work.) Clearly, English has firmly established itself as the need-to-know second language in Japan, as it has in most of the non-Anglo-Saxon world.

English is usually the only foreign language taught at middle and high school, and it is among three compulsory subjects (along with Japanese and math or science) tested on university entrance exams. Yet although many if not most college-educated Japanese end up with a fair command of written English, they are well aware of their low conversational ability. This is sometimes blamed on the different grammatical structures of English and Japanese, and this may well be a factor. For a Japanese student, learning English or any European language for that matter is after all quite a different thing than it is for a European to learn another European language, where at least the structure is similar and much of the vocabulary shares common roots. More fairly, it must be compared to, say, an English student learning Japanese or Chinese, rather than French or Italian.

But there may be a more straightforward explanation for the widespread inadequate command of spoken English: the fact that English conversation is not tested on university entrance examinations and is, therefore, given a low priority in the middle and high school curricula. Some educators argue that including conversational ability in the all-important university entrance exams would swiftly improve fluency.[17] Others advocate the opposite: drop English altogether as a university entrance exam subject, except when the desired course of study specifically demands a certain level of spoken and written English. Such a measure would remove the current animosity against English as an inescapable test subject and restore it to its proper place as an elective study by motivated students.[18]

Another impediment to effective English teaching could be the low academic and social status accorded non-Japanese teachers of English. They are often hired on temporary contracts through employment agencies and as such do not enjoy equality with Japanese nationals, even if they are more qualified. Two full-time foreign teachers I spoke to said that like all foreign teachers they were employed as assistant language teachers and as such were excluded from staff meetings.

They worked as a team with a Japanese teacher of English who left most of the actual teaching to them but sometimes overruled or "humiliated" them in front of the class by changing a set task or disagreeing with a compliment given for "good work" performed.

Foreign Teachers Don't Really Exist

March 7, 2006. Today a German friend introduced me to an American lady who told me that she had just been fired, effective the end of the month, from her position of *gakuen-cho* (president) of a well-known Tokyo high school. She had been with the school for eighteen years, the last eight as *kocho-sensei* (principal), then as president for one year. She receives no pension, as she had always been under contract. Even though she was still in function when I met her, the school's Web site made no mention of her name. This treatment has left her bitter though "unbeaten." "That's the way it is, in Japan," was how she summed up her feelings.

But the root of the problem of poor conversational ability in my opinion is the relentless emphasis on "correct" grammar to the detriment of fluency. The low tolerance for grammatical errors makes many students excessively self-conscious and tongue-tied.

Whatever the flaws in the current methods of teaching English, the larger issues of disaffection (and crime) among the young and a decline in scholastic achievement clearly demand a revamping of the educational system. The government's continued shying away from more liberal educational policies and, instead, its introduction of measures aimed primarily at tightening discipline in the classroom, are matters of serious concern to those hoping for a more enlightened society.

We will have to await the full implementation of the government's program, but it seems unlikely that the reforms—though ostensibly stimulating student participation and lessening somewhat the emphasis on rote learning—will produce a redesigned, more critical citizen. The questioning voice may still not be welcome.

Chapter **33**

Japan's Unfinished Business

In the preceding five chapters, we have surveyed some of the more worrisome aspects of today's Japanese society, which, in the opinion of this writer, may prove detrimental to its future optimal functioning, unless steps are taken to introduce the changes needed to neutralize or lessen their impact.

We discussed the relative unfamiliarity with abstract thinking that often proves a handicap in international discourse. We looked into Japan's high suicide rate and what it suggests about the nature of Japanese society. We examined the call, from the political right, for "more patriotism" and the concern, both at home and abroad, that Japan may be turning nationalistic. The constraints on Japan's officially free press were briefly analyzed. And we presented the conflicting views on needed reforms in Japan's educational system.

Taken together, these things do not paint a particularly rosy picture of today's Japan. And indeed, despite its major accomplishments and attractions, there is much to trouble the conscientious observer. Being exposed day in, day out to the mostly unwritten and sometimes intimidating strictures of this densely organized society, I sometimes despair that it will ever truly open up. At such moments I can't help thinking that the genie is at best only *half* out of the bottle. That it could still be forced back in by a determined Aladdin, back into the confined spaces of patriotism, conformity, unquestioned discipline, deference to authority, and insular self-absorption.

But then I look around me, into the bright young faces in the street, and I think: No, that won't happen, because these young people will not *let* it happen. For they know, perhaps instinctively, that it is that unleashed genie that Japan needs to secure its future in the age of global politics, trade, and communication, and a fast-changing Asia. They may even realize that such a course entails taking risks and that mistakes and setbacks will inevitably occur, but that shame and avoidance of responsibility are unhelpful ways to deal with mistakes. Mistakes, they will learn, make excellent teachers. They help build confidence without arrogance.

Many young and not-so-young Japanese have already demonstrated that they do know some of these things. They understand that greater openness in the political climate and more thinking—and acting—"outside the box" will not only increase their proper self-respect and sense of fulfilment, it will also be beneficial to Japan's future.

But the clock is ticking. Japan doesn't have the luxury to leave its unfinished business untended until this generation of twenty- and thirty-somethings takes over from their elders. The world is changing fast, and Japan must adapt if it is not to be left behind.

Many of its citizens could probably come up with a list of unfinished business for their government to tackle. What makes it on the list will vary with one's interests, age, position, or political views. Most current lists would include pressing issues such as the outrage over the 50 million lost pension records, which has resulted in millions of citizens being deprived, at least for now, of their legitimate social security payments; the recurring quality control scandals in the food industry; the country's $6.5 trillion national debt; and, even more crucially, the threat to its excellent public health care system by plans to open it to market forces that have proved disastrous in the United Kingdom and the United States. The depopulation and decline of the rural areas will also loom large on many lists, as will the rise in teenage crime and the issue of how to counter the sharp fall in the birthrate. Government strategists will place keeping sound relations with the United States high on their list, while the parties of the political opposition advocate attuning Japan's foreign policies more to United Nations initiatives. Economists will want to see government action to reduce dependence on manufacturing by strengthening the service sector and prevent a further widening of the gap between rich and poor, and the consequent shrinking of the middle class.[19]

These are all highly important challenges, some of which are already receiving active attention. But there are three issues of unfinished business that tower above all others, because they are structural in nature and may have a decisive impact on Japan's future. I've brought them up before. In fact, they have been recurring themes throughout these pages. But I want to expand on them here, because to my mind they are of crucial importance to Japan's achieving its full potential.

"Let the Mind Be a Thoroughfare…" (Keats)

First, there is a pressing need—recognized by many Japanese—to liberate the Japanese mind by fostering independence of thought in the schools, at home, in employment, and certainly in academia and the media. People of all ages, but the young in particular, must learn to use their brains imaginatively and critically, and rely less on "mood" and feelings and what others want them to say. Instead of being groomed for a life of obedience and acquiescence, children should be taught how to examine the available options in study, work, social relations, and national priorities, and find what they consider to be the best.

Open discussion, vigorous debate and logical analysis are the classic tools to sharpen the mind and improve communication. They also are an excellent way to combat the complacency that has taken hold of society. Challenged minds are active minds, and active minds will seek answers and ways to improve their own understanding of the world and its dangers and possibilities.

But even in the media these methods are rarely employed. As we can all observe daily on Japanese television shows, there is a woeful lack of hardnosed, focused treatment of almost any subject, from art to politics, from science to social topics. Instead of logical analysis or spirited interpretation, we are likely to get muffled tones of grave assent or admiration by male presenters, supported by the demure smiles of well-groomed studio ladies, eyes cast down, hands correctly resting in the lap. Or, depending on the topic covered and the channel tuned to, the presenters may be deliberately irreverent and joking types wearing funny hats and loud shirts, and their sidekicks barely adult, superficially sexy chicks, known collectively as *talento*, whose petulant tomfoolery is intended to bring some cheer into the unbearable tedium of the proceedings.

Granted, some of the better political and economic talk shows are more serious than these exercises in distraction. But even most of the thoroughly researched and well-funded cultural documentaries produced by NHK are notable for their often uncritical, syrupy atmosphere. The background music is sleep inducing; the voiceover invariably female, soft-spoken, and monotonous; and the commentary respectful, feel-good, and because of a lack of intellectual probing, ultimately non-illuminating. Any intellectual pretension that such programs may have is defeated by their preoccupation with emotions and atmosphere—with casting the right *mood*.

Editors and columnists in the printed media often show a similar lack of analytical skill. They will spend many column inches on a detailed lament of this or that scandal or problem, without dissecting it or suggesting a remedy. A recent, perhaps trivial example occurred in the usually tepid musings of the long-running *Tensei Jingo* (*Vox Populi, Vox Dei*) column of the mass-circulation *Asahi Shimbun* daily. It complained about the dangerous use of sidewalks by cyclists in Tokyo and other large cities, and ended with the wistful question: "What should be done to make bicycles appreciated again?" Not a word about the two obvious solutions that sprung to mind: limiting the cyclists to the road, where by law they belong, and requiring them to wear helmets; or introducing bicycle lanes as was done in Holland and elsewhere.[20]

Does all this matter enough to be cause for serious worry? Not if Japanese society as a whole is content with a future of comfortable obscurity, a future in which Japan, despite its economic importance and technological excellence, remains a bystander on the geopolitical stage. Naturally, such a stance would not be compatible with the status of superpower, however much respected Japan will remain as a member of the G8 and the UN. Non-involvement does not translate into influence, never mind the fig leaf of fat checks.

Of course, Japan's no-war constitution bars it from dispatching troops overseas. It is true that at American urging, it finally bent the rules by contributing some noncombat forces to the conflict in Iraq and agreeing to undertake Afghanistan-related refueling operations for NATO ships deployed in the Indian Ocean, but even these modest efforts are highly controversial at home.

Mostly Japan has sought to overcome constitutional constraints by providing major financial support for such international actions as the first Gulf War, and significant humanitarian and reconstruction aid in Iraq and elsewhere. But the reason that its generosity has been underappreciated must be found less in Japan's inability to commit troops than in its consistently low diplomatic posture, which has so far failed to give it real clout in global affairs. Making this point is not an instance of Japan-bashing—it is, I believe, a fair assessment of present and potential realities.

If there is anything alive in Japan resembling a desire to become a power to be reckoned with (diplomatically and strategically, as well as an inspirational force on the cultural and people-to-people level), then it is essential that national priorities be reordered to aim for a more *mature* Japan, where the mind is developed rather than soothed and challenges are faced rather than hidden from. Where the young are encouraged to work out their own answers to the challenges of life, supported by a government that provides the enabling education and public services, but not the ready-made solutions. For Japan this means a shift away from a culture of expected docility to the potentially far more robust world of informed engagement.

The significance of such a cultural change can hardly be overemphasized. It will invigorate and cosmopolitanize Japanese society and in time not only enhance the nation's status as a leading power, but also serve to revive international confidence in its economy. Encouragement of individual initiative will stimulate the growth of the country's lagging service sector and attract much needed new investment, talent, and employment opportunities. The aggregate of this enhanced economic activity will significantly raise tax revenues, enabling a reduction in the crippling national debt.

If properly managed, such programs will not lead to excessive, selfish individualism. The checks and balances inherent in a vibrant democracy will see to that, as will necessary reminders, in the schools and the workplace, of the crucial importance of teamwork and of our broader responsibilities to society—not by sacrificing individuality, but in harness with it.

Coming to Terms with the Past

The second issue in urgent need of a new direction in Japan is the examination of its twentieth-century history. Most serious observers will agree that there is no such thing as true, objective history. More than perhaps any other discipline, history is highly vulnerable to personal interpretation and political manipulation. History texts are arguments, often revealing more about national perspectives and prejudices than they do about factual events.

Having said that, in a well-functioning democracy, there are adequate safeguards to prevent the hijacking of the historic narrative by one extreme party or another. That does not mean that agreement on what is the "correct" version of history is assured, nor is that essential. Opinions will forever differ on whether or not Japan was provoked into attacking Pearl Harbor, and whether or not America shortened the war by dropping their atom bombs, thereby—as they have argued—saving thousands, if not millions, of lives.

What *is* essential is that hard-to-face facts and controversies are not swept under the carpet, or that one's nation is portrayed, in the textbooks, as self-righteous and blameless, and its past actions as noble or justified. This applies no less to Japan than it does to other major countries. France is now trying to come to terms with atrocities committed during its colonial war in Algeria. Germany has never pretended that its Nazi past was anything but horrific and has earnestly tried to make up for its crimes. South Korea is finally examining the mass killings of communists it perpetrated during the Korean War. China has not made amends for the millions who perished during their Cultural Revolution, nor has Russia for the Gulag. But in the United States, a vibrant democracy despite its many failings, the harsh public examination of the responsibility for the still-raging Iraq war, and the suspected torture at Guantanamo and other detention centers has hardly been out of the news.

If Japan could bring itself to finally open the dossier of their own lost war, and in all sincerity and fairness examine its militarist past with the aim of accepting that, as in any major war, fatal mistakes were made and serious atrocities commit-ted, it would do wonders for its reputation in Asia and around the world, as well as for its own self-esteem. More than endless unofficial apologies for the *meiwaku* ("trouble," "nuisance") caused in the past—the government's standard formula whenever they feel compelled to say *something*—it is a balanced assessment of Japan's twentieth-century history that is needed.

Genuine contrition for atrocities committed is never out of place, and fi-nancial compensation may still be called for in specific cases, but at this stage openness about the past is needed most. Such a conscientious approach, where necessary in a joint effort with the countries concerned, would clear the air and place Japan's undoubted commitment to peace in a new, more convincing light. It would justify it in occupying the moral high ground in Asia, certainly vis-à-vis China, with its own cupboard full of unspeakable skeletons. It might even smooth the way for Japan to a permanent seat on the UN Security Council as a major power in its own right.

I accept that facing up to the past does not come naturally to most minds, least of all to the Japanese psyche, which is more attuned to hiding from painful truths than confronting them. What's more, most Japanese seem to feel that there should be no need to rake over the events of sixty-five or seventy years ago, events that anyhow cannot be changed, whatever ways are found to atone for them now. Such thinking may well have kept Japan from demanding that the United States apologize for dropping the atom bombs on them, acts that must surely be counted among the last century's worst atrocities. Not wanting to endanger the United States–Japan military alliance must have something to do with this reticence. Like-wise the fear of the inevitable tit-for-tat demands that will follow: for Pearl Harbor, Nanking, and whatever else. Let bygones be bygones, seems to be the thinking.

But war victims have long memories, sometimes passed on to their offspring, and often exploited by their leaders for political ends. Whenever the subject is raised, Japanese habitually point to their own victimhood: the atom bombs, the carpet-bombing of major cities, the heavy casualties in battle. Many individual Japanese have shown their contrition over their wartime behavior in China and elsewhere, and one or two Japanese politicians have offered apologies, but by and large, the ruling elite and the people in general have consistently glossed over the atrocities committed, if not actually denied them.

What is needed at this late stage, rather than money or apologies, are two things: official *recognition* of the historic fact that specific atrocities took place and a clear message that those atrocities were committed under a previous regime, one that has no relationship to the democratic society that is today's Japan.

As a business associate of mine has pointed out, such a course of action could have another notable benefit for Japan. In contrast to Germany, where the holocaust and other horrors could be blamed squarely on Hitler and the evil Nazis, Japan has had no such convenient whipping boy for its own bad behavior. The responsible military dictator, Hideki Tojo, was executed by the Americans, together with his henchmen, but the emperor was left on the throne, and many wartime leaders were allowed back in government after the war. This may have obscured the fact that Japan became a true democracy. At least in semantic terms, Japan has not had the clear break with its totalitarian past that Germany has enjoyed.

In British and American television programs about the war in Europe, the bad guys are always Hitler and the Nazis, rather than "the Germans." But when the story is about Japan, then even today, on BBC or CNN, they tend to say that "the Japanese" killed thousands of Chinese in Nanking. "I was born long after the war," sighed my business associate, a highly-educated Japanese woman, "but I sometimes wonder if people think that those 'Japanese' are still 'us.'"

She concludes:

> It is fair to say that most Japanese want to be appreciated by other countries—how much we value peace and harmony over conflict. And how much we suffered during the war and after the defeat. But we will be understood only when today's Japanese generation scrutinizes our wartime history thoroughly, free from fear or favor, from both the Japanese and the foreign point of view. If we can clarify Japan's role during the war, and emphasize that the country was then in the grip of a totalitarian regime, it would not only help repair relations with our Asian neighbors, it would also amount to a formal break in the apparent continuity of wartime and post-war Japan and finally allow us to move on.

Facing the Demographic Imperative

Finally, there is the inescapable question of how to stem or compensate for the precipitous drop in Japan's birthrate and the consequent sharp decline in population in the decades ahead. There are two obvious answers: more babies or immigration. The former is fraught with social and psychological complexities and large financial commitments, and even if successful, will only show results in the long term. The latter is highly controversial, perhaps understandably so, considering Europe's mixed experience with this solution, and Japan's near-homogeneous racial makeup.

Japan's relationship with outsiders has always been a complex one. Although Japanese society as a whole gradually has gotten used to the growing "foreign element" in its midst, personal attitudes to non-Japanese vary. Many Japanese seem far more at ease when meeting and interacting with foreigners, especially well-mannered, well-educated individuals, than was the case in the days of Showa. But there is a clear bias against foreign residents who don't follow the rules or otherwise are too conspicuous in their behavior.[21]

Foreign residents, regardless of their economic or social status, continue to face certain kinds of "soft discrimination" in such matters as airport immigration checks, housing availability, access to certain clubs and public bathhouses, and protection of their human rights. Responding to a question on the latter subject, an October 2007 newspaper article analyzing a government "Survey on the Defense of Human Rights" was scathing. "Why," its (American-born, naturalized Japanese) author wanted to know, "is the government even asking whether non-Japanese deserve [the same human rights protection as Japanese]? Are human rights optional?" The survey revealed that (only) 59 percent answered this question with "yes," another sign of the persistent Japanese ambivalence about the foreign element in their society.[22] Over the past few years, various government agencies and press articles have warned that increased immigration carries the risk of rising crime.

Apprehension over admitting new immigrants into Japan's orderly, civil society is understandable and arguably sometimes justified. Perhaps Japan is taking a cue from certain European countries which, after decades of laissez-faire policies, have been raising their barriers to immigration in recent years. Even non–European Union (EU) foreign residents legally in the EU are sometimes confronted with various kinds of discrimination in such fields as housing, banking, and public services. And the United States, too, has sharply tightened border controls in the wake of 9/11, making many foreign visitors and residents feel less welcome than in the past.

Be that as it may, the sharp decline in the fertility rate, to 1.2 live births per woman in 2007, far below the reproduction rate of 2.1, and the consequent prospect of a rapidly aging and shrinking population, leaves Japan little choice but to rely on immigration to fill the gap, particularly in the agrarian, service, and care sectors. Yet official government policy continues to bar all "immigrants," meaning unskilled and semi-skilled manual workers, from entering the country. The estimated 250,000 foreign laborers working in Japan today are all illegal workers who have overstayed their tourist visas.

By contrast, highly educated foreigners or people with needed skills are increasingly welcomed. One major formal initiative to relieve labor shortages has been in the care sector. Controlled numbers of medical and nursing staff from the

Philippines and other Asian countries are now invited, subject to some command of Japanese language and customs, to come work in Japan, not as immigrants but as temporary workers.

Meanwhile, the designers of robots are working feverishly to produce intelligent substitutes for all kinds of human workers, from cleaners to receptionists to health care helpers in old-age homes. Japan is the world leader in industrial robot technology. It hopes to have a good selection of artificial humans available for duty when the situation turns critical—in five to ten years' time.[23]

Some retirement and nursing homes are already employing robot-like machinery on an experimental basis. One example is a kind of vertical bathtub that can be entered by a patient, wheel chair-and-all, and that offers full washing and drying services with the push of a few buttons. Just like a laundromat—which in fact was the inspiration for the invention.

The Japanese media frequently carry reports of new robots. Much attention was lavished on the attractive information robot featured at Japan's 2005 Aichi World Expo, which answered visitors' questions about the Expo in four languages. Its alluring looks no doubt accounted as much for its huge popularity as its "intelligence."

In spite of such technological advances, an increase in immigrant labor of every kind seems inevitable. Some rural areas of the country have been short of women for years—or at least of women willing to work on farms—forcing farmers to import wives from China and other Asian countries. More recently, the countryside has been suffering from an acute lack of medical staff, prompting the government to consider allowing foreign doctors to practice medicine in Japan, but only in "designated structural reform zones," meaning depopulated and generally depressed areas. But initiatives like these are like drops in the ocean. Without a sea change in the fundamental Japanese mindset against foreigners in general, the stark realities of Japan's demographic bind will turn into a real crisis.

Japan has always found its own ways of coping with setbacks and challenges, as the rebound of its economy in recent years has shown once again. Having said that, the "good old days" of Showa, with its well-nigh homogeneous workforce united by traditional mores and insider codes understood by all, are unlikely ever to return. A more pluralistic society will gradually take its place. It will be less predictable and harder to govern. But it will energize Japanese society in a way that was unthinkable in the days of Showa.

Provided, of course, that the country's reactionaries do not throw a spanner in the works.

The Central Issue

The three areas of unfinished business discussed above represent, in my judgment, the views of many Japanese who are concerned about the sustainability of Japan's prosperity and place in the world—about its very future. But what is the likelihood of such an agenda being realized? Is there perhaps a prerequisite, a sine qua non without which the prospects for real change must be considered remote?

I believe there is: a transformation in the political structure. Initiatives for reform in education, immigration, and dealing with the past would be far more likely to occur, and their reach more comprehensive, if they were preceded or accompanied by a profound change in political philosophy. Or at the very least a fundamental overhaul in the day-to-day workings of government both at the law-making and the executive level.

Given the fact that this book is chiefly concerned with Japanese society and culture—with the occasional detour into economic territory—an analysis of Japan's political system and the mores of its members would not only be out of place, but also outside the competence of this writer. All I want to do here is suggest, from my own perspective, that there is a pressing need for a shake-up of the political scene. Anyone half familiar with Japanese politics knows what an uninspiring spectacle it usually presents, mostly because of the lack of incentives to change inherent in the system. Take for instance the sobering fact that of the 133 *new* Diet members of all parties elected in 2005 to the 480-seat House of Representatives—the lower house of Japan's legislative body—28 percent were second or third generation, essentially hereditary Diet members. What's more, the average age of these 133 fledglings was 52.3.[24] In addition, at just under ten percent, Japan ranks second-lowest of all OECD (Organization for Economic Co-operation and Development) countries, above Turkey, in the percentage of parliamentary seats occupied by women.[25]

But it is not only in dynastic and gender terms that political rejuvenation is called for. Fundamental concepts of governance are at stake. Nothing less than a departure from its ingrained wheeler-dealer culture and a move into the arena of open public debate will meet Japan's democratic imperatives. Such a change cannot be expected from within the existing power structure, where it would conflict with vested interests and ritualized procedure. It would have to come instead from talented young minds willing to trust their own insights and the bundled energies of their own generation in the search for credible alternatives to business-as-usual. Inspiring the electorate to take a more active part in democratic processes would be integral to such a program.

Facing up to its history, freeing the minds of its citizens, finding ways to counter the population decline, and making room for more enlightened politics—these, then, are Japan's chief challenges, its unfinished business.

Realizing such ambitious goals may lead in time to a new era of greatness, a new Golden Age. An age in which Japan's abundant energy, creativity, and genuine love of peace and harmony are no longer constrained by timidity and preoccupation with the hallowed myths of a vanished past—or hamstrung by a stagnant political environment. There is no limit to what Japan could contribute to the world on every level. What are needed are wise and courageous measures to unleash its captive spirit and thus help it come to full flower.

Far from betraying the achievements of the great post-war Showa era, such measures would build on those achievements and enhance them, and in so doing, honor them.

Afterword

Wherever I go in Japan these days I find order and well-dressed people and an abundance of material goods. The streets are safe. The trains are punctual and frequent. The cafés are full. Street protests are extremely rare. Even the out-of-work toe the line. You don't litter. You don't challenge authority. Rules must not be broken, not even bent.

There is a sense of living in a cocoon, cared for, protected from the cold winds of the wider world. No other nation has achieved a comparable state of social contentment, or offered comparable opportunities for unfettered self-indulgence. The words of an old Cole Porter song come to mind: "You're so easy to love..." It's easy to love this fortunate, well-organized, beautiful country and its smiling, well-behaved people. It requires no special effort.

And that, I realize with a shock, is the problem. It's a paradox: something is lacking in Japan because it's perfect. Well, not perfect, but relentlessly striving to iron out the remaining wrinkles in the fabric of society, and very nearly succeeding.

Some years ago I overheard two European women agreeing that they preferred a bastard to a nice guy, any time. Nice guys are boring, they laughed. Bastards are a challenge, but more exciting, and therefore sexier.

No comment on that, but I do agree that the unexpected often trumps the predictable when it comes to experiencing the vital pulse of life. Encountering obstacles, making mistakes, facing—or voicing—dissent, these stimulate the brain. To be shielded from them causes it to atrophy. "From ignorance our comfort flows," as Matthew Prior, English poet and diplomat, already knew in the seventeenth century.

But in Japan unpredictability has always been suspect. Flexibility in dealing with the unexpected was valued much less than dedication to a prescribed course of action. This was especially so in the years of reconstruction and high economic growth. But then single-mindedness was a necessity. In my earlier days here, in the 1950s and 1960s, Japan was a tough, hard-working place, with little leisure and low wages and a national commitment to meeting every conceivable kind of target. There was little room for creative thinking or developing *personality*. The commitment was unified and total, aimed at achieving that noble goal: a good life for all.

For me, coming from Holland, a country with far less rigid patterns of behavior, this absolute devotion to a common purpose was fascinating and strangely inspiring. As a young banker, I came to share vicariously in the glory of new factories built, new car models introduced, export records broken. Loans, no less than oil and raw materials, were a scarce resource, essential for the nation's progress. Banks like mine provided these resources, often having to persuade the distant head office that it was safe to lend to this struggling country. But I was never let down. The "corporate warriors" relentlessly scaled the heights against the odds, planting their flag on every conquered peak. And always paying back their loans.

We, the financial enablers, were often invited to the opening of a new plant or the launching of a supertanker. We were entertained by corporate bosses at grand receptions and intimate dinners at fashionable *ryotei* restaurants such as Kazuo and Hannya-en. At times, we were even received by the prime minister or introduced to members of the imperial family. It was all part of Japan's gigantic, vigorous exertion to lift itself out of poverty and defeat, onto the highest level of prosperity and international recognition. The project's focus was narrow, and it lacked tolerance for deviations, but it was right for the times. It was the Showa way.

Where does that leave the Heisei era, Showa's successor, which began twenty years ago? Why does today's Japanese society, with its increasing diversity and lessened security of employment, somehow seem flaccid and tired? Has success killed the Showa spirit and lulled the majority of Japanese into a state of comfortable torpor?

Many highly educated Japanese remark on the indolence that takes hold of them on returning home from a stay in Europe or North America. "Back in Japan, I stop thinking, because there's no need to think. *Really* think," is how one put it. "Abroad, I was constantly confronted with new challenges, both at work and in private life. Opinions clashed, in the search for the best course of action. Few things are cut and dried. Your own input is crucial. It can be tiring, but it sure keeps your mind working."

Could it be true that the conforming, harmony-seeking, all-noses-in-the same-direction ways of the Showa heyday still dominate this society at a time when they are no longer appropriate? And despite the tumultuous events and profound changes that have taken place since then?

Perhaps Japan is still looking for a viable successor to the obsolete Showa model. But while its leaders ponder the best course to take, they would do well, for starters, to open the windows and let in the air.

Which is what I am doing at this moment. The view from my eighth-floor Tokyo apartment is dominated by the hilltop Renaissance-style building of the

Tsunamachi Mitsui Club, built in 1913, and its extensive gardens, which all but surround my apartment building. I remember attending a lively dinner at the club in the late 1960s, to celebrate some Mitsui accomplishment or other. Now the club and its secluded gardens have become an anachronism in this metropolis of high-rise buildings. As I breathe in the air I watch a lone white heron land majestically on a low tree in the extensive park. It is a sight that should make me feel happy and serene, as it does at times. But today, as on most days, the sight dulls rather than invigorates me.

I notice the wind rising, and rain is predicted. I don an old coat and cap, take the elevator down, and step out into the street, away from the numbing coziness and into the bracing weather. Without an umbrella, because, as my mother used to say, umbrellas are for wimps and Englishmen. Struggling against the brewing storm I feel my brain cells come back to life.

Acknowledgments

This book is in large measure based on own experiences and insights gained during my thirty-year residence in Japan (divided over two periods) as well as on extensive personal research. But I would be remiss if I didn't acknowledge the debt I owe to the many individuals who have shared their knowledge and wisdom with me, favored me with information and suggestions, or generally cheered me along as I made my slow progress to completion. They are too numerous to name individually, and I want to thank them all, in this way, for their generosity and time and interest in this project. I include here most specifically the over one hundred men and women, young and old, who participated in my first-hand survey of 2002 and 2003, which forms one of the building blocks of Part Three of this book, including the students and faculty members of Kansai Gakuin University and a group of graduate students at Kyoto University.

I do want to thank a few men and women specifically, in random order, as each has been helpful in his or her own distinctive way. Shijuro Ogata, Sachio Demura, and Prof. Takashi Ebashi shared their opinions and knowledge of Japanese society with me. Dr. Koji Mizoguchi has shown consistent interest in my work, contributing valuable comments and sharing experiences from his own work as a social scientist. My old friend Prof. Dr. Albert Mok delivered frequent doses of long-distance encouragement, often accompanied by thought-provoking remarks.

I am particularly grateful to my publisher, Eric Oey, for showing early faith in this project, and to my editor, Amanda Dupuis, for her sound advice, all of which have contributed in no small measure to the final shape of the text. A word of thanks is also due to my nephew, Edo van Dijk, an established graphic designer in Amsterdam, who offered helpful advice on design and layout.

This book is dedicated to my partner in many of my endeavors, Hiromi Mizoguchi. Apart from being the translator of my first Japan book, *The Magatama Doodle*—for which she received much deserved praise—and of my monthly essays and other material posted on our Japanese Web site, www.habri.jp, Hiromi regularly provides critical feedback to my writings on Japan, thereby contributing greatly to their accuracy and overall quality. Her interest and participation are invaluable stimuli to my work.

Notes

Preface—Japan: A Case Apart

1. World Values Survey, www.worldvaluessurvey.org.

Part One—A Showa Perspective

1. In 2006 plans were put forward to bury underground the stretch of the expressway that passes over Nihonbashi bridge, as part of an ambitious project to upgrade the area.

2. Martin Web, "A Nation Asleep at the Wheel." *Japan Times*, April 17, 2005, based on an ACNielsen survey.

3. For a thorough examination of Japan in the immediate aftermath of World War II, see John W. Dower's *Embracing Defeat* (New York: W. W. Norton & Company, 2000).

4. *International Herald Tribune*, "Tokyo Governor Visits Disputed Islets," May 20, 2005.

5. *New Internationalist* magazine, issue 352, December 2002.

6. Philip Brasor, "Female Foreigners Are OK in Japan, as Long as They Are Not Asian," *Japan Times*, March 11, 2007.

7. Murasaki Shikibu, *The Tale of Genji*, trans. Edward G. Seidensticker (New York: Alfred A. Knopf, 1976). Other translations are available by Arthur Waley (1926–1933) and Royall Tyler (2001).

Part Two—The Breathless Eighties: From Boom to Bust

1. See Ezra Vogel, *Japan as Number One* (Cambridge, Massachusetts: Harvard University Press, 1979).

2. Timothy Egan, "FOCUS: Investment—Japanese Plunge into US Realty," *New York Times*, November 23, 1986.

3. Christopher Wood, *The Bubble Economy: Japan's Extraordinary Speculative Boom of the 80s and the Dramatic Bust of the 90s* (New York: Atlantic Monthly Press, 1992).

4. David Aldwinckle, "The Japanese Way of Death: a Funeral in Sapporo," Japan Policy Research Institute, September 1997.

5. James Sterngold, "Some Big Japanese Art Purchases Are under Scrutiny for Scandal," *New York Times*, April 23, 1991.

6. Yayori Matsui, "The Sex Tourist's Yen," *New Internationalist*, issue 245, July 1993.

7. BBC News, September 28, 2003.

8. There are many studies of the otaku/shinjinrui phenomenon, both academic and journalistic. For an overview see Volker Grassmuck, "Otaku," *Mediamatic*, 2006, www.mediamatic.net/article-11784-en.html.

9. Hans Brinckmann, "De Post-emotionele Droom van het Moderne Japan," *NRC Handelsblad*, October 7, 1991. Also see www.studio12.gr/cs/cyber.html.

10. Lauren Collins, "Foreign Exchange: Say Cheese!" *New Yorker*, January 22, 2007, p. 31.

11. Charles Bremner, "Surly Parisians Bruise Sensitive Japanese," *The Times* (London), December 19, 2004.

12. Howard W. French, "Ryotei: Vanishing Havens of the High and Mighty," *New York Times*, May 5, 2001.

Part Three—The Magellan Decade: A Post-Bubble X-Ray

1. Patrick L. Smith, "Freer Spirits Take Root in Japan's Firms," *International Herald Tribune*, September 16–17, 2006.

2. James C. Abegglen, *21st Century Japanese Management* (New York: Palgrave Macmillan, 2006).

3. David K. Kaplan, *The Cult at the End of the World* (London: Random House UK, 1996).

4. Koichi Iwabuchi, "Complicit Exoticism: Japan and Its Other," in *The Australian Journal of Media and Culture*, vol. 8, no. 2, 1994.

5. Harumi Befu, *Hegemony of Homogeneity: An Anthropological Analysis of Nihonjinron* (Melbourne, Australia: Trans Pacific Press, 2001).

6. Shintaro Ishihara, *The Japan That Can Say NO: Why Japan Will Be the First among Equals* (New York: Simon & Schuster, 1991).

7. This chapter and the next are based on individual and group discussions, as well as a written survey, conducted by me during 2002 and 2003, when the country was still recovering from the bust, with over a hundred Japanese men and women of all age groups and a wide variety of occupations, in Tokyo, Kobe, and several other locations. About thirty-five of them were students, both graduate and undergraduate.

8. The Ministry of Education, Culture, Sports, Science and Technology (MEXT), "Outline of the Student Exchange System of Japan," 2006. Available on www.mext.go.jp.

9. Hiroko Nakata, "Asian Students Face Slim Job Prospects," *Japan Times*, July 2, 2002.

Part Four—Overcoming Showa

1. BBC News, December 13, 2006.

2. Yasuhiro Nakasone, "Abe, a Return to Conservatism," *Daily Yomiuri*, January 7, 2007.

3. Channel 12 (TV Tokyo), December 20, 2005, "Kekkon Dekinai Otokotachi" ("Men Who Can't Get Married").

4. Tomoko Otake, "Japan's Gender Inequality Puts It to Shame in World Rankings," *Japan Times*, February 24, 2008 (based on Gender Empowerment Measure of the United Nations Development Program).

5. Mieko Takenobu, "ILO: Japan Needs to Correct Gender Wage Gap," *International Herald Tribune/Asahi Shimbun*, May 12, 2009.

6. Kaori Shoji, "In Japan, It's Men Who Want to Be Skinny and Cute," *International Herald Tribune*, November 21, 2007.

7. "Agency Successful Once in 7 Years," *International Herald Tribune/Asahi Shimbun,* February 21, 2007.

8. "JR Exec Defends Punitive Training," *Daily Yomiuri,* February 2, 2007.

9. Eric Prideaux, "World Suicide Capital—Tough Image to Shake," *Japan Times*, November 20, 2007.

10. "Comments on the New Fundamental Law of Education," Japan Federation of Bar Associations, www.nichibenren.or.jp/en/activities/statements/061220.html.

11. Nori Onishi, "Japan to Amend Textbook Accounts of Okinawa Suicides," *International Herald Tribune,* December 26, 2007.

12. Steven Clemons, "The Rise of Japan's Thought Police," *Washington Post*, August 30, 2006.

13. David McNeill, "Softly, Softly," *Number 1 Shimbun*, July 2007, published by the Foreign Correspondents' Club of Japan, Tokyo.

14. Sam Jameson, "Japan's Media Have Not Achieved Their Full Potential," *Number 1 Shimbun,* March 2008, published by the Foreign Correspondents Club of Japan, Tokyo.

15. Mihoko Tsukino, "A Nation Obsessed with Cleanliness: Germ Phobia a Symptom of Social Disconnectedness, Experts Say," *Daily Yomiuri*, November 12, 2006.

16. Masami Murai and Mitsuhiko Watanabe, "OECD Test Rank Shows Decline," *Daily Yomiuri*, December 6, 2007

17. Brian Chapman, "Forging Paths Toward Fluency," *Daily Yomiuri*, April 27, 2007.

18. Mike Guest, "Time to Get English Taken Off the Center Exam," *Daily Yomiuri*, January 29, 2008.

19. Tadao Kakizoe, "Pro-Market Theory Hurts Health Care," *Daily Yomiuri,* May 18, 2008.

20. "What Can Be Done to Make Bikes Appreciated?" *Asahi Shimbun*, May 28, 2007 (translated version in the *International Herald Tribune*, May 29, 2007).

21. Joseph Coleman, "Foreigners, If Conspicuous, Hard to Fit In," *Japan Times*, January 24, 2007.

22. Debito Arudou, "Human Rights Survey Stinks," *Japan Times*, October 23, 2007.

23. Toru Fujioka, "Japan's Answer for an Aging Society: Robots," International Herald Tribune, October 30, 2007.

24. Foreign Press Center Japan, 2005, as quoted on www.nihonsite.com/bol_cons/index.cfm.

25. OECD (Organisation for Economic Co-operation and Development), "Women and Men in OECD countries."

Glossary

Aimai vague; evasive

Amakudari ("descent from heaven") the practice in the bureaucracy of arranging post-retirement jobs for senior officials with companies or agencies they once supervised

Amaterasu o-mikami the "heaven-illuminating great goddess" or sun goddess, in Japanese mythology the highest cosmic power

Anime short for animation, or animated cartoons

Banto senior clerk, employed by merchants or other businesses (outdated)

Bunraku traditional Japanese puppet play

Bushido ("the way of the warrior") the samurai code of honor

Danchi government housing project

Datsu-a-ron ("leave Asia theory") a thesis by the nineteenth-century educator Yukichi Fukuzama which recommended that Japan no longer consider itself an Asian nation, and emulate Western powers instead

Enjo-kosai ("assisted dating") young girls' sexual liaisons with older "uncles"

Freeter an underemployed or part-time worker

Fugu (globefish, also known as pufferfish or swellfish) a delicacy known for its potentially poisonous liver and other parts

Furo traditional Japanese bath, with deep tub

Fusuma wooden-framed, paper sliding door separating rooms in traditional Japanese houses

Gai-atsu ("external pressure") the US or other major powers pushing Japan into taking measures they wanted to avoid

Geisha ("art person") traditional female entertainers

Haiku traditional poem of seventeen syllables

Happi coat traditional brown or indigo cotton coat, emblazoned with a family or shop crest, formerly worn by servants, firefighters, and merchant's assistants

Heisei the era that began in 1989 with the ascent to the throne of Emperor Akihito

Hikikomori ("hidden bats") reclusive urban persons usually in their twenties to forties

Hori-kotatsu a heated, square sunken well in a traditional tatami room, covered by a low table

Ikebana (the art of) Japanese flower arrangement

Izakaya drinking establishment where food is also served

Japan Foundation Japan's principal agent for cultural relations with other countries

Kabuki traditional theater featuring stylized performances, elaborate costumes, heavy make-up, and musical accompaniment, dating back to the seventeenth century

Kaiseki high-end Japanese restaurant food, featuring an array of delicate dishes

Kaisha company; corporation

Kamikaze ("divine wind") suicidal attacks, especially during World War II

Kanryo bureaucracy; officialdom

Katorisenko a green coil that, when lit, emits smoke that repels mosquitoes

Kawaii cute, sweet, adorable

Kayokyoku traditional popular songs

Kisha Club a members-only "club" for journalists, attached to an official agency

Kissaten Western-style tearoom

Ko (also waga) ego, id

Ko o korosu suppression of the self, of one's own ambitions and individuality

Kotatsu charcoal brazier or small electric heater covered with a blanket and topped with a table leaf

Koto Six-foot-long, thirteen-stringed horizontal musical instrument played with finger picks

Kunaicho Imperial Household Agency, responsible for directing the affairs of the royal family

Kyosaku Zen monk responsible for keeping meditating monks alert

Manga cartoon drawings

Matsuri village or shrine festival

Meiji name of the reign of Emperor Mutsuhito, posthumously known as Emperor Meiji (1868–1912)

Meishi business card; name card

Meshi man's word for meal; also, rice

Mochi pounded rice cakes, a New Year's specialty

Mondo Zen question-and-answer

Mono-no-aware ("an empathy toward things") the bittersweet sadness at the passing of all things in life

Neru to sleep

Nihonjinron ("theories about the Japanese") literature that deals especially in terms of national identity and the "uniqueness" of Japanese culture

Noh a form of highly stylized Japanese staged drama with musical accompaniment and the use of masks, dating back to the fourteenth century

Obidome a decorative clasp or brooch for use on a kimono sash

Omakase ("I leave it to you") especially the choice of dishes, to the chef in restaurants

Otaku ("nerd") person with obsessive interests in a specific pursuit such as manga or the Internet, often unsociable and house-bound

Pachinko pinball game

Risutora ("restructuring") re-organization of companies, after the bursting of the asset bubble in the early 1990s

Ryoriya Japanese restaurant

Ryotei up-market Japanese restaurant with private rooms

Saikeirei deep, 90 degree bow; the ultimate sign of respect

Sakoku Japan's (policy of) isolation from the early seventeenth to the middle nineteenth centuries

Salaryman salaried worker

Samisen three-stringed musical instrument played with plectrum

Sangokujin ("third-country nationals") a derogatory term usually referring to Korean (and Chinese) nationals living permanently in Japan; also used in reference to illegal aliens

Satori enlightenment (in the practice of Zen)

Senryu humorous form of haiku

Seppuku the formal term for hara-kiri, or suicide

Setsubun the festival of February 3, New Year's Eve of the old lunar calendar

Shibui adjective meaning restrained, sober, in quiet good taste

Shin-jinrui ("new breed of humans") trendy term used in reference to a category of young people interested only in the superficial pleasures of life

Shinto native polytheistic religion of Japan

Shochu alcoholic beverage usually distilled from barley, with 25 percent alcohol content

Shogun strongmen ("generalissimo") who ruled Japan for several centuries, until the last shogun, Tokugawa Yoshinobu, relinquished the office to Emperor Meiji in 1867

Showa name of the reign of Emperor Hirohito, which lasted from 1926 to 1989; Hirohito is posthumously known as Emperor Showa

Taisho name of the reign of Emperor Yoshihito, from 1912 to 1926; Yoshihito is posthumously known as Emperor Taisho

Talento minor TV or film actress

Tatami woven straw matting used as traditional floor covering

Tokugawa period 1603–1867; same as the Edo period

Umeboshi pickled plum; a traditional workman's lunchbox of rice with a red umeboshi in the center is known as a hinomaru-bento (Japanese flag lunchbox)

Utai Noh chant

Wa harmony, especially in social relations

Wafu Japanese style (as opposed to Western, yofu)

Wakaru understand; agree; accept

Waribashi half-split chopsticks

Washi handmade paper made from mulberry or other fibers (not from rice straw)

Yakuza Japanese gangster

Yoshokuya simple restaurant serving Western food adapted to the Japanese palate

Yofu Western style (as opposed to Japanese, wafu)

Index